Implementing and Managing Telework

A Guide for Those Who
Make It Happen

Bill Fenson and Sharon Hill

Foreword by Timothy J. Kane

Westport, Connecticut
London

Library of Congress Cataloging-in-Publication Data

Fenson, Bill, 1965–
    Implementing and managing telework : a guide for those who make it
happen / Bill Fenson and Sharon Hill ; foreword by Timothy J. Kane.
        p. cm.
    Includes bibliographical references and index.
    ISBN 1-56720-614-X (alk. paper)
        1. Telecommuting—Planning—Handbooks, manuals, etc.   2. Telecom-
muting—Management—Handbooks, manuals, etc.   I. Title: Telework : a
guide for those who make it happen.   II. Hill, Sharon, 1949–   III. Title.
HD2336.3.F46 2003
658.3'123—dc22   2003057974

British Library Cataloguing in Publication Data is available.

Library of Congress Catalog Card Number: 2003057974
ISBN: 1-56720-614-X

First published in 2003

Praeger Publishers, 88 Post Road West, Westport, CT 06881
An imprint of Greenwood Publishing Group, Inc.
www.praeger.com

Printed in the United States of America

The paper used in this book complies with the
Permanent Paper Standard issued by the National
Information Standards Organization (Z39.48-1984).

10 9 8 7 6 5 4 3 2 1

To my parents, family and friends who so unselfishly
provided their patience, enlightenment and
encouragement.

Bill Fenson

To my dear father Norm who monitored and encouraged
my writing from the time I was six years old, and to my
cheerful, creative son Kevin who supported my business
writing efforts both technically and emotionally.

Sharon Hill

Contents

Foreword

Telecommuting, mobile work, hoteling, virtual officing, alternative officing, flexible work arrangements, e-officing. . . . In eight years of helping Global 1000 companies develop, implement, and maintain telework
programs, I have come across countless terms for telework. Why do we
keep creating more and more synonyms for programs that enable people to work from anywhere, anytime? The answer is that organizations
have a great deal of fear and anxiety around the cultural shift required
to make telework successful. My experience tells me that this apprehen-
sion is pervasive among those who manage teleworkers, not among the
teleworkers themselves.

Recently, I sat in the office of a top real estate executive at a very
well-known IT company. We were discussing how the workplace was
changing and how his company could benefit from a formal telework
strategy. The very mention of the word "telework" made him shift in
his chair. "We have people working remotely and some hoteling, but
we do not have a telework program. Telework would never fly with
management at this company." I found this statement ironic, because
nearly one-third of the company's employees were in sales and service,
which required them to be mobile (yes, teleworking) three to five days
per week.

For this company and many others, a large portion of the workforce
is teleworking—from airports, satellite offices, hotels, client sites, and
even home offices. Kinetic Workplace's "State of the Workplace Survey
2001" found that companies who claim not to have telework actually
have anywhere from 8 percent to 21 percent of their workforce
teleworking. Why do so many companies avoid implementing a formal
program? Again, experience tells me that they fear the challenges of
bringing together all of the organizational components required to put

a successful program in place and overcome the anxiety of management. These companies would rather ignore the issue or create various designations for such workers (hoteler, road warrior, remote worker) than confess that they do indeed telework.

This issue will become bigger in the coming years. ITAC found that in 2001, there were approximately 28 million teleworkers in the U.S. With increased competition for labor and greater computing power and bandwidth, this number will increase in the coming years.

This book is a great tool for those companies seeking to overcome the fear and anxiety of implementing and managing a formal telework program. Bill Fenson and Sharon Hill take aim at the key challenges to telework and provided a sound and manageable path forward so that companies can put processes in place to benefit from today's increasingly mobile workforce.

Timothy J. Kane
President
International Telework Association
and Council (ITAC)
Director, Virtual Work Practices,
Deloitte Consulting

Preface

The mission of this book, to provide managers with a guide to successful implementation of telework and effective day-to-day supervision of teleworkers, would not be complete without our readers' understanding of the roots, the reasons, and the results of the telecommuting initiative sweeping the globe. Our primary focus will be threefold: helping you with your decision to offer telework, your preparation for contingency telework, and your implementation of a successful formal telework program.

While we do encourage you, in this day of ozone depletion, floods, earthquakes, and now even terrorism, to implement at least a contingency telework plan, we know that you will need to think long and hard about your decision to implement a formal telework program.

Our information will help with that decision, as well as with both types of implementation. We will look at the history of and catalysts for telework. We will then explore the frontline management how-to's—determining which positions and which employees are telework candidates and the day-to-day process for effective supervision. We'll also guide you through the senior executive implementation issues—safety, security, costs, benefits, legislation, labor union resistance, written policies and guidelines, and the like.

The meat of our publication is the tips offered by the executives we have interviewed—those supervisors, managers, CEOs, and consultants in the United States, Canada, England, Ireland, Scotland, Wales, Japan, and Portugal who gave of their time and expertise to guide others in the management of teleworkers. Their quotes and information are interspersed throughout the book. We also offer extensive information from various labor union representatives explaining their attitudes towards telework.

In Chapter 1, "It's Broke, But We Can Fix It!" we look at the problems facing you, the employer—the issues such as recruitment, retention, finances, and real estate—and discuss how telework can help resolve these problems. We explain what telework is and who is doing it.

Chapter 2, "In the Beginning," explains the who, what, when, where, and whys of telework's history. We'll see what "got the telework ball rolling" and why other firms and organizations began to offer telework to their employees.

Chapter 3, "Keeping It On the Up and Up," offers a glimpse into the legislation that supports telework or dictates its growth. We also discuss the potentially litigious side of telework. From employment lawyers and telework consultants we have garnered advice on the legal issues surrounding offering a telework option to your employees—topics such as wage and hour issues, discrimination, information or equipment theft, ADA compliance, taxes, confidentiality, protected communications, and non-compete covenants.

Chapter 4, "Feeling Safe and Secure," discusses home safety and security issues. With the prominence of doing business online, and the expansion of telework, the old view of computer security, "keeping the bad guys out," needs to expand to include the concept of "letting the good guys in." Much information is available on remote computer security; a small portion can be readily understood by those of us who are not network technicians, system administrators, or programmers, but rather "mere mortal managers."

We've gathered the best and the friendliest of what we found through research, personal interviews, tours, and demonstrations with the experts and software firms. The result is our telework implementation "security guidelines." You'll also find suggested publications, Web sites, and security and antitheft products and devices.

Chapter 5, "Home Away from Home," focuses on the second most prevalent form of telecommuting, telework centers. We discuss their history and their struggle to survive. We discuss the newest hybrid, telecommunity centers, also taking a look at executive suite products, services, and vendors. We explain hoteling and talk about its importance in your telework program's financial success.

Chapter 6, "An Organized Response," addresses labor union response to and attitudes about telework. We talk about several major unions and their experiences with firms that offer telework. We take a look at several contracts and the telework guidelines drafted by labor union representatives.

Chapter 7, "Preparing for Disaster," explains the term *contingency telework*. We talk about earthquakes, floods, fires, and terrorism and about how telework can respond to these emergencies. We walk you through the process of preparing your firm's contingency telework.

Chapter 8, "The Implementation Process," focuses on our seven-step process for implementing telework. We explain exactly how your firm determines your goals and how to quantify them; how you choose the people to run your telework program and how you decide who can telework; we point out the online, written, and vendor resources available to assist with your telework implementation; we show you how to begin, run, and publicize your pilot program; how to determine what equipment and supplies are needed; and how to evaluate the results and determine whether a formal telework program is right for your firm.

Chapter 9, "Clearing the Hurdles," is a guide to avoiding problems that can sabotage your telework success. We talk about the four key issues and ways to avoid the problems inherent in each. We explain how to keep the lines of communication open between teleworkers, non-teleworking coworkers, and managers. We discuss the reasons for management resistance and point out ways to overcome it. We talk about telemanagement training—changing your managers' supervisory process from management by sight to management by performance.

We offer two Appendices. Appendix A includes sample labor union agreements, an understanding of which can avoid some very serious confrontations for those of you with organized workers. Appendix B includes sample telework documents—applications, agreements, guidelines, policies, assessments, self-assessments, surveys, evaluations, and home-office safety evaluations.

The Glossary defines and explains terms and titles included in this book.

Acknowledgments

This book could not have been written without the input of many wonderfully helpful managers, executives, vendors, consultants, and longtime telework advocates who selflessly shared their expertise and experience so that others might introduce this work/life option to their firms.

First and foremost, we wish to thank Helen Birkmann and Tim Brascheid of MKL.NET, without whose computer expertise and hours of contribution and patient explanations of technical security issues our security chapter would not have happened, and attorney Kathleen Bray, who spent many hours composing advice on telework employment law issues for us.

Others who were especially giving of their expertise and their time are Jennifer Alcott, director of three Washington, D.C.–area federal telework centers; Professor Miles Davis of Shenandoah University; MATAC's Michael Dziak, president of InteleWorks; Etienne Gentin and Ben Taube, former and current environmental managers for the city of Altanta; Bruce Holmes, director of public safety at Clayton State University; Jack Heacock, former president and current board member of ITAC; Timothy Kane, president of ITAC and head of Deloitte Consulting's virtual work practices; Angela Schwers, human resources vice president at Pearson Education; Keith Segerson and Russell Miller, directors of the Mason Enterprise Center and Fairfax Telework Center; Dr. Helen Solomons of Harrison Associates; Professor Pauline Stamp of Hartwick College; and John Vivadelli, ITAC board member and founder and CEO of Agilquest.

We also wish to effusively thank Bradley Alge, management professor at Purdue University; Jane Anderson of MITE; Mark Anderson of Smart Computing; Teresa Antunes, general manager of InterWorks;

Shari Aponte with Regus; Kyle Arteaga of Reuters America; Leif Limkilde Bloch, executive consultant for HK; Marcia Branco and Harvey Levitt of Decision One; Caroline Cheales at Surrey County Council; Dee Christenson of Washington State University; Kathy Clinton of Auto Desk; Steve Clairborne at Frank Russell Company; David Creelman, knowledge manager for HR.Com; Sherry Cronin at Prudential; Melissa Crook of Bell South; Ian Culpin of Martech Int'l. and eWork 2000; Sherry Doggett of Health Alliance of Cincinnati; Nick Doty, editorial director for Techies.Com; Geoff Fernihough, former CEO of the Faulkner Group; Kevin Fitzgerald with the law firm of Nixon Peabody; Bob Fortier, president of Innovisions Canada and the Canadian Telework Association; Anne Giese and Jennifer Milre at CSEA; Steve Gibson, founder of Gibson Research Corp.; Art Goes, president of PRM Inc.; Debra Goldman of the Communication Workers of America; telework pioneer Gil Gordon of Gil Gordon Associates; C. Andrew Head, attorney with Holland & Knight, LLP; Don Hawk of Tech Target; Ron Helgeson and Anne Losby at Sopheon; Wendy Herman of Nortel Networks; Paul Hershenson, president of Art & Logic, Inc.; Noel Howell at UNI, T. J. Johnson of the Washington State Department of Transportation; Dr. Wendell Joice of the General Services Administration; Kent Kappen at Placeware, Inc.; Professor Andrea Kavanaugh of Virginia Tech; Toni Kistner at Network World; attorney Charles Knapp with Faegre & Benson LLP; Mark Kranowski of Service Employees International Union Local 660; telework guru June Langhoff of Langhoff Associates; Leo LaPorte and Catherine Brett of TechTV; Pierre Lebel of the Public Service Alliance of Canada; Barbara Leitz of Allina Hospitals; Glenn Lovelace of TManage; Yvette Lucio , telework project manager for i2 Technologies; India McClellan and Grace Sorian-Abad of 3Com; Neil McClocklin and Steve McPherson, former and current Workstyle Consultancy Group Managers at BT; Janice Miholics, vice president of Global Work/Life Strategies for Merrill Lynch , Pat Mokhtarian, Professor of Engineering at U.C. Davis; Allyson Nikulicz of MacMillan Communications; telework legend Jack Nilles of JALA Inc.; Neal O'Farrell, CEO of Hackademia; Alan Paller of SANS Research Institute; Shelly Rappaport with NEPI/eCommute; Brigid Quinn with the U.S. Patent and Trademark Office; Kimberly Reason of The Bon Marche; John Roach and Paul Hindo of Royal LePage; Asim Saber, CEO of Willow CSN; Anne Katherine Schon, Landwell attorney; David Siesel of Lucira Technologies; Dr.Wendy Spinks, management science professor at the Science University of Tokyo; Peter Skyte, national secretary for Amicus/MSF; James Michael Stewart, attorney, with LANWrights; Sharon Stockwell of Washington State's Smart Moves; James Sykes of Assurant Group; Peter Thomson of Future Work Forum; telework consultant Colin Tierney; attorney Darrell Van Deusen, with the firm of

Kollman & Saucier, P.A.; Brian Walther and Yuko Nakase of Pasona, Inc.; Anthony Whitehurst of National Telecenters, Inc.; Graham Wing of PCI Net; and Jeff Zbar, SBA Small Business Journalist of the Year.

We also much appreciate the assistance of the folks at HQ Global Workplace who took the time to show us around their Atlanta office. We also thank Janet Jones of Janet Jones Works and Renate Mengelberg of Canby Telecommunity Center, who taught us about telecommunity centers, and AT&T's Joe Roitz, Allearnatives' Debra Dinnocenzo, Auxillium West's Jeff Moe, and TMA Group's Diane Davidson and Billy Higgins, who so generously allowed us to use their wonderfully thorough online telework materials.

For their continued telework support and their contribution to our book we wish to thank the following legislators: Governor Mark Warner of Virginia, Virginia Congress member Frank Wolf, Maryland Delegate Joan Pitkin, Calgary Assembly member Jon Lord, and Noel Treacy, Ireland's Minister for Science, Technology and Commerce. Government agencies and their representatives to whom we owe a debt of gratitude for their generous contributions to our book's material are the states of Arizona (Telework Arizona), California (TGA), Colorado, Florida (Dept. of Management Services), Oregon (Office of Energy), Washington (Cooperative Extension Service and Dept. of Transportation), and Wyoming; the federal contributors we thank include the U.S Air Force Reserves, General Services Administration, Office of Personnel Administration, and the Environmental Protection Agency.

We are also grateful to Dr. Barbara Bailey and Virginia Lockridge of WGUN Radio in Atlanta for allowing us to visit their "To the Point" program and talk about our book.

Much thanks also to Eric Valentine, former editor of Quorum Books, who with exceeding patience answered our myriad "new-author" questions and gave back so much gentle guidance.

It's Broke, But We Can Fix It!

It's an old adage that a firm's most valuable assets walk out the door every night. Employees, increasingly referred to as human or intellectual capital, are the key to a company's financial success, and retention of this intellectual capital is crucial to revenue. But, as Thomas Stewart of *Fortune* magazine warns, there is and will continue to be an employee—more especially an *executive*—shortage. He points out that the baby boom generation has entered its fifties and over the next few years will be retiring in large numbers. Younger generations, fewer in numbers, will not be able to fill the vacancies. The number of people between the ages of thirty-five and forty-four will fall by 15 percent over the next fifteen years.[1]

The concern becomes how to expand your reach to qualified candidates, how to become the employer of choice, and how to retain the valued employees you already have. When cost-cutting and smaller candidate pools translate to unfilled or underfilled positions, how do you increase the productivity of the staff members you have?

Another problem faced by managers and executives is that of reducing the need for real estate—not just for financial reasons. The real estate market faces high volatility, in part due to firm restructurings, closings, and downsizings, and can and does change its vacancy rate and/or pricing very quickly. Firms unable to grow without adding to their space may have to forego expansion or incur drastic cost increases to do so.

One very vivid example of this volatility is the area of Ottawa, Ontario and its Kanata suburb. As recently as April 12, 2001, Paul Hindo, vice president of real estate services firm Royal LePage Commercial, Inc., explained of the local area, "There is simply not any more land or office space available." The high-tech west end of the million-population city, the area known as Kanata, was growing at an exponential rate, bringing with it a low vacancy rate in Ottawa of 2.3 percent, and in Kanata of zero, a pricey situation for any firm wishing to increase its space.

Not so just one year later. By May 2002 many of these high-tech firms, such as Nokia, Cisco, and Nortel Networks, had downsized, bringing with it a space availability of 1.5 million square feet, translating to a 25 percent vacancy, a vacancy rate change of 25 percent from one year earlier.

The point this example drives home is that the less dependent your firm is on increased real estate space for growth, the less your expansion and your firm's success will depend on factors you cannot control, such as price and availability changes and the volatility of other firms.

Another problem encountered by firms and private citizens everywhere is disaster. Not a day goes by that we do not hear about devastating floods, fires, and earthquakes. They happen to organizations and industries as well as households. What do we do if we are permanently or temporarily wiped out, or even if our phones, computers, and other communication devices are unavailable?

Nothing exemplifies this issue better than the horrific 9/11 event in 2001, with dozens of firms' offices (including even the U.S. Army's Pentagon location) or the firms themselves wiped out, with hundreds of casualties. How would our companies recover from such an event? Are we ready?

More prevalent on employees' minds than in decades past is the issue of work/life balance and quality of life. Record numbers of double-income households and working single-parent households exacerbate the problem of "having a life"—giving quality and quantity of time to our families and to ourselves. People put in longer work hours and commute greater distances in heavier traffic, creating worse smog than ever before. Our employees are going to demand that we resolve their work/life problems, or they will look elsewhere.

Mark Parkinson, principal occupational psychologist for the UK's Morrisby Organization, says that, much as in the United States, the UK population is aging fast and that very shortly the majority of workers will be women. "The latter could be the clincher," Parkinson believes. "The pressure to restructure work in order to integrate traditionally female roles will in itself force more flexible work practices into the system—a uniquely biological and potentially extremely positive pressure."[2]

What can we do to help our employees and ourselves increase personal and family time and still get the job done? How do we keep this planet safe and its citizens healthy?

Of course, we're all concerned about smog and congestion. Not only do air pollution and the stress of traffic congestion pose health risks, but this issue hits employers right in the pocketbook, as we all take longer and use more gas to get to and from work and as our employees begin to miss work and use their employer-provided health benefits. As employers and community members, our firms are increasingly mandated by federal legislation to get our employees out of their cars, reducing smog, congestion, and wear and tear on aging highways.

This book is about one solution to these myriad problems. This book is about telework.

WHAT IS TELEWORK?

In researching telework, we found almost as many definitions and interpretations as there were authors and experts. Most documents began, "for purposes of this article, our definition is. . . ." In other words, we're still in the process of figuring it out. To serve the greatest needs, we have adopted the most general definition: *telecommuting*, or *telework* (or, what the U.S. federal government refers to as *flexiwork*), is an employment situation in which all or part of the work is accomplished from other than the employer's work site or primary office location.

Jack Nilles, the "father of telecommuting," differentiates between telecommuting and telework. His definitions follow:

- *Telework:* Any form of substitution of information technologies (such as telecommunications and/or computers) for normal work-related travel; moving the work to the workers instead of moving the workers to work.
- *Telecommuting:* Periodic work out of the principal office, one or more days per week, either at home, a client's site, or in a telework center; the partial or total substitution of information technologies for the commute to work. The emphasis here is on the reduction or elimination of the daily commute to and from the workplace. Telecommuting is a form of telework.[3]

The three primary forms of telework are work-at-home, telework centers, and mobile telework. Much of our book will focus on work-at-home telework, as that is the mostprevalent and the most requested by employees. But let's take a short look at the others.

Telework centers, which we will focus on exclusively and in depth in Chapter 6, provide employees with an opportunity to leave their home environment but yet reduce the lengthy commute to their employer's office. Typical telework centers are built in geographically convenient areas by governments, real estate venture capitalists, or nonprofit agencies. Telework centers provide workstations and computer and other business services that can generally be rented on an ongoing basis or for day-to-day use by employers.

Mobile telework simply indicates that employees or entrepreneurs work from anywhere—hotel room, airport, restaurant, and client's firm—wherever their work takes them. Many firms have already implemented mobile telework for some staff members—most typically, outside sales— without having recognized them as teleworkers.

WHO'S TELEWORKING?

You may believe in telecommuting or you may have had telecommuting supervision thrust upon you. Whichever the case, you need to succeed. It is our conviction that success comes with understanding and "buy in"; and from everything we have researched, from the managers with whom we have spoken, it becomes clear that supervisors *must* get on board the telecommuting train. From our talks with Glenn Lovelace at TManage, we discovered Sage Research's findings that 70 percent of all U.S. organizations with over 5,000 employees and 43 percent of all U.S. firms with under 1,000 staff have in place, or have plans to initiate, telecommuting as an employment option. Chances are that if you supervise in the United States, you will supervise telecommuters.

Sherry Doggett, director of corporate transcriptions for Health Alliance of Cincinnati's Help Line, initiated their telecommuting program and firmly states that she has no supervisory resistance to teleworkers because she simply does not hire supervisors who do not support telecommuting. " If you're going to survive in finding folks you have got to take this [telecommuting] leap," she states.

Telecommuting is far from just a U.S. venture, however. According to Statistics Canada, one million Canadian employees were teleworking as of 1997, a growth of 40 percent since 1993, with an estimated 2002 high of close to 1.5 million.

ETO, European Telework Online, in its 1999 "Status Report on European Telework" states that more than 9 million Europeans now telework. "Telework is gradually becoming a normal way of working for most Europeans at some stage in their working lives," begins this exhaustive study. "Telework is not an objective in itself," it affirms, "but an indicator of changes in all aspects of working life and a convenient focus for understanding them."[4] Its "New Ways To Work" 2000 report projects an increase to 10 million teleworking Europeans.[5]

Denmark, among Europe's most highly invested users of IT and PCs, has had a surge of interest in telework, with recent estimates of 13.1 percent of the workforce telecommuting. According to Leif Bloch, in his July 2000 report to trade union HK, Denmark vies with Sweden for top position as having Europe's most intensive and highly invested use of IT and is "among the vanguard of Nordic nations and leads Europe, and often the world, in terms of take up of ICTs and new forms of work like telework." He explains the advance can be credited to "strong governmental leadership coupled with active partner cooperation in terms of labour market policies and the development and use of new technology . . . for example . . . the rapid spread of telework framework agreements at the workplace."[6]

Noel Treacy, Ireland's Minister for Science, Technology and Commerce, established his country's National Advisory Council on Teleworking in April of 1998, advocating the implementation of telework policies in all publicly funded organizations of 2002.[7] The Irish Central Statistics Office says there are now almost 40,000 teleworkers in Ireland. Some 39,000 people spend their whole working week at home, communicating with the office by electronic means. Others use a home-based computer with a telecommunications link for at least part of the week.[8]

In Germany, telework is booming. More and more organizations have identified telework as a new way of working, and the country has experienced over the last five years by far the highest telework growth rate in all of Europe. The average annual increase in the number of teleworkers has been 34 percent, as compared to the overall European growth rate of 17 percent. As of 2000, Germany had the greatest number of national teleworkers—2 million of the 10 million European total.[9]

Japan may be the most radically changing example of a teleworking implementation need. Dr. Wendy A. Spinks, director of the International Flexwork Forum and assistant professor at Josai International University, in her "Telework in Japan: A Status Report" clearly states that "As with any other change in the status quo, telework does not exist in a vacuum from the larger political, social and economic currents which affect national life. If anything, because changing how we work is linked so closely to our value systems, it is imperative that we consider its development, and indeed its future potential, in the light of the broader backdrop." She goes on to clarify that the Japanese employment market is undergoing significant change as both information and communications technology (ICT) and demographic trends converge to shake up the status quo. Japan's population is aging faster than any other industrialized country.[10]

These demographic trends mean that Japan's corporate sector must learn how to incorporate more women and elders into its hitherto monolithic male force. Moreover, any such diversification of the labor pool inevitably means the diversification of work arrangements, as both European and North American experience attests. "Slowly but surely," Spinks continues, " [Japanese companies] are coming to see that telework and its flexible principles are no longer a question of like or dislike, but a means for surviving the demographic and technological shakeup that is currently hitting them."[11]

In May 2002, Japan Labor Bulletin reported that the number of IBM Japan's teleworking employees increased from 300 to 2000, making the firm the first Japanese company to have thousands of employees working from home. Previously offered to their research and development employees, the telecommuting option is now available to IBM human resources, accounting and marketing department workers with the title of deputy chief (non-managerial post) or above and at least one year of employment.[12]

In October 2002, Japan's Business Federation (Nippon Keidanren) clarified the country's telework progress: "Some 170,000 persons are doing home-based work using information and telecommunications equipment, while engaging in child-care and nursing."[13]

The federation, a comprehensive economic organization born in May 2002, is an amalgamation of two groups—Japan Federation of Economic Organizations (Keidanren) and Japan Federation of Employers' Associations (Nikkeiren). Its 1,584 members represent 1,268 companies, including 79 foreign-owned firms, 126 industrial associations, and 47 regional employers' associations. In response to concerns about the country's dismal employment situation and prolonged recession, the federation compiled the "Japan Business Federation's Emergency Employment Measures Program." Still in the implementation stage, the program includes strenuous telemanagement efforts including remote worker "vocational training and leasing information and communications equipment."[14]

FYI . . .

Many organizations and sites have emerged in the last few years to support, inform, and advise about telework. Two of the best are the International Telework Association and Council (ITAC) and its counterpart Telework America (www.telework.org) and the Canadian Telework Association (www.ivc.ca). You would do well to bookmark these sites as excellent resources for all the latest news on telework-related issues, such as legislation and statistics. European Telework Online (www.eto.org) is an excellent resource for international information and will direct you to telework sites in dozens of other countries.

Another avid telework support group, the Telework Consortium, is the brainchild of the Software Productivity Consortium (www.software.org), a nonprofit partnership of industry, government, and academia. Members include Sun MicroSystems, AT&T, Lockheed Martin, Raytheon, Lend Lease, UniSys, Xerox, Motorola, British Standards Institute, and Information Technology Association of America and government affiliate members Ginnie Mae, Los Alamos National Laboratory, and NASA. Academic partners include George Mason University, Carnegie Mellon, Johns Hopkins, and Virginia Tech.

The Telework Consortium's mission is to improve remote collaboration and security through ultra-high bandwidth and virtual presence. To that end, their programs include creation of a telework demonstration laboratory designed to show a recommended work-at-home workstation and software and secure connectivity and support and assistance with telework pilot programs. Do take a look at their site, and especially the webcast of their kickoff meeting October 26, 2001 (www.teleworkconsortium.org). Held in Herndon Virginia at the Center for Innovative Technology, the meeting included an ITAC award presentation to Congress member Frank Wolf of Virginia for his legislative contribution to telework. Speakers included Joseph Cunningham, president of DynCorp; Werner Schaer, president and CEO of the Software Productivity Consortium; and Dr. William Mullarie, former office director of Internet Systems for DARPA, the group responsible for bringing us the Internet.

WHAT'S SO GREAT ABOUT TELEWORK?

Can this newest work/life option really help solve our congestion, recruitment, and financial problems? Can it really give our workers more time with their families and bring them into our firms happier and more motivated, which translates to more productive?

Yes, it certainly can. And telework has myriad other benefits as well.

We spoke with one of Canada's political leaders, Alberta assembly member Jon Lord, who shared his conviction of telework's benefits for all:

> Telework is much bigger than people might think. In fact, telework is global in its implications. It dispels the negative aspects of the Industrial Revolution—that created the big cities, and then filled them with large numbers of huddled, impoverished workers, dependent on the limited

factory jobs, unable to travel far, bereft of alternative choices, who then started to organize out of desperation.

Third-world countries, and their citizens, who are still in that situation, now have a choice. Telework presents an unprecedented opportunity for economic development for third world and rural peoples everywhere.

In past decades, choices were limited. Employees had to be there physically; they had to live close by because of the commute. But now, with telework, they don't have to anymore. The rural folk who had been left behind—the poor, the oppressed, the damaged, the disabled—all have new, low-cost and unprecedented opportunity to get aboard the information highway without ever having to leave their homes, to now forge a better life for themselves. Anyone else in society that wants to has a choice of returning to more traditional ways of life out in the country—but can still keep that big-city income as well.

The result? Happier employees, stable communities, better-adjusted children, parents who are around, neighbors who are around. A gentler way of life.

No doctors nearby? Telehealth. No schools? Teleteaching. No lawyers, bankers, consultants? Electronically they are almost next door. With a little determined investigation, the technology is there now or will be very soon, to do just about anything anywhere in terms of information transferal using telework technologies. Live where you want, work where you want, though the two may be a world apart.

Teleworking is fun, it is healthy, it is much more productive. Teleworking is the future.

FYI . . .

With a substantial increase in recruitment success and an $800,000 real estate savings in one year alone, Merrill Lynch's Janice Miholics states their success simply: "Telework has become the key cornerstone of our work/life strategy."

Virginia's newly elected governor Mark Warner is as enthusiastic about telework as was his predecessor, Governor Gilmore:

As a businessman, I have been involved for many years in looking for creative solutions to Virginia's transportation problems. Innovative business thinkers have long recognized the benefits of telecommuting. Telework is an important solution in helping increase productivity and improving the overall quality of life for families in Virginia as we reduce the amount of time people spend sitting in traffic during their commute to and from work. I've been a strong advocate of Telework!Va, a pilot public-private telework partnership for businesses in Northern Virginia. As more employers and their workers embrace telework, I will be looking for ways to broaden opportunities for all Virginians, including those who live and work in our rural communities, to participate in this growing trend.

The U.S. military supports telework also. At the 1999 International Telework Association and Council (ITAC) Sixth Annual International Conference, Major General Terrence Dake, U.S. Air Force Materiel Command, received the Telework Leadership Award for the U.S. Air Force Reserves' outstanding achievements in the area of telework. Since 1995 Major General Dake (now retired) has strongly supported the use of telecommuting by AFMC reservists to accomplish a wide range of important mission needs. Under the leadership of General Dake, the AFMC reserve program successfully piloted the use of telecommuting. Since 1995 the more than 2,000 reserve officers assigned to AFMC and its components have been afforded telecommute opportunities to complete a multitude of project tasks while not physically located at their unit of assignment. The positive experience by the AFMC reserves shows that proper management of the telecommuting process provides quality, task-oriented products while saving time and money.

Telecommuting significantly improves the capability of the Air Force Reserves to be responsive to the exigencies of the active forces by effectively expanding the timeframe so the reservists are available to work on projects anywhere at anytime.

Telecommuting proves particularly valuable in carrying out time-critical projects in direct support of military activities across the globe. Telecommuting may also serve to improve retention and can help ease time conflicts with the reservists' civilian jobs. The telecommuting alternative is expected to significantly enhance reservists' contribution to realizing the AFMC Workforce 2005 objectives.

In presenting the award, ITAC's president Jack Heacock affirmed that "Major General Dake's vision and advocacy of telecommuting was instrumental in providing a valuable tool to enable Reservists to augment thoroughly the active forces."[15]

One recipient of the Clean Air Council 2000 PACE awards in Atlanta, Georgia, is Clayton University in the town of Morrow, an Atlanta suburb of 5,000 residents. Bruce Holmes, Clayton's director of public safety and head of Clayton State's clean air efforts for the past several years, has spent many hours creating, managing, and overseeing ozone reduction programs in addition to his duties as chief of police.

Holmes spoke to us extensively about Clayton's innovative telecommuting program. In discussing its 1999 implementation, he said that non-ozone attainment "ignited the rocket" but real estate restrictions were also a concern. The city of Morrow has no public transportation, and employees are spread everywhere, with different schedules.

The alternative work situation that makes the most sense is telework. He is proud and enthusiastic about their telework program and its success, clarifying that their work environment, "just about as paper-less as you can get," is very e-mail based.

"Lots of our folks are in intelligence productivity," he explains, "and we have seen a 15–25 percent increase in productivity" (through teleworking).

The Massachusetts Telecommuting Initiative determined that, over-all, telecommuters were as productive as, or more productive than, non-telecommuting workers; were happier, more dedicated employees; and were better able to balance the pressures of work and family lives. Their telework also reduced vehicular air pollution, highway conges-tion, and transportation fuel use. In addition, the study's interviews and performance data led them to the conclusion that "the major obstacle to implementation of telecommuting appears to be the lack of information about, and experience with, the benefits of telecommuting on the part of managers."[16]

What other firms offer telework? Which of your fellow human-resource professionals have "been there and done that?" The following list includes those managers and executives who gave of their time and expertise to share with us how their telework began, why it began, what they learned, and how it all worked out. Throughout the book we will call on them time and again to share their telemanagement failures as well as their successes, so that you might learn from their experiences. The following list clarifies what firms have provided the information, how many teleworkers they employ, and what percentage of their workweek is spent telecommuting.

- Half of Allina Metro Hospital's 68 medical transcriptionists work from home full time.
- 67 percent of Auto Desk's 3,500 employees telework, most part time, although some programmers work full time from other states.
- While Merrill Lynch has just eliminated 4,000–5,000 jobs and their numbers are not exact, they have typically had a telework percent-age of 5 percent, or approximately 3,500 globally, primarily in the United States; they are now implementing in the UK, the Asia Pacific Rim, and Brazil.
- BT (British Telecommunications) has 40,000 teleworking employ-ees on an ad hoc basis and 7,000 contractually based to work from home. Every job and personal work style is different. Some work 100 percent at home; 90 percent typically work 2–3 days at home and the other days somewhere else (one of BT's many touch-down offices, with a client, or with a partner).

- At Faulkner Group in Chapelizod, Ireland, their pilot program includes 4 of their 65 workers, all of whom work 100 percent from home, although they do make periodic office visits.
- Health Alliance of Cincinnati employs 70 medical transcriptionists, all of whom telework full time, working a minimum of a 32-hour workweek. At first they were required to work in the office one day a week; that requirement has now been reduced to appearances at regular quarterly staff meetings. Most, though, voluntarily come to the office approximately once a month.
- The State of Florida's Department of Revenue employs the majority of the state's telecommuters. Of the agency's 5,400 employees, 259 telework; 54 percent telework 4 days per week, 28 percent telework 1–2 days per week, and 18 percent telecommute full time.[17]
- Of i2's 5,000 employees, 700 work from home, a large portion 3 or more days each week.
- Of Hewlett Packard's U.S. staff, 6–10 percent work at home at least once a week.[18]
- At Fred Hutchinson Cancer Research Center, 10–15 percent of its research center staff work from home one day a month or more.[19]
- The Washington Department of Transportation employs 6,500, with 45 working from home. Over 1,000 telework from a satellite office closer to their home or customer base.[20]
- Sopheon Resource Network Corporation employs over 250 in 8 offices in 5 countries. While many employees who are laptop enabled do occasional hoteling or mobile officing, in the Minneapolis office over 20 percent of the 90+ staff are full-time teleworkers residing in various parts of the country.
- Half of Tmanage's 100 employees telework, with 30 of those doing so full time.
- Siemens' telework program involves one-fourth of their Enterprise Network Division's 1,300 U.S. employees, some of whom use hoteling as a telework option.[21]
- Art & Logic, a Glendale, California, software engineering firm, is almost completely work-at-home. All 35 of its engineers and programmers and 2 of its 3 executives work at home full time, while the other executive works at home half time. The only 2 full-time office employees are its comptroller and office manager.
- Of Pearson Education's 10,000 employees, 25 percent commute, mostly part time, some only one day per week; 500 employees telework full time.
- Willow CSN, a Virtual Call Center, has 1,600 "CyberAgents," independent contractors rather than employees. All work from home.
- All of Kinetic Workplace's 15 employees telework most of the time.

- Nortel Networks, a global Internet and communications leader headquartered near Ontario, Canada, employs 5,000 telecommuters worldwide, 4,000 of whom telework full time; the others work varying portions of their week from home, depending on the position.
- InterWorks, Inc., founded in Portugal in 1997, provides a platform of products and services with integrated systems solutions. Of its 30 teleworkers, 3 are employees working at a satellite office, 11 are work-at-home employees, and the others are mobile collaborator/consultants, working at various off-site locations. InterWorks anticipates opening a telecenter this year. In general the teleworkers spend 40 percent of their workweek outside the office.
- Caroline Cheales, Project Manager, Flexible Working, for Surrey County Council in the UK, says that of the 24,000 employees only 30 are permanent full-time teleworkers, but approximately 700 do so on a part-time basis, while 200–300 others "hot desk," with this number increasing as the hot-desk areas increase. One telecenter location opened in 2000, one in 2001, and an additional one in 2002, along with six smaller satellite locations. Many other employees are mobile workers also—social workers, highway engineers, and so on.
- Pasona, Inc., a temporary employment agency whose home office is in Tokyo, Japan, provides its employer clients with 15,000 registered telecommuters.
- Washington Mutual began its teleworking option for 28 appraisers in August of 1998. Within a year it had grown to nearly 200 working at home full time—38 percent of the staff! Its goal is 50 percent of appraisal staff working at home full time.[22]

YES, BUT WHAT'S IN IT FOR ME?

While there is not always agreement on the statistics, there *is* general consensus within the community of teleworking experts and experienced managers that teleworking offers several unique though not always quantifiable benefits.

Ecological Advantages, Such as Reduction of Air Pollution and Gas Consumption

Did executives just get together one day and determine that they cared about Mother Earth and wanted to save her from smog and air pollution? No, like other progressive human endeavors this one was legislated. The federal government stepped in with the Clean Air Act Amendments of 1990.

Essentially the law said that states and municipalities whose air was becoming a health hazard—"severe ozone attainment levels" is the term used—would lose federal funding for road maintenance and construction if they did not find ways to improve their air quality. Cities such as Los Angeles, Atlanta, New York, and Seattle, whose smog levels are often dangerous, must, for the sake of their residents, their tourism, and their federal road construction funding, improve their air quality.

The government's solution, entitled Reactive Transportation Demand Management (RTDM), incorporated traffic resolutions such as compressed workweeks, flextime and staggered work hours. Telework has proven to be a strong part of the workable solution as well.

The United States Departments of Energy and Transportation project significant energy and environmental benefits to teleworking by the year 2010, including yearly estimates of savings of 2 billion gallons of fuel, 43,200 metric tons of hydrocarbon emissions, and a $19.9 billion decreasse in highway construction costs.[23]

The International Telework Association and Council's 1999 study of teleworkers found that on non-telework days, 87 percent of teleworkers drive to work alone. On average, each employee saved 33.2 commute miles each time she or he teleworked, which translates to 28.5 pounds of pollution emissions saved in just one day by just one person. If each person teleworked two days a week, the annual result would be a reduction of 2,850 pounds of pollution for each teleworker.

In the Metropolitan Washington region, the Council of Governments implemented a Telework Resource Center in June 1996 to provide information, training, and assistance to individuals and businesses to further in-home and telecenter-based telework programs. Between January 1997 and June 1999, the program reduced 34,910 vehicle trips and recorded a 606,908-vehicle miles reduction. This amounted to 0.96 ton daily reduction in NOx and a 0.50 ton daily reduction in VOC.[24]

In recent years, the city of Atlanta instituted an Ozone Alert System to encourage people to telecommute on days when the city is at risk for high levels of ground-level ozone. In early 2001, Etienne Gentin, then environmental project manager for the city, explained at length what the state of Georgia and the city of Atlanta have implemented to tackle the smog issue.

In 1998, Georgia's Voluntary Ozone Program was three tiered: the first tier, called Impact Operations, included guidance to residents on voluntary programs during the May 1 through September 30 smog season. These programs included refueling cars after 6 p.m., eliminating the use of oil-based paints, and the elimination as possible of such gasoline-use operations as filling potholes. State and city educational programs included seminars at City Hall from such organizations as

Smog Free Georgia, MARTA, and the Bicycle Club, as well as written reminders on city paychecks.

"This past year," Gentin explained, "Atlanta gave birth to its telecommuting program. Its infancy includes a goal of 100 teleworking DPW workers this session [May–September 2001]. These workers will be full-time employees, and will continue their telecommute status beyond the smog-high months. We've been awarded a Gold Level Participant status," he stated proudly. He went on to explain that the state awards participating cities according to their efforts and their success in implementing smog-reduction plans such as telecommuting; the gold level is second only to the platinum, and it indicates a city working hard to clean up its air quality.

In April 2002 we returned to Atlanta for an update on its telework progress. Speaking with Ben Taube, the city's current environmental project manager, we learned that Atlanta has recently earned the state's highest environmental award—platinum—for its monthly reporting to the state EPA on city employee commuting habits. Taube shared that the following year's city goal was to take its telework program from pilot to citywide implementation, opening it up to all but a very few municipal positions.

FYI . . .

NEPI (the National Environmental Policy Institute) has a pilot program called eCommute now in Denver, Houston, Los Angeles, Philadelphia, and Washington, D.C., whose mission is to alleviate congestion and smog through reduction of vehicle trips. The company incentive, besides employee and community benefits, is that the firm earns "pollution credits" to be used in trade. For more information about the program, visit http://www.ecommute-nepi.org/newindex.html.

Alleviation of Traffic Congestion

While the population grew 22 percent in the nation's largest urban areas in the past 15 years, traffic congestion grew by an astounding 235 percent.[25]

According to the National Environmental Policy Institute (NEPI), traffic congestion in many states has become the number-one daily problem for commuters. Their December 1999 report, a collaboration with the International Telework Association and Conference, states emphatically: "Telework should be incorporated into the workplace culture if we are going to overcome the increasing and exacerbating commuter crawl on our nation's highways." The real cost of traffic congestion was tabulated: In four national and six council urban areas the cost of driving studies found that total driving costs range from 45 to 84 cents per vehicle mile. These costs, when applied to a major metropolitan area, indicate that the true cost of driving may be approximately $13–$24 per round trip commute or $3,250–$6,090 annually per commuter.[26]

If you would like to calculate your own commute's "true cost," see the Washington State Department of Transportation's Smart Moves site, http://www.wsdot.wa.gov/smartmoves/truecost.htm.[27]

FYI . . .

We tried our own commute-cost calculation, based on a one-way trip of 35 miles. The true cost that was returned (using 1999 figures) used a per mile cost of .421 cents for economy car and .4962 cents for a luxury car. This works out to a monthly expense of $294.70 and $347.34, respectively, and yearly figures of $3,536.40 and $4,168.08. (Keep in mind that as we write this in New York State in June of 2002, a gallon of regular gas is now at an all-time high of $1.46.) The calculator also provides startlingly negative emission figures for this daily commute: 64.68 pounds of hydrocarbons per year, 462 pounds of carbon monoxide, 27.72 pounds of nitrogen oxides, and a whopping 8,400 pounds of carbon dioxide.

According to David Spivey, executive vice president of the Asphalt Paving Association of Washington, in discussing his states' problems: "We're finding out that traffic jams are more than just major headaches and time-wasters for commuters. Our growing gridlock also creates safety hazards, causes increased pollution emissions, and threatens to siphon off the economic gains Washington has made over the past decades."[28]

A representative of Virginia, in the state's Washington, D.C., metropolitan area, Congressmember Frank Wolf is unequivocal when voicing his belief in telework: "There will never be enough roads or bridges to adequately handle the population growth in this area. Therefore, we must explore 'Information Age' solutions in addition to 'Industrial Age'—brick and mortar—solutions." He goes on to emphasize his belief in telecommuting as a gridlock solution:

> Traffic congestion in the Washington metropolitan area is horrendous. Like you, I sit in traffic every morning and evening to and from work. I often tell my constituents—and my colleagues in Congress—that I conduct a field hearing on the area's transportation problems every day. . . . Traffic

congestion has become a quality of life issue for almost everyone living in the region.

. . . I believe there is a way to [resolve this congestion issue], and it won't cost millions of dollars or involve building miles and miles of new highways. It's called telework.

Improvement and Enhancement of Management Skills

Several experts with whom we met in person—Professor Miles Davis, assistant professor of management of Shenandoah University; Michael Dziak, accomplished telework speaker, author, and consultant; Bruce Holmes, telework program coordinator at Clayton University; and Dr. Helen Solomons, human resource consultant and president of Harrison Associates—all shared a conviction that managers often do not manage well.

Dziak and Davis agreed that many managers are products of MBA training through the 1980s that believed in an industrial management philosophy that held that if employees were at their workstation, they had to be working. Holmes agreed, mentioning his frustration that Clayton's managers are often presented with new MBO ideas but within 90 days slip back into the old way of doing things.

Dziak emphasized that while there is no "magic" in telework, "It does amplify pre-existing deficiencies in organizations." He concluded, therefore, that firms benefit from offering telecommuting because "telework is pushing the issue and becoming the catalyst to force managers to learn how to manage well."

FYI . . .

Executives at Faulkner Group believe that telework is not really just about saving money, but rather about more flexible working, a saving more difficult to quantify. What the firm considers one of the most important aspects of the eWork initiative has been the introduction of a more strategic and planned way of managing and ultimately a greater focus on target setting and reviewing.

Targets are set for the sales staff. They come in to the office once a week to discuss what they have done and put together the following week's plan. Faulkner has seen *greater discipline in management and operations* and *an increase in sales* as a result. The company believes that the full impact of the pilot cannot be measured but just knows that it is having a positive impact.

Competitive Advantage in Attraction of Employees

Offering employees the ability to telework also gives employers an important competitive advantage. In "Bridging the Gap: Information

Technology Skills for a New Millennium," the Information Technology Association of America rated telework as the number-one benefit for high-tech workers.[29] The 1999 Telework America National Telework Survey by Joanne H. Pratt Associates affirmed that 53 percent of the teleworkers interviewed indicated that working at home, at least part of their work week, would be "important" or even "extremely important" in their consideration of a new employer. [30]

FYI . . .

Telework has proven an asset for Nortel Network's recruitment and retention issues, especially when recruiting a specific hard-to-find skill. Often the candidate does not wish to relocate to a Nortel Networks site, and offering telework makes it possible for the firm to employ the candidate.

Increases in Employee Satisfaction, Resulting in Increased Employee Retention

---

FYI . . .

Willow CSN has had phenomenal success since its inception in 1997. "We strongly believe that the invested workforce is a motivated workforce," says Kathleen Bocek, vice president of people resources at Willow CSN. Today more than 1,600 Cyber Agent customer service representatives provide remote call-center services to household names such as AAA motor clubs, Alamo Rent A Car, Gap Inc., GE Financial, HSN (formerly Home Shopping Network), 1-800-FLOWERS.Com, Staples, SkyMall, and Office Depot. "As our clients begin to experience the superiority of our model in terms of return on investment, flexibility and quality, they inevitably send more calls to us," says CEO Asim Saber, who notes that the company handled 42 million minutes of calls for clients through March 2001, compared to 22 million minutes in the same period last year. Willow currently has a database of 5,500 applicants for the Cyber Agent training program. Their turnover is less than 10 percent, as opposed to a call-center industry standard of almost 68 percent. Able to draw from a pool of entrepreneurial-spirited candidates as well as the disabled who find it difficult if not impossible to commute to an office location, Mr. Saber's conviction is that "you can never go wrong if you treat people well."

What employees tell us they include in their benefits list, the list that makes their employer the employer of choice, include:

- Flexibility of work schedules
- Reduction in commute time and costs
- Casual dress, resulting in reduction of wardrobe expense
- Ability to work around family needs and with body's natural biorhythms
- Reduction in stress
- Reduction in auto insurance expense
- Increased job satisfaction due to increase of responsibility and trust
- More work accomplished in less time, due to fewer interruptions
- Expansion of job opportunities
- Opportunity for the "trailing spouse," to continue employment, enhancing family relations and financial issues
- Ability to work during temporary or permanent disabilities
- Even in the case of telework centers, telework often results in a reduction of lunch expense due to the ability to travel home for lunch

---

FYI . . .

Sherry Doggett at Health Alliance of Cincinnati recalls one teleworker for whom the firm's flexibility works extremely well. This employee has been with the firm for over six years, works 5–7 a.m., takes her children to school, returns to work 9 a.m.–11:30 a.m., picks up her kindergartener, works 1:30–3:30 p.m., leaves to pick up her older children from school, and then returns to her work at 8 p.m. until she is finished.

AT&T's 1997 telecommuter survey discovered that 36 percent of the employees would seek another work-at-home job if their employer decided to discontinue their work-at-home option.[31] Pacific Bell also studied the telecommuting issue and, in its 1999 report on telecommuting, determined that companies offering formal telework programs reduced their employee turnover by up to 30 percent.[32]

The *Journal of Accountancy*[33] offers a process by which to calculate your own firm's cost of employee turnover. Estimating total cost at 93–150 percent of an employee's annual salary, the minimum cost breaks down as 50 percent of the cost to the learning-curve loss, 33 percent to recruitment, and 10 percent to training. To figure your firm's turnover cost, multiply the number of employees lost annually due to work/life issues, multiplied by the average salary and then by 93 percent for the minimum loss or 150 percent for the maximum. These figures indicate your annual work/life turnover loss, or *the amount you could save* by retaining these same employees through telework and other flexible work options.

During our interviews, managers of telecommuters *without exception* listed recruitment and retention as the number-one or number-two reason for the institution and continuation of telework in their firms, with most prioritizing retention above recruitment. A significant majority stated emphatically that numerous valued employees would have left their firms had it not been for the telework option. Even executives who admitted some concerns about the accuracy of improved productivity from teleworking employees still affirmed that they needed to continue and even formalize the telecommute process, because if they did not they would lose good employees and could fail to recruit others.

Angela Schwers, vice president of human resources for Pearson Education talks about their 2,500 telecommuters (25 percent of their workforce): "Without telework, we definitely would have lost people. A lot of people are sticking around because of the telecommute program. We are seeing a little more loyalty because it's offered."

Another human resource executive emphasizes that his retail company cares so much about employees, their attitudes, and being an employer of choice that it conducts periodic work/life surveys of its employees. Survey results provide continuing input on creating the best place to work and continually enhancing employee satisfaction.

Emphasizing that it makes good business sense to acknowledge that people have lives and families, the retailer admits that offering work options is inexpensive and not totally unselfish. "We know," he explains, "that it results in more loyalty and less absenteeism."

Neil McLocklin, former head of BT Workstyle Consultancy Group, says that teleworking is his firm's "key to recruitment and retention." One of the reasons, he said, that BT premiered teleworking was that "people wanted to do it. The real drive," he states "is now about giving people flexibility as a weapon in the war for talent."

Reduction in Costs for Facility Expansion and New Real Estate

Reduction in facility costs is easily quantified, and examples abound of the savings possible. IBM, for example, saves $75 million per year by having 10,000 employees mobile, and has documented 40 percent to 60 percent reductions in real estate costs.[34] Florida's Departments of Environmental Protection, Highway Safety and Motor Vehicles, and Labor and Employment Security, combined, eliminated over 6,300 square feet of office space during one fiscal year. The Department of Labor and Employment Security closed its Cocoa Beach office as a result of telecommuting, saving the state approximately $56,000. The Department of Revenue has been able to cut by almost half the amount of office space needed for auditors in the Miami area.

FYI . . .

Washington State Department of Transportation has the lowest employee turnover of any state agency, largely due to the work options offered to DOT workers. Their telework program has seen a 400 percent increase in participants since its inception. Results of telework pilot program surveys indicate increased employee performance, enhanced job satisfaction, and increased recruitment and retention. Management also sees work options such as telework as an aid to increasing office capacity. One work group now uses staggered schedules and telework to accommodate five people in a space that originally held two. WSDOT's main building in Olympia, intended to house 450–500 people, presently accommodates 650 workers. More staff is being encouraged to combine work options with sharing workspace now that the building has reached the maximum occupancy.[35]

The state of Arizona offers some guidance on quantifying the benefits of telework. Guesstimating the potential for telework's reduction of leased office space requirements, they point out that the reduction depends on the space occupied by the employee, the rental cost for the floor area required, and the slight increase in space required for shared office space for telecommuters when they are in the office. Their computation includes an assumption of an average reduction of 130–140 square feet per remote user per year.

The math looks like this: The number of mobile workers × 135 sq.ft. × annual cost/square foot × .75 (assuming that one-fourth of the office space requirement remains intact for hoteling). The result is the potential annual reduction in rent due to telework and hoteling.

Reducing the need for more real estate space is not just a financial issue. In some areas there is simply no more land or office space available, or the change is so volatile that an employer must not depend on availability of space for its growth.

FYI . . .

Telework is a critical part of Washington Mutual's plan to become the nationally preferred low-cost mortgage provider. The telework policy has a direct effect on the bottom line, with the elimination of rental charges and cubicle occupancy costs for the teleworkers saving $166,000 each year. In addition, productivity is up. Because of a new incentive plan and the more efficient use of time that telework allows, the average production per appraiser increased 24 percent within a year.

Reduced Parking Requirements

This is an advantage realized by the employer, the employee, and the community at large, especially in downtown or midtown large company situations, where providing parking space requires reduction of green space or historic buildings and the expensive construction of additional parking garages. It may also alienate and anger nearby residential neighbors who lose parking space in front of their homes to area employees. Employees may often incur parking charges, and after-hours walks through these neighborhoods may be a safety issue. The employer may also incur an additional charge for expansion and maintenance of its own parking area.

One example of this issue and how it affected a number of groups was the expansion a few years back of a California newspaper's midtown office location. With no suitable nearby property available, company executives realized that in order to complete the facility's much needed expansion they would have to reduce their parking lot space by half. Employees' cars spilled over into nearby neighborhoods.

One angry resident, tired of not being allowed to park in front of her own home, took matters into her own hands. "She actually took 2×4s," explained a former newspaper employee, "and drove nails into them and set them on the ground in front of her curb. We got mad, so each day one of us would pull up in front of her house, get out of our car, remove the boards, and park there anyway."

The employer's solution was to provide bus and light rail passes for employees. The city's excellent light rail system, with park 'n' ride locations and well-thought-out connections to the area's bus stops and routes, stopped every 15 minutes at the newspaper's back door. The light rail purchase ($40/month value) was so popular that the pilot program was expanded permanently. They have now added telework to their commute alternative options.

FYI . . .

Air Touch Cellular has approximately 130 inbound call-center representatives working full time from home. Their telework program was launched in 1997, partly as a result of a real estate crunch. By freeing up these workstations and allowing employees to work from home they have alleviated tight employee parking and avoided an increase in real estate needs.[36]

Expansion of the Labor Pool

The expansion of the labor pool, an important component of recruitment, is another benefit of teleworking, not only because it makes possible the recruitment of those such as the disabled who were formerly unable to seek employment, but also because of the ever-increasing average age of our society's members and their resulting decrease in activity and "commutability." Telework also expands the labor pool to include job candidates geographically distant.

Dee Christensen, telework project manager for Washington State University, talks about this issue. "We love to do research," she explains of WSU. Affirming her conviction that "telework is a great economic development and recruitment tool," she shares that WSU is currently conducting a pilot project in three remote Washington State locations. She tells us of an employer that has hired 15 teleworkers from one small town and is planning on hiring a total of sixty teleworkers from the same locale.

"This is a great boon to the town," she says. "The employer is delighted, the wages are slightly lower and they saved quite a bit in real estate costs, too. From the over 200 applicants they picked the sixty best and felt they could have hired each one they interviewed."

In October 2002 the U.S. Department of Labor awarded a $1 million grant to the Boston, Massachusetts-based National Telecommuting Institute (NTI), for the operation of a 3-site national telework demonstration project. The grant's purpose is to increase telecommuting employment opportunities for people with disabilities.[37]

NTI began as the job placement division of Helping Hands, a nonprofit disability organization established in 1982. The division was re-organized and incorporated under the name National Telecommuting Institute in 1995. In 1997, NTI became the first virtual school ever accepted for candidacy accreditation status by the New England Association of Schools and Colleges. Working in partnership with employers who have agreed to "go virtual" NTI prepares qualified individuals with disabilities for work primarily as customer service representatives. Equipped with voice and computer connections, the institutes' clients provide service for customers of companies such as Sprint, 1-800-Flowers.com, AAA, Staples, QWest, MCI, The Gap, Home Shopping Network, Ticketmaster, Alamo Car Rental, Lens Express and the AT&T Language Line.[38]

Reduction of Nonproductive (Water-Cooler) Office Time

While some may say that water-cooler time is an informal learning ground, the fact is that a great chunk of a workday can be taken up by nonwork interaction. Though some of this interaction is to be expected and can even be good in moderation, its reduction is undoubtedly time effective. If you are not having face time with others, the quality of your communication with them— by phone, email, instant messaging, fax—

will tend to be much more scheduled, organized, on-task, and work oriented.

Expansion of Service Hours

Once telework has provided your firm the opportunity to employ or retain employees who relocate or already reside in other areas—East Coast U.S. employees with West Coast employers, for instance—the hours and even days available to your firm and your clients can now conveniently increase without requiring unusual work hours of your employees.

FYI . . .

The Frank Russell Company, whose motto is "employees first, clients second," has three times won Washington "CEO Magazine's" Best Place to Work award. Implementing telework was not that difficult, as their staff and clients were already scattered around the world. One executive, Frank Russell's manager of international assignments, works in Tacoma but reports to a supervisor based in London. She is responsible for transfers of staff from one country to another, including negotiating the terms, shipping belongings, and obtaining work permits. She works from home several times a month, usually on Fridays when the phone is quiet because it is already Saturday at offices in many other countries. "I can get more done in the same amount of time, and it's more relaxing," she says. "I take home work that involves reading, writing, creating spreadsheets, and answering emails."

The manager states that she is a more loyal employee because of the combination of benefits, flexibility, and trust her employer offers. "I've been here eleven years. Once in a while I wonder if I should look elsewhere, but the opportunity to flex my hours and work at home are part of the formula that always ends up on the Russell side."[39]

Improved Productivity

Examples abound that teleworking increases productivity. Evidence of this increase was offered as early as 1984, when Pacific Bell introduced their Los Angeles telework program to alleviate traffic congestion during the Olympics. Statistics indicated a 10–20 percent productivity increase.[40] ITAC's Telework America 2001 employer survey results concur. Over 70 percent (72.4%) reported that working at home slightly or greatly increased productivity; 19.5 percent reported that it remained the same; only 6.5 percent reported a slight productivity decrease since working at home.[41]

Another productivity testimonial comes from the Massachusetts Telecommuting Initiative. Created to study the impacts of telecommuting on 50 Massachusetts employers (300 respondents), this 1995 state Division of Energy Resources and Highway Department report stated that 87 percent of telecommuters, as well as 82.6 percent from a subsequent 1996 phone survey, reported improved productivity and overall work performance over the prior year. Of the supervisors, 100 percent reported improved or sustained productivity and 96.7 percent reported improved overall performance for telecommuters over the prior year.[42]

Telework also increases total production,[43] because teleworkers tend to work more hours and at times that are best suited to their lifestyles and body rhythms. Morning people often get the chance to work in the early morning, while night owls can work after dark if they wish. They also can use the time typically devoted to commuting to actually produce work.

FYI ..

Bruce Holmes at Clayton University shares an initial telework "problem" that actually had its plus side. The increased productivity of the teleworkers increased the burden on fellow workers. One woman who used to turn in one report on Tuesday, a second on Wednesday, and a third on Friday was now completing all three reports by Tuesday because she worked at home. It overburdened those who followed up. As a result, the university initiated its Ladder Program. Now, if Jane telecommutes on Monday, Bill, the follow-up, telecommutes on Tuesday—all because they are accomplishing so much more working from home!

Barbara Leitz, operations manager for Allina Metro Hospital Medical Transcription Services, also affirms that an important aspect of the success of a telework program, and in measuring that success, is the productivity of the employee who telecommutes. In this sense, medical transcription is a good fit for telecommuting because it requires specific deliverables. Medical transcription productivity is measured by minutes of dictation per hour.

For Allina's medical transcriptionists who telecommute, the time normally spent commuting to and from work can be used for working, and the production of each employee has increased. These employees who telecommute are also free from many distractions that occur in the office, thus adding to productivity. The increase in productivity is measured simply by comparing the number of lines completed per hour when telecommuting to the number of lines completed per hour when working in the office.

In 1998, 38 percent of the hospital's transcriptionists telecommuted full time and produced 46 percent of the total work volume. Allina's current work-at-home productivity increase over on-site staff is approximately 15 percent. Allina readily attributes productivity and production increases to more time actually working and less time commuting, doing other small projects in and around the office, and socializing with others in the office.

However, not until a few years in to the program did they notice the long-term personal benefits telework offered to employees. The hospital found that those medical transcriptionists who teleworked had high job satisfaction, increased loyalty to the company, and no intention of changing jobs. Not only did the hospitals experience better bottom-line production results and cost efficiency, but they saw increased employee satisfaction, which eventually translated to improved bottom-line results as well.

Reduction of Absenteeism and Tardiness

Absenteeism clearly decreases when employees telecommute. Telework America's 1999 survey quantifies the issue. They discovered that office employees are often absent because they have to meet family and personal obligations during the business day. Eighty percent of teleworkers indicated that they have had to take time during the normal workday for doctor or dentist appointments, while 34 percent have taken time to meet workpersons coming to their home (cable, phone, plumbing). Forty-nine percent have taken time for banking or legal affairs, car repair, family events, or household emergencies; while 72 percent of teleworkers with children take time off for school and after-school functions and 44 percent when a child is sick. A few are obligated to assist adults such as elderly parents by driving them to appointments or caring for them during illness.

Teleworkers reported an average of 45.3 occasions of absenteeism per year, equaling 165.1 hours, or about 22 working days. Only about one-third of these could be scheduled in advance.

In studying these numbers the survey points out that if teleworkers were to take a full day off to deal with personal and family needs, they would be absent from work fully 45 days. But because each occasion, except for caring for a sick family member, takes only 2–4 hours to complete, the teleworker has the balance of the day, that is, about one-half day per event, to work in the home office. Actually, the numbers are even more promising than that, as 54 percent of teleworkers indicate that they work the same or more hours on days that they work at home while managing personal and household matters that keep them out of the office.

The bottom line for employers? Based on the average salary reported by teleworkers combined with the average number of days absent on which teleworkers are able to work from home, the survey indicates that employers can save 63 percent of the cost of absenteeism per teleworking employee, or $2,086 per employee per year. Without teleworking, absenteeism would cost $3,313 per year per employee, assuming each employee takes one full day at a current salary/wage rate for each day managing needs associated with absenteeism.[44]

In regard to more long-term absenteeism—that caused by temporary disabilities—the U.S. Department of Labor Statistics reported 2.8 million injuries and illnesses in private industry workplaces during 2000 that resulted in lost workdays (from recuperation away from work or restricted duties at work, or both).[45]

In its eleventh annual "Unscheduled Absence Survey," human resource firm CCH, Inc., reported that employers ranked telecommuting the second most effective means for alleviating absenteeism, with 42 percent of those surveyed saying they offer the telework option at their firm.[46]

FYI . . .

Telecommuting has definitely worked for BT. According to Neil McClocklin, former head of the telecommunication giant's Workstyle Consultancy Group, "We have reduced our real estate by millions of pounds, we have increased the flexibility of our workforce, *we have 93% of our employees returning from maternity leave* (highest in the UK, with the next highest 80%), we have reduced travel by 20,000 miles each year."

Maximizing of Potential by Broadening of Responsibilities

Typically, the employees asking for and chosen for telework are your most self-directed, self-motivated employees. Thrown into the at-home-alone or work-from-afar situation, they are for the first time confronted with the need to fix their technical problems and make decisions on their own or to decide to contact the employer. This empowerment can be a very satisfying facet of telework for self-directed employees.

> **FYI . . .**
>
> Telework has been a boost to Washington Mutual's efforts to recruit real estate appraisers. Typically independent personalities, many of whom have been self-employed, appraisers have been difficult to bring on board. The autonomy of telework, without the expense and risk of owning their own business, has appealed to these much-needed appraisers, who otherwise might not have been eager to work for an institution.

Assistance in Compliance with ADA and Other Statutes

The Americans with Disabilities Act (ADA), protects U.S. employees who have a qualifying disability by requiring employers to reasonably accommodate the employees' disabilities, as long as it does not result in substantial hardship to the employer. The legal implications of this are discussed in depth in Chapter 3, "Keeping It On the Up and Up," but it's clear that telework offers an opportunity for an employer to comply with the requirement while also expanding their labor pool to the physically disabled, the agoraphobic, those in remote areas without a vehicle or access to a car, and the elderly who may be mentally competent but lack the physical stamina for a lengthy commute.

Some communities, in an effort to comply with the CAAA, have legislated employer efforts. Arizona's highly congested Maricopa County, for instance, requires that all employers with 50 or more workers at one site are required to reduce employee trips each year, submitting plans and data to show their compliance. The state of Arizona requires each of its agencies, boards, and commissions to have at least 15 percent of its employees in Maricopa County participating in telework.

> **FYI . . .**
>
> The Florida legislature established a telecommuting pilot program for its state employees in August of 1991. The state's Joint Legislative Information Technology Resource Committee recommended telework as a means to increase productivity, enhance work quality, and reduce costs. They also suggested it as a way to help recruit and retain personnel and increase accessibility to state employment, especially for individuals who have a disabling condition.[47]

Financial Incentives

Oregon's Office of Energy, in its 1995 plan for telework implementation, devised a cost comparison chart that contrasted the expenses involved in retaining on-site employees and telecommuting workers. This table, also available on their site, www.energy.state.or.us /telework, is reproduced below. While the figures are outdated and may not be accurate for a particular region, it does clarify that the cost to an employer of maintaining an in-house worker is greater than that of maintaining a teleworker.[48]

Reduction of traffic and introduction of telework is not only an air quality ozone issue. Numerous states, as well as the federal government, are not only penalizing noncompliant areas with reduction or removal of road construction financial assistance, but are also rewarding firms who keep their workers off the roads.

Tax and other financial incentives are now being offered at various government levels in growing numbers to employers and even to employees for the introduction of telework and other alternative-commute options.

As telework's expansion continues, the legislation evolves. What is described in this chapter as proposed or pending may or may not become legislation before this book is on the shelves. Other incentives may be introduced and passed. The discussion does provide a good overview, however, of the political and legal support for the telework issue. You will want to take a look at your state or region's legislative Web site or keep in touch with your legislators to encourage telework tax incentives and other rewards and to keep abreast of the changes in

Cost-Benefit Analysis of Telework vs. On Site

	On-Site	Teleworker
One-Time-Only Expenses		
Workstation	$3,891	$4,577
Software	$450	$600
Furnishings	$4,950	$2,475
Other Equipment	Overhead	$750
Telephone Equipment	$200	$150
Extension Installation	$0	$240
Annual Expenses		
Facility Rental	$2,100	$1,050
Supplies	$110	$100
Phone Maintenance	Included in facility	$300
Fee for Off-premise Extension	$0	$480
Total	$9,491 + $2,220 per year	$8,792 + $1,940 per year

legislated rewards. Your best U.S. starting point is the Library of Congress Web site http:\\www.thomas.loc.gov.

The state of Virginia may well have the most far-reaching telework legislation in the United States, if not globally. Signed into law by then-governor Jim Gilmore, Telework!VA is a public/private telework partnership for businesses located in the northern part of the state. Launched as part of Governor Gilmore's Innovative Progress Initiatives and receiving continued support from the current governor Mark Warner, Telework!VA provides financial incentives for businesses to start or expand a formal telework program, up to $35,000 over two years! This new capital match program, administered through the Department of Rail and Public Transportation by the Metropolitan Washington Council of Governments, provides monetary incentives, technical assistance, and training for telework from both home and telework centers.[49]

Frank Wolf, Virginia's representative in the U.S. Congress, introduced House bill 1012, the Telework Tax Incentive Act, March 13, 2001. Pennsylvania Senator Rick Santorum simultaneously introduced its Senate counterpart, S.521. The legislation, if approved, would provide a $500 tax credit for purchase and installation of electronic equipment for a teleworker's home office and could be credited to either employee or employer, depending on who absorbs the expense. Both bills are currently in committee.[50]

Another terrific state telework program is Connecticut's Telecommute CT! While it does not offer any direct monetary rewards, we have included this program under financial benefits because the program's free services constitute a considerable savings to Connecticut employers. For more information peruse their Web site at http://www.telecommutect.com.[51]

Arizona's Governor Janet Napolitano has partnered with the Phoenix-area Valley Metro, the former Regional Public Transportation Authority. The program, Telework Partnership, like Telecommute CT, does not offer immediate financial reimbursements or grants but does provide free implementation and management assistance. Additionally, the state's Project Adopt provides refurbished home-office equipment free of charge to qualifying firms whose employees wish to telework. Applications to receive equipment as well as contact information should your firm wish to donate equipment is available at Valley Metro's site, http://www.valleymetro.org/Rideshare/Telework/project_adopt.htm.[52]

May 11, 2000, was a landmark day for the state of Maryland, when its Parris Glendening became the first governor to sign into law state funding that employers were to pass on to employees who give up a parking spot at work. It is also the first U.S. law that extends tax credits to not-for-profit firms such as hospitals and schools, when they pay for employee transit or "reward for not driving" incentives.[53]

Minnesota Representative Andrew Westerberg has been the chief author of two important telework bills. The first, still in committee, was introduced as HF 1513 and would provide for public service announcements encouraging telecommuting and for monetary incentives to firms that allow their employees to telework. This legislation recommends that the Departments of Public Safety and Transportation, in consultation with the U.S. Weather Service, authorize the release of public service announcements that a telecommuting day is being called no later than 6 a.m. or a predetermined beginning of morning drive time.

The announcements would encourage employers to call for their telecommuting checklist, discuss telework benefits, describe the telecommuting day concept, and direct individuals to a Web site that would offer additional information. A proposed pilot project included in this bill would appropriate some general fund money to provide grants to employers for equipment and other expenses incurred when offering telework to employees. The funds, limited to 10 employers, $1,000 maximum each, could be used to set up a new "teleworksite" for purposes such as:

- Telephone or cable installation or improvement
- E-mail or Internet service-provider fees
- Telephone, cellular, or wireless services[54]

Westerberg's most recent legislation, introduced March 8, 2001, proposed an initial $100 per employee tax credit for the charges incurred in setting up at-home telework, to be followed by a $50 per month tax credit for each month the employee continues to work at home. Passage of this bill does not look promising, although it may be reintroduced.

New Jersey Assembly member Michael Patrick Carroll introduced a state telework tax credit bill, No. 3436, to the state legislature April 19, 2001. The bill has been referred to the State's Assembly, Commerce, Tourism, Gaming and Military and Veterans' Affairs Committee. The law would provide corporation business tax and gross income tax credits for employers who allow their employees to telecommute. Employers would earn a credit equal to 1 percent of the portion of wages and salaries paid to employees for the part of the workweek that they regularly telecommute.[55]

U.S. Senator Rick Santorum, Pennsylania's representative and author of the 1999 National Telecommuting and Air Quality Act, announced on July 14, 2000, that the city of Philadelphia was to receive $250,000 to continue its telecommuting initiative. This bill also provides equal funds to Houston, Chicago, Los Angeles, and Washington, D.C.[56]

The Oregon Office ofEnergy offers a 35 percent state tax credit and low-interest loans for telecommuting equipment—computers, fax machines, modems, phones, printers, software, copiers, and the like. In order to qualify, employees must work at home or at a satellite office or telework center near home, to reduce vehicle miles traveled for the work commute a minimum of 45 days per year. Projects that reduce business-related employee travel by at least 25 percent also qualify.

North Dakota House Bill 1035 became law in March of 2001 and offers substantial monetary incentives to state agencies and their individual teleworkers. It stipulates that the proposal [reimbursement request] must contain a comparison of the estimated annual costs of locating the employee away from a central office setting within the agency to the estimated annual costs of locating the employee in a central office setting within the agency.

A state agency head who submits a proposal that is approved by the suggestion incentive committee and implemented by the state agency shall compare the actual costs directly relating to the telecommuting program for the twelve-month period, beginning with the month the proposed change is instituted to the estimated costs if the program would not have been implemented. The state agency is entitled to receive 10 percent of any savings identified in the report as a resulting from implementing the telecommuting program for the twelve-month period up to a maximum of $2,000.

The state employee who is located away from a central office setting of the agency is entitled to receive 20 percent of any savings identified in the report up to a maximum of $2,000.

Reduced Business Disruptions Due to Natural Disaster, Bad Weather, Power Outages, Transit Strikes, and Other Unforeseen Events

Telework consultant Jack Heacock, board member and former president of ITAC, discusses telework's value in response to the 2001 World Trade Center terrorist attacks: "We (U.S. especially) can use technology to make better use of our abundant geography and reduce the number of lucrative targets for those wishing us harm. A sad commentary on mankind—but we do have the means to better protect and defend ourselves. Widespread telework and remote work strategies can go a long ways towards reducing threats!"

For the sake of your company's survivability in time of disaster, your employees need to avoid banding together. The fewer employees in one location, that is, the greater the number of places from which your firm and its staff members can accomplish work tasks, the better the chances your organization will survive catastrophe.

Another transportation benefit of teleworking can clearly be seen in the area of Vancouver, British Columbia, where unsuccessful negotiations between Coast Mountain Bus Company and the Canadian Auto Workers Company shut down mass transportation for several months, increasing rush hour volume by 80,000 cars. The area's 70,000+ telecommuters helped ease the problem, however.[57] One local employer, whose 10 employees have been telecommuting since well before the transit strike, put it this way: "Because of telework the transit strike was a non-issue for our firm."

Canadian Telework Association's "Telework Guys" point out the problems created by eastern North America's great ice storm of 1998 and the snowstorms of 2000. They remind us that the effects included power outages for millions of residents and workers. In some cases, tens of thousands of federal workers were prevented from getting to work, some for days. However, they recall, telework allowed thousands to continue working. Most homes either were not cut off or had intermittent power while their office buildings were unreachable.[58] More on this issue can be found in Chapter 7, "Preparing for Disaster," where we discuss contingency telework as a response to emergency situations.

FYI . . .

Neil McClocklin, former head of British Telecommunication's Work-style Consultancy, raved about his firm's ability to respond to natural disaster, due to its teleworking arrangements. BT, one of the world's leading providers of telecommunications services and one of the largest private sector companies in Europe, offers local, long distance, and international telecommunications services, mobile communications, Internet services, and IT solutions. BT serves 28 million exchange lines and more than 7 million mobile customers in the UK, as well as providing network services to other licensed operators. Its presence worldwide includes operations and joint ventures in countries such as France, Spain, Japan, Germany, New Zealand, and Latin America. McClocklin explains his company's ability to respond to disaster this way: "In the UK we seem to have 'travel disasters' of some sort every month—rail crashes, petrol boycotts, underground strikes. With two thirds of our people able to work from home this barely affects us."

Reduction in Health and Life Insurance Costs

More than 142 million Americans—75 percent of the nation's population living in counties with ozone monitors—were breathing unhealthy amounts of ozone air pollution (smog), in the third straight year in which the toxic pollutant reached fully half of the American public, according to the American Lung Association's State of the Air 2002 report. Of those living in the 678 counties monitoring ozone, the vast majority of the most vulnerable lived in the nearly 400 counties receiving an "F," including nearly three-quarters of the seniors and more than 70 percent of children who had an asthma attack in the last year. The findings are compounded by the reality that, because of a series of legal and management delays, states are relying on weak federal clean air standards in place since 1979.

Among those metropolitan areas scoring "F," the 10 most ozone-polluted areas are Los Angeles-Riverside-Orange County, CA; Bakersfield, CA; Fresno, CA; Visalia-Tulare-Porterville, CA; Houston-Galveston-Brazoria, TX; Atlanta, GA; Merced, CA; Knoxville, TN; Charlotte-Gastonia-Rock Hill, NC-SC; and Sacramento-Yolo, CA.[59]

Work-at-home employees can help keep themselves well by avoiding the communicable diseases rampant in a crowded workplace setting. There's another side to that benefit coin as well. The fact that teleworkers work at home offices when not in tiptop shape—for instance, with just a bad cold—keeps them from spreading their germs to others and still keeps the work schedule intact.

There's even the possibility of saving lives. Videoconference vendors with whom we spoke talked about 40–400 percent increases in the number of calls for their services in the aftermath of September 11, 2001, as corporate representatives and their employees feared air travel. Indeed, the elimination of the need to leave home to meet with others could save your life and the life of your teleworking employee.

The fewer health and life insurance benefit reimbursements and services provided to your employees, the less need your insurer has to increase your rates.

FYI...

An interesting aside to this issue, and one that can also significantly impact absenteeism as well as the cost of health benefits, is the advent of telemedicine. With telecommunications technology that has created the telemedicine workstation, doctors can provide vital, cost-effective, and confidential medical services to virtually any location, rural or urban, national or international. Patients can now benefit from the latest knowledge, technology, and treatment while remaining under the care of their hometown health care provider.

By providing specialty clinical consultative services via telemedicine, health care providers can improve access to medical care for patients residing in rural regions of medically underserved communities.

There are two types of telemedicine workstations. The *store-and-forward* variety allows the user to asynchronously transfer files (images, video or audio clips, medical records, etc.) from one location to another without the use of live, interactive audio and video. Store-and-forward workstations are generally used for radiology consults and medical consultations that do not require interaction between a patient and a physician. *Interactive* telemedicine workstations allow the user to interact with the remotely located patient by using live audio and/or video technologies. Most interactive workstations provide more than just videoconferencing by integrating a multimedia electronic patient record into the telemedicine platform. A multimedia patient record permits the reviewing physician to review information from current or previous encounters at the time of the patient interaction. It also permits the reviewing physician to store information from the encounter for later review.[60]

Reduction in Workers' Compensation Insurance Costs

The telework response to the World Trade Center and Pentagon disasters, for instance, not only reduces the threat but may be close to a necessity for those employers who need to continue workers' compensation insurance but now house over 100 employees in the same location.

In a January 9, 2002 edition of the *Wall Street Journal,* reporters Christopher Oster and Michael Schroeder passed along Standard & Poor's reported information that workers' compensation insurance rates are expected to increase as much as 50 percent nationwide, even causing some insurers to stop offering coverage to large companies.

Clarifying that Standard & Poor estimates a $4 billion loss to insurance carriers, the *Journal* article explains that brokers and agents are now required by most insurers to list any location with more than 100 employees; because workers' compensation insurers are, in most states, the only insurers not allowed to exclude terrorism from coverage, their response, in order to survive, may well be to deny insurance to firms housing 50–100 or more employees in one location.[61]

Safer Communities

While it seems obvious that if numerous neighborhood residents are visibly at home vandals and thieves will invade elsewhere, it is also true that your children and your employees' children, with a parent in attendance, will be less likely than their latchkey peers to stray into unsafe or illegal activities.

Community Economic Revival and Employment and Population Stability

While a large metropolitan area is impacted by a decrease in traffic congestion and smog when its firms' suburban employees telework, the smaller outlying communities can also realize enormous benefits from this stay-at-home practice. Teleworkers contribute to the revitalization of their outlying home communities.

A well-placed telework or telecommunity center can allow residents to retain or secure a position with a firm in a metropolitan or inconveniently located area while continuing to work in close proximity to their rural homes. This would tend to retain retail, service, and food vendor revenue in the smaller struggling community.

Economically struggling former manufacturing areas or seasonal resort areas might also be able to retain or attract numerous year-round residents and some of the former tax base lost to high-tech or service industry areas.

Telecommuting can be a very attractive venture for cold-climate locales such as the Mid-Atlantic and Northeast areas, continually losing population and their tax base to the high-tech Northwest or warm southern regions of the United States, as well as esthetically attractive resort communities who need to retain year-round residents. The answer may lie in luring residents who can work for anyone from anywhere.

Colorado ski communities such as Steamboat Springs and Telluride actively seek to attract professional telecommuters to their communities. By design, high-paid professionals will live in the towns and communities. The towns do not have to create industrial infrastructure or deal with industrial pollutants, and the areas maintain a highly educated, well-paid populace. Creating these communities requires providing telecommuters with access to a commercial airport, overnight mail services, and computer-based digital switching for telephones.[62]

PUTTING IT ALL TOGETHER

To conclude our look at the positive impact of telework for employers, let's go back to the question "What's so great about telework?" and see what other firms have to say:

The majority of Clayton University teleworkers are in intelligence productivity. The school has seen a 15–25 percent productivity increase since telework started. Telework has also helped with retention. There is a feeling of trust, which builds loyalty. Bruce Holmes explains that the most important aspect of teleworking has been its impact on employees' home life—breakfasting with families, meeting the children when they get home from school. Teleworkers can start work at 4 a.m., take a couple of hours off when the kids are at home, whatever they wish.

Pasona, Inc., explains that one major benefit of its telework initiative is that it has allowed people who are unable or uninterested in traditional temporary staffing work styles to register for work. Access to a new pool of potential workers is naturally a boon for Pasona. The fact that Pasona offers a menu of choices places the firm in a better position to attract the best workers. The agency's Home Office Network is placing it in the lead, at least domestically, in the home-based/off-site temporary staffing market.

Sopheon Resource Network's use of telework has contributed to improved employee morale and made flexible work arrangements an employee benefit and a competitive advantage. Productivity and retention seem to be the same as for in-house employees, however. The teleworkers themselves are very satisfied with the personal benefits of the program. Teleworking has allowed several employees to stay with Sopheon although relocating, and reduced the two-hour commute of several others. Some teleworkers contend that there are fewer distractions when teleworking.

Over 82 percent of the state of Florida's telecommuters reported that their productivity increased; 41 percent of their supervisors reported an increase in productivity and work quality, while over half perceived no change.[63]

At Health Alliance of Cincinnati, telework is a big success, primarily due to their increased ability to recruit and retain employees.

At Faulkner Group, the belief is that the "advantages are so obvious that the pilot only went to underline them." The company believes that it is getting more out of people by allowing them to work at home, people are not spending hours driving to and from work, and they are probably spending that additional time working. Key benefits include being able to offer flexibility to staff and helping to keep good staff. Telework also saves on time and money for advertising and interviewing, as well as saving office space.

At Surrey County Council, telecommuting has been very beneficial. The people who opt to do it like it very much. So far the council has been able to recover significant capital from the release of unwanted premises and expects to realize considerable savings in future property costs.

For InterWorks, teleworking is a success story. The philosophy of the company and its business revolves around telework. It has helped them recruit and retain. Teleworkers appreciate the more autonomous situation and that creates motivation. The increased responsibility also brings more professional commitment from the telecommuters. As General Manager Teresa Antunes says, it "makes them believers." She emphasizes that the company saves money by renting space that their own workers used to occupy and by productivity increases as workers spend less time in traffic and more time at work.

At KCTS Television, telework is a recruitment and productivity success. Their turnover is 3 percent, compared to an industry standard of 9–14 percent. Their at-home workers rave about telework's ability to assist them balance their job and family lives, reducing their use of sick time and increasing productivity, as they are able to better concentrate at home.[64]

Deutsche Telekom's pilot program was a complete success, with 97 percent of the telecommuters wishing to continue their telecommuting, 64 percent feeling they achieved more independence, 55 percent saying they acquired new skills, and 75 percent saying it improved their working conditions. The firm's human resource management determined that teleworking encouraged a management culture of trust, led to increased employee satisfaction, and helped to boost their competitiveness and that its continuation would secure jobs.[65]

The U.S. government's Office of Personnel Management reports resounding success with the federal "flexiplace" telework program. In its May 2001 study, both managers and employees mentioned productivity.

Most employees believed that productivity has increased as a result of their teleworking. They attributed that increase most often to having uninterrupted time to read and think, and many of them planned their work accordingly. Some of the supervisors also reported productivity improvement, while the majority reported no loss in productivity.

Almost all interviewed employees said that they felt more relaxed and less tense as a result of not having to commute one or two days a week. Most said that having a break from rush-hour traffic had made a significant impact on reducing their tension levels. Many supervisors also mentioned that teleworking employees seemed less "wired" and often improved their relationships within the office because of their more relaxed attitude.

The employees all appreciated the commuting time they saved. Avoiding the commute gave them extra time to be with their families, run errands, or go to doctor's appointments and made a significant difference in their quality of life.

Most of the employees reported that their electronic access to email and information was the same from home or the telecenter as it was from the office. Some had to purchase their own equipment or use excess computers, others had to pay for phone lines, but all felt that whatever they invested was worth the trade-off. One of the managers stated her conviction that anything the agency spent on computer equipment was worth the productivity and well-being gains for the teleworkers. She affirmed that she supplied identical equipment to her teleworking employees.

Both employees and supervisors said that they had to work harder to maintain relationships. Some employees had to cajole coworkers into calling them at home, because the coworkers' tendency was to hold work until they got back into the office. Some supervisors reported that they had to be especially aware of including teleworkers by phone when they had meetings in the office. Some employees said it required more effort to keep in communication with coworkers, so they made it a point to catch up when they were in the office. All reported some difficulty, but nothing that could not be solved by paying attention to it.[66]

Chapter 1 answered the question asked of our contributing managers: "How and why did your telework start?" The more important question, of course, is "Did it succeed?" In numerous FYI's throughout this story we've focused on specific success stories. Here are several others:

At InterWorks there are plenty of successes. "But," states Teresa Antunes, "there is a particular case I would like to share: that of Lina R., who was a technician for the marketing area of a multinational in the pharmacy industry."

On May 2000 another company bought the company where she worked, and a general feeling of unsettlement permeated the company. Her superiors always regarded Lina as a devoted collaborator, professional and creative, but from that moment on, she started to lose interest and began to consider an alternative. She chose to become a teleworker after a long interview with InterWorks.

Lina initiated her activity as a teleworker extremely afraid, mostly because she was not certain of what the future would bring her; at the same time, she was extremely willing to acquire new knowledge and commit deeply to the post she was about to occupy. Lina occupies the post of Webmaster of the sites of InterWorks and started working from her home without any previous experience in this area. All the information concerning the company and her role was given to her. She was advised of all the difficulties that could arise because she worked at home.

"We advised Lina to use all the necessary means to avoid foreseeable problems, namely to practice some sport, to have a break each two hours, to avoid exceeding five–six hours of work, to have lunch with friends or colleagues, to eat breakfast out every day (making her dress for going out) and to do a weekly plan of work and fulfill it. Lina followed the directives, participated in training courses for Webmasters and did not come across any problems in the performance of her professional activity. On the contrary, she started to enjoy a quieter life with more time available to her friends, and her motivation in her work reached its peak. Lina is now responsible for the contents and changes in the design of telecentro.pt and the telecentro.org, assuming some translations of the contents. If you could talk to Lina you would tell for sure that the telework has changed her life in terms of a personal and professional fulfillment."

Pearson Education's first teleworker is still working from home full time and is one of their most productive employees. Another editor works diligently full time from Texas (Pearson is in New Jersey).

Neil McLocklin of BT enthused: "We have thousands of success stories. I guess key is the voluntary basis of our programme, backed up by a much higher level of service offered to telecommuters than other staff (e.g., technical support, IT fault repair, home furniture, etc.)."

The U.S. Office of Personnel Management offers several federal employee success stories. Here are three:

1. Two information technology specialists, GS 13–14, with the National Agricultural Statistics Service (NASS) have been teleworking one day a week for the past three years, one from home, one from a telecaster. NASS conducts hundreds of surveys and prepares reports covering virtually every facet of U.S. agriculture. The biggest problem is in attracting and retaining a knowledgeable staff. The work they do is at the cutting edge of computer technology, and the competition from the private sector is fierce. A supervisor said that he jumped at the chance to permit employees to telework, because he believes that it is a tool for retaining his excellent staff at a time when salaries are not competitive. He permits his staff to telework one day a week, either from home or a telecenter. Tuesdays are set aside for all employees to be in the office. Because of the nature of their work, his employees already have the latest computer equipment in their homes, so their only direct cost is to install and pay for an additional phone line. He sees no downside to telework. There have been no problems within the staff or with the customers. Service is the same whether the specialist works from the office or from another location. Most important, his staff is happier. Some of them live 40 or 50 miles from the office, and avoiding that commute is a significant improvement in their workweek.
2. A contract specialist (GS-12) for a regional office of the General Services Administration (GSA) has worked two days per week for 11½ years from a telecenter near her home. Contract specialists

spend the majority of their time negotiating contracts with furniture manufacturers for the Federal Supply Schedule. Each journey-level specialist works independently with the vendors to negotiate the best possible price for the government, and then follows the contract over its life span (generally five years). When the employee initially requested permission to work two days a week from a telecenter near her home, the supervisor reported that she was uncomfortable with the request. The employee was a high performer, who could be counted on to skillfully handle special projects. She also had information technology skills that she used to help others in the office.

However, the supervisor decided that her initial reaction was unfair to the employee, who wanted to avoid her time-consuming, 65-mile commute to the office. Because the supervisor believed that the potential benefits to the employee (reducing stress, allowing for more time with her family, reducing traffic in her community) outweighed her initial misgivings, she approved a formal agreement to permit the employee to work on Tuesdays and Thursdays from a telecenter located ten minutes from her home.

The supervisor reported that her misgivings were unfounded. There were short-lived start-up problems to enable the employee to seamlessly access email and the office databases, but once that was accomplished, the change has gone smoothly. Always accessible, the employee uses voice mail at both locations to let callers know exactly how to reach her. Because she is on a flexible work schedule, she emails her supervisor upon her arrival at the telecenter to let her know her schedule for the day. When there are meetings scheduled on the telework days, the employee either conferences in by phone or adjusts her schedule so she can be there in person.

In addition to the personal benefits to the employee, the supervisor reported organizational benefits as well. The employee is less stressed on the days that she is in the office because she has had a day off from her commute. She is more upbeat, and her attitude positively influences others in the office. The two days at the telecenter allow the employee more uninterrupted time to think about projects, and the supervisor reported making assignments to take advantage of that extra concentration time.

3. A human resources specialist, GS-13, with the Office of Personnel Management has worked full time from home for three years. The employee works in one of several field divisions that evaluate the operation of personnel management programs in federal agencies and conduct nationwide studies of human resources policies and programs. Although the work involves ad hoc teams of evaluators

that conduct on-site reviews at the various agency field or head-quarters locations, they conduct much of the planning and follow-up work by phone or email. The division has a staff of 20, mostly in one office location. However, the telecommuting employee's duty station is in a different city.

Because his predecessor approved the arrangement, the supervisor was not involved in the decision to permit the employee to telework full time from his home. However, the current supervisor is very pleased with the arrangement. Not only does it save the cost of leasing office space in the employee's high-cost duty station, but having an employee at a remote duty station avoids the travel costs associated with sending an employee to that area to conduct on-site work. That the employee works from his home is transparent to the division staff. He is always available, responsive, and particularly sensitive to keeping others informed when he will be away from his home office. The supervisor reported no downside to the arrangement, attributing its success to the employee, his senior status as an evaluator, and his excellent work habits. The supervisor said that such an arrangement would be problematic with someone who was not at the full journey-level, without the experience, discipline, and independence that the current employee brings to the job.[67]

Art & Logic, Inc. had begun its telework program with the intent not to extend beyond North America. One employee, however, a U.S. resident, decided when his German wife became pregnant that it would be important for them to live near her family in Germany. He has scheduled his work time so his hours coincide with the Glendale, California, home office hours. With his email and phone set up there is no way to tell he is not local.

NOTES

1. Thomas Stewart, "Shortage of Executives Starts 'War for Talent,'" *Financial Times,* London edition, February 1, 2000, p. 8.

2. Mark Parkinson, "Flexible Workforce and the Role of the Personnel Manager," *Facilities* 14 (12/13), 1996, pp. 45–46.

3. Jack Nilles, Jala International, Inc. [database online 4 April 2001], http://www.jala.com/definitions.htm.

4. Peter Johnston and Maarten Botterman, "Status Report on European Telework, New Methods of Work 1999," European Telework Online [database online Telework99.doc, August 1999] http://www.eto.org.uk.

5. eWork 2000, "Status Report on New Ways to Work in the Information Society." The range of telework penetration across European countries is enormous, with Spain finding itself at the tail end with 2.8 percent of the employees

working as teleworkers and Finland at the top with almost 17 percent teleworkers. Germany finds itself in the European midfield and exactly at the European average. The number of 1999 teleworkers by country is as follows:

- Ireland, 61,000
- Denmark, 280,600
- Finland, 355,000
- Spain, 357,000
- Sweden, 594,000
- France, 635,000
- Italy, 720,000
- Netherlands, 1,044,000
- England, 2,027,000

From these 9 million teleworkers, 2.9 million are regular home-based teleworkers, 3 million are occasional ones, another 2.3 million belong to the group of mobile teleworkers, and 1.4 million are self-employed. ETO also reported that while two-thirds of European firms with 500+ employees already practice telework, only 12 percent of firms with 10 or fewer employees offered a telework option.

6. Leif Limkilde Bloch, National Reports Denmark Euro-Telework [database online, July 2000], English translation at http://www.telework-mirti. org/dbdocs/national.doc , p. 9.

7. Noel Treacy, "Address at the Launch of Telework Ireland's Teleworking Manuals and the Relaunch of Their Website, at Buswell's Hotel," Telework Ireland [database online, May 25, 2000], www.telework.ie.

8. Canadian Telework Association [database online, 2003] http://www.ivc. ca/studies/Euripean.html.

9. Peter Johnston and John Nolan, "eWork2000: Status Report on New Ways to Work in the Information Society," September 2000, p. 68.

10. As of April 1997, the 15 and under population stood at 19.52 million, 10 million male, the lowest on record and the tenth consecutive drop, with the over 65 population accounting for 15.4 percent.

11. Wendy Spinks, "Telework in Japan: A Status Report," presented at Telecommute '97 in Orlando, Florida, November 2, 1997.

12. Japan Institute of Labour, "IBM Japan Increase Number of Employees Working From Home," Japan Labor Bulletin, May 2002.

13. Nippon Keidanren, "Japan Business Federation's Emergency Employment Measures Program" [database online October 23, 2002] http://www. keidanren.or.jp/english/policy/2002/066.html.

14. Ibid.

15. Jack Heacock, presenter and ITAC President, 1999 ITAC Awards Luncheon, Sixth Annual International Conference, "Telework: A Virtual Revolution," Seattle WA, October 5, 1999. The AFMC pilot test of telecommuting was integral to the development and approval of Air Force Instruction 36-8002, *Telecommuting Guidelines for Air Force Reservists and Their Supervisors*, initially published June 1, 1998 (see appendix B). This regulation allows assigned reservists to work in an official capacity away from the official duty location in either active duty or inactive duty status. Together, the military supervisor and the reservist agree on the telecommuting arrangement required to complete a specific project or task and then prepare a contract to ensure the work performed by the reservist is completed in a safe and effective environment. In the past,

before telecommuting, reservists typically performed duty over consecutive days or weeks to lessen the cost of travel to their military unit.

16. Donahue Institute, University of Massachusetts, "Summary Report of Findings for the Massachusetts Telecommuting Initiative."

17. Florida Department of Management Services, "Review of the State Employee Telecommuting Program," State of Florida [database online, December 1997], http://www.eog.state.fl.us/dms/hrm/telecom/97telerp.html.

18. Washington State University Cooperative Extension Energy Program, in collaboration with Commuter Challenge, "Telework Resource Kit" case study, April 1999.

19. Ibid.

20. Ibid.

21. Ibid.

22. Ibid.

23. NEPI, December 1999. NOx, oxides of nitrogen, is the sum of nitrogen oxide and nitrogen dioxide. VOC, or volcanic organic compounds, generally refers to gaseous, non-methane organic compounds with vapor pressure.

24. DOE report, "Energy and Emissions Consequences of Telecommuting," U.S. Dept. of Energy [database online], www.energy.gov., p. 27.

25. *USA Today*, November 1999, cover story.

26. K.T. Analytics, Inc., and the Victoria Transport Policy Institute, May 1997. These estimates are based on the following components:

- Direct User Costs—incurred by individual users and paid directly from their personal resources. Range is 34–44 cents per vehicle mile.
- Public Infrastructure Costs—include expenditures of governmental highway and public works departments and government expenditures on behalf of drivers incurred for functions such as traffic police and cost of court and correctional agencies that can be related to automobile use. These costs are 2–3.5 cents per vehicle miles, and are usually recovered through road user charges like gas and tire taxes, tolls, parking revenues, and sales and property taxes.
- Private Parking Costs—include the costs of parking at trip destinations and cost of residential facilities. These costs range from 3 to 5 cents per vehicle mile. Automobile users do not pay these costs directly; rather, they are recovered by the private sector through increased costs of goods and services, lower wages, and other means.
- Congestion Costs—include costs due to congestion in terms of incremental delays and incremental vehicle operating costs caused by congestion. These costs are collectively borne by the users as a group, and range from 2 to 15 cents per vehicle mile depending on the level of congestion.
- External Accident Costs—include costs incurred by others and not paid by the responsible party, including costs paid in excess of insurance payments, cost paid on behalf of uninsured motorists, costs of pain and suffering, and cost to society of lost productivity due to injuries and fatalities suffered by non-responsible parties. These costs range from 1 to 6 cents per VMT.
- Pollution Costs—include costs of health and other damages to people and other entities, including loss of productivity, pain, and suffering and damages to habitat, due to ground-level mobile source air pollution; economic and health costs of global warming due to greenhouse effects; cost of noise pollution; and other environmental costs (water pollution, waste, etc.). These indirect costs, which range from 2 to 11 cents per VMT, are borne by society at large and are unpaid by the driver.

27. The annual Smart Moves campaign was initiated by Oil Smart in 1990 by a group of concerned citizens in the greater Seattle area, in response to the Persian Gulf Crisis. The original intent, to reduce dependency on foreign oil, provided a focus on reducing vehicular use, especially SOVs (single occupancy vehicles.) The Smart Moves theme for 2001 centered on a magical theme "Making Driving Alone Disappear." The challenge was to use a commute alternative at least once during the month of April. Six counties participated statewide, with over 12,000 participants. Executives were asked to take the challenge, and their names were featured in full-page thank-you ads in local papers around the state. There were also children's contest and radio campaigns featuring prizes for trivia questions, live interviews, and live TV stories.

28. U.S. Newswire, "Traffic Congestion Threatens State's Economy, Quality of Life," April 3, 2001.

29. Harris N. Miller, President ITAA [database online, June 21, 2000], http://www.itaa.org/workforce/events/wfwc1.ppt.

30. Joanne Pratt for the International Telework Association and Council, "1999 Telework America National Telework Survey, Cost/Benefits of Teleworking to Manage Work/Life Responsibilities," October 1999, ITAC, p. 9, [database online], http://www.telecommute.org/twa/twa1999/twa_research_exec_summary.doc.

31. June Langhoff, "The Telecommuter's Advisor: Real World Solutions for Remote Workers," (Newport RI, Aegis Publishing Group, 1999), p. 21.

32. Pacific Bell, "Telecommuting 99–Where We Are" [database online], http://www.pacbell.com/Remoteaccess/0,1217,00.html.

33. Arlene Johnson, "The Business Case for Work-Family Programs," *Journal of Accountancy*, August 1995.

34. Glenn Lovelace, "Telework: A Source of Strategic and Competitive Advantage for Your State," July 10, 2000, p. 5.

35. Washington State University Cooperative Extension and Commuter Challenge, "Telework Resource Kit."

36. Ibid.

37. U.S. Department of Labor, "Secretary of Labor Announces $14 million in Grants to Support New Freedom Initiative [database online October 3, 2002], http://www.dol.gov/opa/media/press/odep/ODEP2002571.htm.

38. National Telecommuting Institute, Inc. [database online], http://www.nticentral.org/info.page1.htm.

39. Washington State University cooperative extension and commuter challenge, "Telework Resource Kit."

40. D. S. Bailey and J. Foley, "Pacific Bell Works Long Distance," *HR Magazine*, August 1990, pp. 50–52.

41. Telework America, U.S. subsidiary of ITAC [database online, 2001], www.telecommute.org.

42. The Donahue Institute, University of Massachusetts, "Summary Report of Findings for the Massachusetts Telecommuting Initiative," p. 3.

43. As opposed to productivity, which is work per time period, typically per hour; production is the measurement of the total accomplished. For example, a person who produces 24 widgets in 8 hours would have productivity of 3 per hour, but production of 24.

44. Pratt, "1999 Telework America National Telework Survey," p. 6.

45. U.S. Department of Labor Bureau of Labor Statistics, "Workplace Injuries and Illnesses in 2000" [database online, 2000], www.bls.gov/iif./home.htm.

46. For the 11th annual *CCH Unscheduled Absence Survey*, human resource professionals from U.S. companies of all sizes and across major industries were

surveyed. Results of the survey appear in the October 24, 2001, issue of *CCH Human Resources Management Ideas & Trends*, a newsletter for HR professionals. For further information, see www.cch.com.

47. Florida Department of Management Services, "Review of the State Employee Telecommuting Program," December 1997.

48. Oregon Office of Energy, "Example of a Cost-Benefit Analysis of a Telework Program in an Oregon Business [database online June 20, 2003], http://www.energy.state.or.us/telework/cost-ben.htm.

49. http://www.telework.va.org. To qualify, businesses must be private Northern Virginia firms, either for-profit or not-for-profit, with a minimum of 20 employees. Participating teleworking employees must be Virginia residents. The program reimburses at a variable percentage of lease costs and consultant/technical assistance expenses. No purchases are eligible for reimbursement. Eligible expenses include, for example, computer equipment, answering machine, fax, modem, printers, telephone equipment, telework center fees, consultant services, scanner, telephone line charge and installation fees, to a maximum reimbursement of $3,500 per teleworker, or $35,000 total, whichever is less. Reimbursement includes 50 percent each of equipment and space lease and 100 percent of consultant's fees. Participation in the Telework!VA pilot program must result in a formal company telework program that provides the opportunity for qualified employees to telework from home or a telework center. The following minimum criteria apply:

- Telework from home—a minimum of eight days each month. This must result in the reduction of eight employee round trips per month during normal business hours (7 a.m.–6 p.m. approximately) from their home to the primary business location.
- Working from a telework center—a minimum of one telework station for two days per week, or eight daily reservations per month. These centers are open 24 hours a day, allowing three employees per workstation to participate if desired. Participation must result in the reduction of a minimum of eight employee round trips per month during normal business hours from their home to the primary business location. Travel to the telework center cannot be a longer commute for any teleworking employee than travel from their home to the primary work site.

50. Frank Wolf, U.S. Congress, "Teleworking Will Help Ease Traffic Congestion," March, 19, 2001, press release.

51. Telecommute Connecticut [database online], http://www. telecommutect. com.

52. Valley Metro [database online], http://www.valleymetro.org.

53. The employer tax credit is worth up to half of what the employer pays towards an employee's transit or vanpool costs, with a ceiling of $30 per month per employee. Employers are also eligible for the credit if they boost the employee's pay by the fair value of a parking space that employees pledge not to use, typically $3 or more per day. This law took effect January 1, 2001.

54. The bill reads, in part, "The legislation finds that:

1. Minnesota is frequently subjected to weather conditions that create significant road congestion;

2. On days of bad weather, significant time is lost to the economy as workers are unable to get to and from work in a timely manner;

3. Significant economic losses are incurred on days of bad weather in time, property damage, and personal injury;

4. Technology is changing the workplace both in terms of where work is done and how it is done;

5. Traditional transportation costs continue to rise with little opportunity for adding capacity to the system while costs of electronic travel are rapidly decreasing with a decentralizing potential for settlement patterns within the region; and

6. The cost of government operations will be reduced significantly if the growth in telecommuting can exceed the increase in vehicle trip generation.

"Therefore, the legislator finds that it is in the best interests of the state, its agencies, and the communities they serve to establish criteria by which a telecommuting day will be announced whereby employers will be encouraged to have their telecommuting-compatible employees telecommute. This will remove a percentage of traffic from the highways, which will result in a directly proportional reduction in accidents and time loss. This process will also communicate the state's interest in encouraging telecommuting, which will decrease the likelihood of congestion on any given day."

55. For a credit to be allowed, the employee working at home must regularly telecommute pursuant to a structured plan approved by the employer. The credit will be calculated based upon the portion of wages or salary paid to the employee while the employee telecommutes. For example, for telecommuting two out of five workdays per week, the credit of 1 percent will be calculated based upon 40 percent of the remuneration paid to the employee, which is derived from 40 percent of the regular workweek that the employee telecommutes.

56. Senator Santorum's 1999 legislation allocated $500,000 to study the feasibility of providing incentives for companies to allow their employees to telecommute in five major metropolitan areas, including Philadelphia. The law created a pilot program to examine the feasibility of an emissions credit trading and exchange system. The program, administered by the National Environmental Policy Institute in consultation with the EPA and the Departments of Transportation and Energy, has established a steering committee, comprised of members from the public and private sectors, to oversee the design of the pilot program at the national level. Phase II will market, implement, and evaluate the program over a two-year period.

57. Jeff Lee, "Commuters Brace for Big Transit Strike," *Vancouver Sun*, April 12, 2001, cover page.

58. Bob Fortier and John Edwards, "Don't Let a Winter Storm Disrupt Your Work—Let Telework Make Your Day," Canadian Telework Association [database online, May 2, 2001], http://www.ivc.ca/part45.html.

59. American Lung Association, "State of the Air 2002" [database online], http://www.lungusa.org/air2001/summary02.html.

60. University of Virginia Office of Telemedicine [database online 2002], http://www.telemed.Virginia.edu.

61. Christopher Oster and Michael Schroeder, *Wall Street Journal*, "Workers' Comp Gets More Expensive for Employers in Post-Sept. 11 World," January 9, 2002.

62. Git and Dunning, "The Employee Perspective," *American Demographics Magazine*, June 1995.

63. Florida Dept. of Management Services, "Telecommuting: A Guide for Managers and Employees Considering Telecommuting," http://fcn.state.fl.us/dms/hrm/telecom/telegde.html.

64. Ibid.

65. eWork 2000 awards [database online], http://www.etw.org/2000/HTML/Awards/Nominations/index.htm.

66. OPM Office of Merit Systems Oversight and Effectiveness, "Telework Works: A Compendium of Success Stories," U.S. Government Office of Personnel Management [database online, May 2001], http://www.opm.gov/studies/FINAL-TELEWRK.txt.

67. Ibid.

In the Beginning

Government has played a significant role in the start, growth and promotion of telework. In the United States, for instance, both the federal and state governments have been instrumental in legislating and rewarding the introduction of telecommuting and other work/life options. They have also produced excellent written resources, such as many of the sample telework documents in Appendix B.

The U.S. government allowed federal employees to telework as early as 1957, when the Comptroller General approved the payment of salaries for some federal employees for work done at home.

Dr. Wendell Joice, in his GSA publication *The Evolution of Telework in the Federal Government*, stresses the importance of telecommuting in U.S. government history. "The history of Federal telework reflects the evolution of *one of the most significant and progressive changes in work conditions for Federal employees*," he states (emphasis added).

> "Beginning during the last decade of the 20th century," Joice explains, "the Federal telework movement reflected that period's interest in workforce impact on family, environment, and general quality of life. It was also one of the most important barometers of the transition of the industrial age to information age human resources and workplace management."

Joice calls the introduction of federal telework a classic study of the struggle for change in a twentieth-century bureaucracy and points out that through this government telework emphasis, "the efforts of a relatively few resulted in a potential impact on the work lives of 1.8 million Federal workers."[1]

Jack Nilles, whom we introduced in Chapter 1 as the "father of telecommuting," began his career as a federal government employee—a rocket scientist in the U.S Air Force space program in the 1960s. In that position he began teleworking between Los Angeles and Washington, D.C. From there he segued into a research position for the University of Southern California, studying the effects that telecommunications and its resulting telecommuting opportunities had on transportation issues. In 1973 he directed the first telework demonstration project and coined the words *telework* and *telecommute*. (His association's site, www.jala.com is an excellent telework resource.)

Another term often considered synonymous with telecommute, or possibly the public-sector version of a telework arrangement, is *flexiplace*, coined by Frank Schiff, the concept's oft-proclaimed origina-tor. As chief economist for the federal government's Committee for Economic Development, Schiff wrote a *Washington Post* article in 1979 that encouraged the government to look at management practices, union rules, and federal laws and regulations on telework. During this energy-crisis era, he envisioned creation of a federal flexiplace environment as a means of improving productivity and saving costs and energy. Schiff then defined *flexiplace* to "encompass not only work-at-home but also such other flexible location arrangements as satellite work centers." He believed that in contrast to such terms as telecommuting, the word flexiplace "stressed increased flexibility in the location of work, whether or not this is based on telecommunications equipment."[2]

FYI . . .

Gil Gordon is another telework legend whose Web site you'll defi-nitely want to bookmark. Though irreverently describing himself as a "teleworker who among other things is responsible for laundry and household chores," Mr. Gordon is truly recognized around the world as a leading telecommuting expert and a pioneer in the field. Since 1982 he has worked with public and private sector employers in the United States, Canada, Europe, Japan, New Zealand, and Australia to plan and implement successful, bottom-line–oriented telecom-muting programs. He edits the newsletter *Telecommuting Review* and has written or co-authored several books on the subject. His superb site is www.gilgordon.com.

WHAT STARTED THE TELEWORK BALL ROLLING?

As with so many other innovations, telework was born of necessity. Workers just started doing it because it made sense. At some point in their lives they needed employment but also needed to be elsewhere than at the home office—and they were valued staff members, whom their employers needed to retain.

FYI . . .

Sherry Cronin, director of human resource policy and strategy for Prudential, shares how their teleworking program came into being twelve years ago. "We had a great employee whose mother was terminally ill and wanted to die in her own bed. She became our first telecommuter." Ms. Cronin goes on to tell about others. One spouse's job was taking the family from Newark to Denver. Prudential, not wishing to lose this valuable staff member, set her up as a telecommuting New Jersey employee who now actually lives and works in Colorado. Another New Jersey employee is actually a Boston-relocated telecommuter. All were situations of family necessity, and all were valuable employees retained only through telecommuting.

Companies also began offering telework options in response to the decreasing labor pool and the need for innovation that would present their firms as the "employer of choice." Telecommuting became another option to keep workers off the roads, especially at peak commute times, and also an effective response to natural disaster.

FYI . . .

The first federal government–wide flexiplace project, led by the President's Council on Management Improvement task force partnership of OPM and GSA, was initiated in 1990. Earliest participants were the Animal and Plant Health Inspection Service of the Department of Agriculture, the Equal Opportunity Commission, and the Department of the Interior. This flexiplace pilot program was created in response to 1988 reports by the Department of Labor and the Office of Personnel Management predicting a "slowly emerging crisis of competence." The dire message was that the federal government, with wages, incentives, and working conditions less than competitive with the private sector, could expect a deterioration of competency levels without implementing new steps to counteract this. Telework was seen as a potential "drawing card."

As mentioned before, government initiatives for the most part preceded private sector telework programs. As early as 1980 the states of Washington and California and federal agencies such as the General Services Administration (GSA), Environmental Protection Agency (EPA), National Aeronautics and Space Administration (NASA), and the Air Force provided invaluable information through their telework pilot programs and the resulting telework centers. The EPA, for example, implemented a six-month flexiplace pilot study in July of 1989 in Research Triangle Park, N.C., as a federal government effort to respond to issues of improving productivity, reducing costs, and saving energy.

The state of California began its two-year telecommuting pilot project in January of 1988, with 200 teleworkers, 150 nonteleworking "control group" participant workers, and 100 supervisors and managers. Teleworker effectiveness during this pilot met or exceeded expectations, telework quality of life was enhanced, and the results-oriented management techniques they implemented proved to be effective for teleworkers as well as other employees. With these successes, as well as their finding that major capitol investments were not necessary to implement telework, California's governor issued two executive orders—to implement telework expeditiously to help offset the state's growing congestion problem and to encourage the use of telecommuting as an emergency response to the Bay area Loma Prieta earthquake of 1989.

FYI ...

California's San Francisco/Marin County region now claims the country's largest concentration of telecommuters, partially because the area lies on a major earthquake fault line—the San Andreas. In the aftermath of earthquakes, numerous companies that have implemented telework have been able to resume their firm's normal operation quickly, and employees have often continued their telework habit.

On October 17, 1989, at 5:04:15 p.m. PDT, a magnitude 6.9 earthquake severely shook the San Francisco and Monterey Bay regions. The epicenter was located in Watsonville, near the Loma Prieta Peak of the Santa Cruz Mountains, approximately nine miles northeast of the coastal resort area of Santa Cruz, and just 60 miles from San Francisco. The effects were felt as far away as Sacramento.

This earthquake severely damaged the EPA Region 9 office building in San Francisco, displacing 800 employees.

EPA responded by establishing a temporary office for eighty employees and work-at-home arrangements for the remaining 700+ workers. By March 1990, 60 percent of the displaced employees were back in traditional temporary workstations, while the other 40 percent continued in flexiplace, awaiting the opening of a new office building.

EPA conducted several studies of this experience, learning quite a bit about the feasibility of telework as both a permanent solution and an emergency response strategy, and continues to use flexiplace.[3] The extensive lessons they learned about effective implementation of telework can be found in Chapter 7, "Preparing for Disaster."

Seven other states and the congested California counties of Contra Costa, Los Angeles, San Diego, and San Bernardino quickly followed the San Francisco lead with their own telework pilot programs, President Bush included telecommuting as part of the national transportation policy, and telework was included as a legitimate means of complying with the state's clean air mandates.

The Washington State Department of Transportation in 1993 embarked on a campaign to encourage work options such as telecommuting. Charged with overseeing the state's Commute Trip Reduction Law, the department decided to lead by example. It was also convinced that encouraging work options fit hand in glove with finding more efficient ways to get work done while retaining and recruiting top-performing employees.[4]

In 1990, the U.S. federal sector began its exploration of the impact of working from home or a telecenter by establishing the Federal Flexible Workplace Pilot Project. "Flexiplace" was designed to experiment with and evaluate the impact of alternative workplaces on quality of life issues. The pilot was sponsored by the President's Council on Management and Improvement and was co-directed by the Office of Personnel Management (OPM) and the General Services Administration (GSA). As an outgrowth of the pilot, in 1993 GSA received funding for the first telecommuting centers. They were established as satellite work locations that would serve as surrogate offices for workers who had excessively long commutes. There are now telecenters in California, Georgia, Illinois, Maryland, Minnesota, Ohio, Virginia, and West Virginia.[5]

In 1994, a presidential memorandum directed agencies to establish a program to support flexible family-friendly work arrangements, including telecommuting and satellite work locations. OPM and GSA were asked to work with agencies to expand flexible work arrangements, revise regulations that are barriers to such work, and develop any necessary legislative proposals.

Since its inception in 1990, telework has become an important part of the federal government's work/life programs. The government has taken great strides toward meeting its original goals—to save energy, improve air quality, reduce congestion and stress on roads and bridges, and enhance the quality of family-friendly and other initiatives for federal workers. According to the OPM 2001 report, the telework experience "has been successful in many agencies, encompassing a wide variety of jobs and work situations."[6]

FYI . . .

In May 2003, the U.S. Office of Personnel Management published a telework manual for government supervisors. While designed for federal employees, the guide is also valuable to private sector managers who need assistance with telework management or implementation. Entitled "Telework: A Management Priority—a Guide for Managers, Supervisor and Telework Coordinators," the manual is available online and can be downloaded as an html or Word document. The topics addressed include telework studies and training materials; teleworker selection, monitoring and appraisal; telework history and benefits; home-office safety guidelines and telecenter locations.[7]

Recipient of a 1999 ITAC award for its support of telework, the GSA's Federal Technology Services has had a telecommuting program since 1994. When preparing to move to a new facility in 1999, the agency used its technological expertise and its involvement with telework to build an innovative facility in Northern Virginia, to house 75 percent of its projected personnel.

Their Willow Wood computer system accommodates a mobile workforce, giving all FTS employees the flexibility to use laptops while at remote locations or teleworking from home or local telework centers. The new facility features workstations that allow for plug and play. Workers can share a cubicle on alternate days. Additionally, all communication systems, including the phone system and laptops with docking stations, are designed specifically to accommodate teleworking. This facility's innovations enabled FTS to greatly increase the number of employees teleworking at any one time and realize tremendous savings in real estate.[8]

The U.S. Environmental Protection Agency, the federal "spokesagency" for the government's efforts to improve our nation's ecology, is partnering with leading U.S. companies, the Department of Transportation's Federal Highway and Transit Administrations, and state and local governments to cut air pollution and improve public health through the new Commuter Choice Leadership Initiative.

One strong factor in the program's success is its encouragement of telework. In the program's announcement, EPA described the initiative as "part of an effort to redefine the meaning of the 'comprehensive employee benefits package' so it includes a Commuter Choice benefits package. The Commuter Choice benefits package helps American workers get to and from work in ways that cut air pollution and global warming pollution, improve public health, increase worker productivity, and reduce expenses and taxes for employers and employees."

Some of the commuting options promoted through the initiative include parking space cash-out (trading an employer-provided parking space for the cash equivalent), transit fare subsidies, telecommuting, compressed and flexible work schedules, car and van pools, and biking or walking to work.

EPA and the program's proponents believe employers' participation brings them increased ability to recruit and retain, increased productivity, reduced employer tax burden due to recent changes in the tax code targeting green commuting, reduced facility and parking costs, improved brand image due to public recognition by EPA and its partners, and improved community relations through reductions in traffic, air pollution, and parking spillover into residential areas. Current participants include the states of Georgia and Maryland and the city of Fort Worth and the firms Calvert Group, Geico, Intel, Kaiser Permanente, Nike, Pitney Bowes, and Walt Disney Company.[9]

The United States is certainly not the only federal government acting as a telework driving force. The European Commission's first interest dates from 1989, when the governments of the member states began to realize the potential for economic impact of advanced communications on rural areas and remote regions. A white paper, *Growth, Competitiveness, Employment, Challenges and Way Forward in the 21st Century*, launched in 1993, set the priorities for moving Europe to the information society. The top focus was work. The enormous growth of unemployment in the European Union (500,000 information society jobs were vacant because of a lack of skilled people in the labor market) reinforced the need for a new focus on greater flexibility in employment.

In 1994 a high-level group of industrialists recommended a ten-step action plan to stimulate employment, the first step of which was telework. The plan was adopted by the council. In 1998 the member states wrote the Fifth Framework Programme for European Research and Technology Development. Its telework efforts were two pronged.

The first focus was the enhancement of "eWork." This term is used to describe Internet software technology-enabled (IST) work practices, encompassing not only telework but also more flexible work in new office environments, in which new information and communication technologies play a major role. To that end, the states' priorities became to improve their IST applications, networks, software, and services, making them more readily available and training more citizens in their use. They also focused on ways to enhance data security and privacy and to prevent fraud and dissemination of illegal and harmful content.

The committee created a European Telework Agenda, to enhance their second focus—bringing the information and training to the European citizens. Each year since 1995, all of Europe has participated in Telework Week, now called eWork Week.

The annual week-long practice includes over 500 events, averaging an attendance of 60,000 people. Over a thousand press articles have been published each year in national, regional, and trade publications; and hundreds of radio and television programs about telework have been broadcast. The topics include technological solutions for the networked organization, social impacts of telework, integration of the disadvantaged into the workplace, new work legislation in response to telework, and ways to gain a competitive edge by introducing e-work.[10]

The commission's annual efforts have been fruitful. In Denmark, for instance, a recent collective agreement between the minister of finance and the Danish Central Federation of State Employee's Organisations sets the framework for telework options for 100,000 employees in county boroughs and municipalities—the National Association of Local Authorities in Denmark, the Association of County Councils in Denmark, the city of Copenhagen, the municipality of Frederiksburg, private day care centers with which the county councils have contracted, and natural gas and other joint companies of the counties and municipalities. The purpose of the agreement is to "increase the flexibility of the way work is planned, to overcome barriers to mobility, and to open up the prospect of making voluntary agreements with a view to performing work at home which is usually carried out at the conventional place of work."

The basic points of the agreements include the following:

- The county or municipality and the representatives for organizations with collective bargaining rights define the terms of termination.
- Upon expiration of the agreement, the employee has the right to return to the same job or another job with the same or similar specifications.
- Telework is voluntary.

In the UK the regional government of Surrey County Council introduced telework in 1997 after the success of their pilot telecenter in the town of Epsom. According to Caroline Cheales, project manager for flexible working for the council, this paved the way for their 1998 expanded Surrey WorkStyle Program, offering a number of telework options, including not only work at home but also 15 satellite locations. The motivations, she explained, were a growing interest in new ways of working, the need to make substantial savings to prevent cuts in frontline services, and the need to ease pressure on Surrey's overcrowded roads.

Cheales shares a humorous story that demonstrates not only how little need we may sometimes have for face-to-face meetings, but also how traffic congestion has contributed to the rise of telework. She relates:

> Two of my colleagues who work at home and at a variety of locations across the country had arranged a meeting at one of our area offices. They traveled up from home and hit terrible traffic conditions. They could see each other in their respective cars, stuck in the motorway traffic. As time ticked by it was clear that they were not going to make their meeting. Whilst speaking on the phone to arrange another time and place to meet they decided to go through the main points from their cars. By the time the traffic had cleared they had completed their business, had no need to meet physically and were able to go on to their next appointments.

Geoff Fernihough, CEO of Faulkner Group, shares that his staff's teleworking was unplanned and initiated by the request of one worker they needed to retain. A major packaging material supplier out of Dublin Ireland, Faulkner Group began its teleworking concept with a woman who served as credit control manager. Faced with losing this valued employee at the time of her child's birth, Faulkner offered her work-at-home status, with ad hoc office visits. She accepted. This "eWork pilot," as he terms it, was subsequently extended to three area sales managers.

Other contributors have something to say about their reasons for introducing telework, as follows. 3Com's California employees began telecommuting in the mid-1990s. Faced with Bay area commuting problems, 3Com began offering satellite office and work-at-home options. Pearson Education's telework started seven years ago, when the firm made the decision to move its New Jersey office to another part of the state and needed to retain employees who were not prepared to relocate.

Sopheon Resource Network Corporation began its formal telework pilot program in 1994 when faced with the loss of two valued headquarters personnel. One was to be a trailing spouse; the other simply did not wish to continue the 100-mile round-trip daily commute. The pilot was originally only offered to researchers living outside the Minnesota Twin Cities area. Merrill Lynch, whose home office is in New Jersey, began offering telework in 1992 as a result of the Clean Air Act Amendment, and in response to an employee survey in which workers asked for tools to balance work and life. Retention is the driver now.

Abbott Northwestern Hospital (now a consolidation called Allina Metro Hospital with Abbott, United, and Mercy/Unity Hospitals) began its telework pilot program for medical transcriptionists in 1993. They saw it as a way to save space, time, and money and as a recruitment tool in the Twin Cities, Minnesota, market, which was suffering a shortage of experienced medical transcriptionists.

Prudential's employees began informally telecommuting 12 years ago in response to personal and family needs of employees. Their national telework program was formalized in 1998.

According to Kathy Clinton, of Auto Desk, employees have been teleworking "since day one" (Auto Desk's founding in 1982). The first to embrace telework was their multimedia division, called Discreet, with a separate office in San Francisco. The number-one catalyst was recruitment, as they simply could not attract some highly talented people without offering telework. In the IT department the vice president requested that a large percentage of the staff telework in an effort to decrease real estate costs.

The two catalysts for i2's telecommute implementation were real estate costs and the wishes of their employees. While telework began as early as 1999, Project Manager Yvette Lucio says it did not really catch on until early 2002, when reimbursing teleworkers for home office expenses began.

Art & Logic's founder and president Paul Hershenson tells us that the firm began with at-home work because the three founders had been doing it that way with their former employers. When the firm grew to 10 employees, all in the L.A. area, they considered an office. After listing all the percs and niceties each wanted in an office, however, they just laughed and decided no structure would be able to accommodate that. It was not until Hershenson and his family became annoyed about faxes ringing at home all hours of the night that they decided to acquire an office.

United Kingdom's Automobile Association has had a number of employees handling calls from their homes since 1997. Since the busiest time for calls is typically during work commute trips, 7:30–11:30 a.m. and 4:30–8:30 p.m., they needed a staff that could easily respond to this split shift requirement, without having to commute to the office twice in one day. Home working seemed the answer.[11]

In a stressful industry with a hot job market, The Bon Marche introduced work options such as telecommuting in 1996 to help retain employees. Japan's Pasona, Inc., began offering teleworking contractors to clients in 1998. They noticed that since the use of computers in work was increasing, so did the number of people who wanted to work from computers in their homes.

According to Gene Puckett, deputy director of the state of Utah's Division of Information Technology, their May 13, 1998, inception of telework was designed to relieve employees of the daily commute to the office. They also recognized the benefits of energy conservation, better employee morale, increased productivity, and increased employee retention.[12]

Yorkshire Water, in the Irish Dales, began its teleworking option in the mid-1990s, in response to its need to offer 24-hour emergency accessibility to its reservoir, treatment plant, and water mains clients.[13]

Teresa Antunes, general manager and founder of InterWorks, Portugal, explains that telework was an option from the company's inception in October of 1997. "Because I have become a teleworker myself," she says,

> my 6-year-old son, who was systematically taken ill, is, nowadays, a healthy child and the pressures that I indirectly passed on to him during the time I was working with a company have ceased to exist. It is difficult to put into words what a mother feels when she has to face a traffic jam for one hour, literally "dump" her son at school, only to return to another traffic jam and arrive at work absolutely exhausted. On top of that, she still has a hard day's work ahead of her! She leaves work even more exhausted, returns to the traffic jam for another hour, trying to make it to her son's school as soon as possible, picks up her son, returns to the massive traffic jam and at home has another series of tasks to attend to. And the following day won't be any different! Is this the quality of life a woman dreams of?

Nortel Network started its telecommuting trials in 1995 with 230 users; its teleworking staff grew to 1,100 in 1996, 4,000 in 1998, and 8,000 in 1999. Wendy Herman, Nortel's media relations representative, explains the company's current philosophy:

> Being an Internet and networks company building the high performance Internet, we recognize that anywhere, anytime work is an important element of a global corporation and a reality in the new economy of work. Our teleworking program is not a contributor to employee satisfaction and productivity but provides a showcase for the leading-edge technology that we sell.
>
> For several years, Nortel Networks has grown the number of people involved in what we call "virtual teaming" so that it is now very common within the company. It is not unusual for an employee to be in one location and have all other members of his/her team located elsewhere, either in North America or around the world. As such, team members often seldom meet face to face with each other, depending instead on email, teleconferences and frequent telephone exchanges to do their work.
>
> Because of this, working at home is more seamless to our approach to work than at many other companies, since jobs are not location specific. Being at home or in an office, depending on the job function, isn't a factor for many employees. We organize work around the right people for the team regardless of where they are located.
>
> Besides the "virtual" office aspect, we have found through surveys of telecommuters that their job satisfaction increases when telecommuting and they are more productive. Telecommuters often indicate that at least half of the time saved from not having to commute to an office is dedicated to work. As well, telecommuting enables employees, especially those with families, to better balance professional and personal lives.

NOTES

1. Wendell Joice, Ph.D., *The Evolution of Telework in the Federal Government*, Office of Governementwide Policy, U.S. General Services Administration, February 2000, p. 5.

2. Ibid., p. 6.

3. Ibid., p. 7.

4. Washington State University Cooperative Extension, and Commuter Challenge, "Telework Resource Kit."

5. Ernst & Young, *Federal Interagency Telecommuting Center Pilot Project: An Analysis and Review of the Telecommuting Centers in Greater Metropolitan Washington, DC*. In 1997 and 1998 Ernst & Young analyzed the success of the first 14-center 1993—1997 pilot project in metropolitan Washington, D.C. An 11.25 million dollar federal venture, this pilot project program opened seven telecenters in Maryland, six in Virginia, and one in West Virginia. As of November 1997, 380 federal teleworkers of 14 federal agencies had used 322 workstations in these telecenters. In general, the report gave the pilot project flying colors for its success, with the exception of its one goal of reduction in real estate costs. Teleworkers reported improved quality of life, more time with families, and less time in traffic, while the government reported estimated road wear savings of $119,000–$213,000, as well as savings from congestion reduction, accidents, and pollution of $119,000–$759,000. Where the program did not yet succeed was full utilization of the centers. For some centers that did not rent unused time or space to non-federal firms or organizations, the telecenters were viewed as extra real estate that the government must support. One financially successful center, however, contracted with the local municipal government to allow resident use.

6. U.S. Office of Personnel Management Office of Merit Systems Oversight and Effectiveness, *Telework Works, A Compendium of Success Stories*, May 2001.

7. United States Office of Personnel Managment, "Telework: A Management Priority—A Guide for Managers, Supervisors, and Telework Coordinators" [database online May 8, 2003], http://www.telework.gov/documents/ tw_man03/ tw_man.asp.

8. FTS is also setting up hoteling workstations in their other FTS locations in Falls Church, Virginia, and Washington, D.C. The GSA IntraNet has a presence at these locations, and remote users can tie directly into the servers at Willow Wood. Employees are encouraged to drop into a workplace nearest them or to work at home. FTS's immediate goal for teleworking is 25 percent of their workforce. That is up from their current telework participation of 7 percent.

9. U.S. Environmental Protection Agency update, October 12, 2000. For documents see the Office of Transportation and Air Quality Web site: http://www.epa.gov/otaq/transp/comchoic/ccweb.htm.
Commuter Choice Leaders commit their organizations to:

- Appoint a commuter coordinator
- Centralize and simplify all employee commuter information
- Regularly inform employees of their commuting benefits
- Offer employees at least one core commuting benefit (telework, transit fare subsidies, etc.)
- Offer employees at least three other commuting benefits
- Report their progress to the EPA

EPA has committed to helping the Commuter Choice Leaders and their employees in the following ways:

- Appoint a contact account manager for each Leader organization
- Provide public recognition to Leaders for their efforts in reducing stress, traffic, costs, and pollution
- Inform future potential employees of the commuting benefits of working for Leaders
- Develop and provide assessment tools that help Leaders determine which commuting benefits and commuting information would provide the greatest value
- Develop and provide analytical tools to help Leaders calculate and assess the impact of their commuter benefits package
- Help Leaders identify companies, non-profit organizations, and other government entities that offer commuting-related products and services that contribute to employee commuter benefits
- Host conferences and produce materials to help Leaders share commuter benefit information
- Limit the number of Leaders so each gets a significant voice and attention during the leadership phase
- Help the Leaders share their success with other employers that may want to offer a Commuter Choice benefits package once the Leadership phase has completed

10. Peter Johnston and John Nolan, "eWork 2000: Status Report on New Ways to Work in the Information Society, " Sept. 2000.

11. UK Online, "Working Anywhere, Exploring Telework for Individuals and Organizations," p. 25.

12. Gene Puckett, deputy director in the Division of Information Technology Services for the state of Utah, is author of the state's 1998 telecommuting policies and guidelines, revised October 2, 2000, and found at http://www.its.state .ut.us/contents/resources/policiesprocedures/polprofiles/pptwo02.prn.pdf.

13. UK Online, "Working Anywhere: Exploring Telework for Individuals and Organizations," p. 7.

Keeping It
on the Up and Up

It's now time to peruse the laws and legal issues that effect an employer's successful and litigation-free implementation and administration of a telework program. In this chapter we look at the mandated introduction and promulgation of telework, highlight some of the political support for telecommuting in the United States and globally, and focus on the legal aspects of offering telework to your employees.

As telework's expansion continues, the legislation evolves. What is described in this chapter as proposed or pending may or may not become legislation before this book is on the shelves. The information does offer a good overview, however, of the political and legal support for the telework issue and will head you in the right direction to discover the legal outcome of this issue in your area, as well as federally and globally.

LEGISLATED OVERVIEW

The legislative impetus for teleworking in the United States was most probably the Clean Air Act Amendment (CAAA) of 1990. This legislation significantly amended the Clean Air Act of 1970 and placed renewed emphasis on transportation planning in order to maintain existing air quality and achieve air quality improvements. Teleworking within state and federal agencies, as well as in private firms in poor-air-quality areas, was a direct result of concerns for the loss of federal funding on critical area projects.[1]

Senator John Kerry of Massachusetts and Congressmember Mark Udall of Colorado introduced the Small Business Telecommuting Act on March 14, 2000. This legislation directs the administrator of the Small Business Administration (SBA) to create a pilot program in a maximum of five SBA regions at a maximum total two-year cost of five million dollars. Money would be appropriated for developing educational materials, conducting outreach to small business, and acquiring equipment for demonstration purposes. In addition, the bill directs the administrator to undertake special efforts for those individuals with disabilities who are small business owners and employees. Finally, it requires the SBA to prepare and submit a report to Congress evaluating the telework pilot program.

The state of Virginia's "Telecommuting Incentive Act" took effect July 1, 2001. The law compels the secretary of administration to direct the formulation and promulgation of policies, standards, specifications, and guidelines for information technology concerning telecommuting by the employees of state agencies. The head of each state agency is directed to develop a telecommuting policy in accordance with the statewide policy to be developed by the secretary of administration, to maximize telecommuting without diminished employee work performance or service delivery. The secretary of administration is also directed to advise and assist state agencies in developing the state agencies' telecommuting policies, and the secretary may provide advice and assistance to a local government or a private sector employer upon request.[2]

One of the most vocal telework proponents is another Virginia legislator, Congressmember Frank Wolf, who in March 2001 called for a federal telework czar to see that legislation requiring more telecommuting in the federal workplace is implemented. "This is the law. Agencies who aren't compliant ought to be held accountable," he affirmed. U.S. law now dictates that federal agencies must establish policies allowing eligible employees to telecommute. Legislation also requires the Office of Personnel Management to implement a telework program in which 25 percent of federal employees telework at least part of the time by April 2001.

The 1999 Special Legislative Award of the International Telework Association and Council went to Delegate Joan Pitkin of Bowie, Maryland. A 24-year legislative veteran representing the Twenty-third District in Annapolis, Ms. Pitkin is a member of the House of Delegates Appropriations Committee and has worked for many years to address critical transportation needs in the region. Having served on the influential Appropriations Subcommittee on Transportation and the Environment, she also serves on the Prince Georges County Oversight Committee on Transportation. Delegate Pitkin has helped shape state policy regarding travel on the information highway, specifically through legislation to create both a telecommuting advisory committee, and subsequently a state telecommuting pilot program for state employees.

Passage of that bill in 1994 created a statewide telecommuting program, reauthorized in 1998 and again in 1999 in the General Assembly. In 1999, Pitkin was able to build on earlier efforts to increase the level of participation of state employees in the telecommuting program through a telecommuting workgroup, setting in motion an incentive program to enable teleworkers to acquire home computers and to establish additional telework and workforce development centers. Through her legislation, Maryland secured a telework consultant to manage and market these state telecommuting programs, conducting training for managers and teleworkers.

Pitkin successfully lobbied the Metropolitan Council of Governments and the Maryland Departments of the Environment and Transportation to "prioritize telecommuting in their joint regional efforts to meet the requirements of the Federal Clean Air Act." In addition, she encouraged the governor and the Maryland Department of Transportation to set up a grant program to further telework in the private sector, helping to mitigate air quality problems in the Greater Washington metropolitan region.

Pitkin was also successful in obtaining federal funding and the General Services Administration's assistance for a new telework center at Bowie State University, with more planned at strategic locations around the state. Through partnerships with the Maryland National Guard, she is leading the effort to implement a statewide plan at the sites of twelve Guard facilities. The plan, funded and equipped by the federal government, will provide technical support to state agencies for telecommuting, video conferencing, and distance learning capabilities in the Guard's Distributing Training Technology Centers.[3]

Maryland's 1999 telework legislation requires the state's Department of Budget and Management to establish telework programs in every state agency. The legislated goal, 10 percent of all agency eligible employees participating in telework, should result in the elimination of eight million vehicle trips annually within four years.

Senator Byron Sher, Stanford (Bay area), California, state representative, is sponsoring State Senate Bill 826 which proposes to amend the provisions of legislation that governs how a $4 per vehicle registration surcharge in the Bay area could be spent. While this may seem a small figure, the annual revenue is over $20 million, some of which would be earmarked for telecommuting support expenditures.[4]

North Dakota's Senate Bill 2026, introduced at the last legislative session, would require each state agency to prepare an information technology plan annually based on guidelines developed by the department and provide information technology goals, objectives, and activities for the current and next two bienniums. These plans would address the feasibility of telecommuting by selected employees, including positions that are suitable for telecommuting, travel and space needs, and information needs for supporting telecommuting and must include a list of information technology assets owned, leased, or employed by the entity.

According to Copenhagen attorney Katherine Schon, Denmark's employment relationships are governed through legislation and partly through collective agreements. Her country attaches far greater importance to collective agreements than other industrialized countries. No legislation addresses telework specifically, which means that the general legislation relating to employment and working environment also applies to telework. However, a number of bargaining records of collective agreements particularly govern telework.

The Employment Standards Act of Ontario, Canada, sets the minimum wage for home workers as 110 percent of the regular minimum wage, due to costs incurred by home workers such as Internet access and utilities costs. The legislation also dictates that employers must pay home workers at least the same rate of pay as workers doing the same job at the employer's office location.

Belgium's 1996 Law on Homeworking compels the employer to draw up and sign a homeworking contract with each teleworker and provide the necessary home equipment. This equipment will remain the property of the employer. The law further states that without such an agreement the employee has the right to claim 10 percent of the gross salary as a business expense. As the cost of the purchases is considered the employer's business expense, the company pays no tax or social security payments on it.

TELEWORK LEGAL ISSUES

While keeping abreast of telework-related legislation is important, employers must also be aware of the complications and potentially litigious situations that could arise in offering telecommuting options to their employees. Some of the issues to be considered include the following:

- Workplace safety and work-related injury
- Information theft
- Equipment theft or damage
- Discrimination and constructive dismissal
- Fair Labor Standards Act wage and hours issues
- Americans with Disabilities Act
- Taxes
- Insurance implications
- Confidentiality and security
- Conversion of property by terminated telecommuter
- Protected communications (LMRA)
- Noncompete covenants

Let's look briefly at each, keeping in mind that most of our legislative focus will be within the United States. With the one exception of Denmark, most European employment standards and rules (other than workplace safety) are determined by collective agreements rather than governmental legislation. For guidance on European attitudes toward the following subjects, your best sources of information are the sample agreements shown in Appendix A.

Workplace Safety and Work-Related Injury

Duluth, Minnesota attorney Kathleen Bray, experienced representative for employers and writer and presenter of seminars on matters involving workers' compensation and employment law, offers an overview of the U.S. issue from the federal government standpoint.[5] She explains that the furor over home-based worksites began with a November 15, 1999, Interpretation and Compliance Letter issued by OSHA to a Houston-based business. The employer asked OSHA for guidance on the employer's obligations under the OSH Act (Occupational Saftey and Health Act of 1970) for home-based offices, the extent of compliance required, inspection procedures, and record-keeping requirements, among other general issues.

Interestingly, OSHA's letter was quietly posted on its Web site, and no attention was brought to it until the media picked up on it shortly after the first of the year, and a brief frenzy began. Because of the misunderstanding created by the letter, it was withdrawn as a formal policy directive on telecommuting. Instead, OSHA Directive CPL 2-0.125—Home Based Worksites, was posted, which is available on OSHA's website at www.osha.gov. Although OSHA has backpedaled from its original guidance on telecommuting and home-based worksites, it is unlikely this is the last word from them.

Ms. Bray explains OSHA's telecommuting philosophy: "In all of its telecommunications, OSHA emphasizes its support of 'family-friendly, flexible and fair work arrangements.' "[6] Because of the changing nature of the workplace and the increasing availability of work from home, OSHA believes it has the responsibility to ensure "safe and healthful conditions" for all employees, regardless of where they work. In clarifying OSHA's formal position on telecommuting, OSHA's assistant secretary, Charles Jeffress, made a statement to the Senate Subcommittee on Employment, Safety, and Training, on January 25, 2000, which provided in relevant part:

1. We believe the OSH Act does *not* apply to an employee's house or furnishings.
2. OSHA will not hold employers liable for work activities in employees' home offices.

3. OSHA does not expect employers to inspect home offices.
4. OSHA does not, and will not, inspect home offices.
5. Approximately 20 percent of employers, because of their size or industry classification, are required by the OSH Act to keep records of work-related injuries and illnesses. *These employers continue to be responsible for keeping such records, regardless of whether the injuries occur in the factory, on the road, in a home office, or elsewhere, as long as they are work-related.*
6. Where work other than office work is performed at home, such as manufacturing operations, employers are responsible for hazardous materials, equipment, or work processes which they provide or require to be used in an employer's home.
7. OSHA will only conduct inspections of hazardous home workplaces, such as home manufacturing, when OSHA receives a complaint or referral.[7]

Ms. Bray adds that OSHA has asked the National Economic Council to convene an interagency working group to further examine the issue. The group will include members of the Department of Commerce, the Small Business Administration, and other agencies. Further rulemaking or guidance, she concludes, is likely to follow.

This legislative clarification does not, however, relieve federal agencies from responsibility for the safety of their flexiwork and homeworking employees. The Federal Employees Compensation Act of 1993 states that government workers are covered by workers' compensation for work-related injuries that happen when they are working at home. The Office of Personnel Management states "Agencies should make sure that the telecommuting employee's worksite meets acceptable standards. Some agencies (require) employees to complete a self-certification safety inspection form. Onsite inspections (with adequate notice to the employee) are another option."

While OSHA has clarified that its responsibility does not include inspection of the homes of teleworkers for compliance with federal safety standards, there are still state workers' compensation laws to consider. OSHA's recommendation is that employers educate their employees about the ways to avoid work-related injury, such as good ergonomic habits. Their site offers much ergonomic guidance for both employer and teleworker at http://www.osha.gov/SLTC/ergonomics/index.html.

(For further home safety and ergonomic tips, see Chapter 4, "Feeling Safe and Secure." A sample home-safety inspection form, the MITE Telework Office Evaluation, is found in Appendix B.)

For general workers' compensation advice, we again turn to attorney Kathleen Bray:

Although each state varies in its workers' compensation laws, generally, if an employee is injured in the course and scope of work activities for her employer, the employer is liable for workers' compensation benefits. This premise is unchanged, simply because the injury occurs at a home office rather than on the employer's premises.

It may be more difficult, however, to determine whether the employee was acting within the scope of the work activities, or whether the injury arose out of his work activities, as opposed to personal activities, because of the lack of supervision and the sometimes overlapping activities when working from home.

Bray advises that as an employer, you need to ensure a safe work environment, but obviously, she clarifies, you cannot monitor the home-based worksite as easily. She says that assisting the employee with setting up the workstation at home, providing ergonomically correct equipment, and periodically evaluating the employee's use of space and equipment are smart risk-management steps to take. As a condition of telecommuting, she suggests, you may want to consider a pre-telecommuting home inspection, to confirm that the employee's home space safely accommodates or can be modified to safely accommodate the equipment and space required.

Bray also clarifies that the information provided by her in this chapter is general in nature and "should not be used as a substitute for professional service and advice. Readers should consult with their legal counsel before taking any action on matters covered" by her in this chapter.

The Transportation Management Association Group states in their *TeleManagers Handbook* that the home office must provide a safe and healthy environment in which to work. It clarifies that in terms of worker health and safety, if an injury happens in the course and scope of employment, then it will definitely fall under workers' compensation. They advise limiting employer risk not only by clearly defining where the home work is to occur and the hours of work in the telecommuting agreement but also by indemnifying the employer against any claims from third parties who happen to wander into the work area.

The TMA handbook also points out that for workers' compensation to apply, the worker must be in a designated work area during the agreed-upon work hours when the injury happens. Their opinion is that the employer has the right to regularly check the workplace to evaluate whether it is in a safe and efficient condition, but that reasonable advance notice should be provided to the employee, and the inspection should be limited to the work area. They state it is legally permissible to photograph the conditions of the home workspace provided that the right to photograph is included in the telecommuting agreement.[8]

Jack Nilles's organization, JALA International Inc., offers a nifty telework Web site, whose e-mail was flooded with inquiries about OSHA's jurisdiction over work-at-home safety. He responded:

> *What's New?* For decades we have been telling clients that it is import-ant that teleworkers' home offices be kept at least as free from hazards as traditional offices. We have also generally recommended that there be some written agreement between employer and teleworker that specifies their respective responsibilities, including workplace safety issues. In essence we have been saying obey the spirit of OSHA regula-tions but don't get hung up on details (such as exit signs) that apply to traditional workplaces but not to homes. *What accident risk?* The vast majority of teleworkers are very conscientious and responsible people. They can be relied on to keep their agreements including maintaining their home offices in safe condition. Furthermore, most teleworkers consider that teleworking is a privilege, not a right. Hence, they take special pains to ensure that they continue to earn that privilege. *We do not know of a single successful case being brought by a teleworker against an employer on the basis of work safety violations—and we've been watching this since 1970!*[9]

Copenhagen attorney Katherine Schon explains that in Denmark the rules of the Danish Working Environment Act also apply when work is performed from the employer's home (referred to in Denmark as "out-work"). This implies that the employer is under an obligation to ensure that the outworking employee performs the work in a proper manner as regards security and health. Under this act the employer should ensure that the workplace—office furniture and the like—is of such a standard and design that injuries do not occur. If necessary, the em-ployer must visit the place of outwork in order to ensure that the requirements are met.

UK employers have a general duty to protect the health, safety, and welfare of their employees under the Health and Safety at Work Act of 1974, which applies whether employees are working in a conventional office or remotely. This general duty is qualified by the principle of "so far as reasonably practicable," in other words, the duty is to be balanced against the time, trouble, cost, and physical difficulty of taking mea-sures to avoid or reduce risk.

The UK's Management of Health and Safety at Work Regulations of 1992 also requires employers to do a suitable and sufficient risk assess-ment of all the work activities carried out by their workers, including work from home or elsewhere. The risk assessment must identify the hazards that are present and then assess the extent of the risks. The legislation notes that hazards can arise from electrical equipment and video display units (VDUs) from equipment and fitting in the room where the work activity is taking place. These may include the work-station, seating, lighting, heating, or ventilation.[10]

Information Theft

You, as the employer, can be held legally responsible for your company's paper as well as electronic information even while it is retained in a teleworker's home. If misuse were to occur—by the teleworker or other persons to whom the information was made available in the teleworkers' home—the result could be litigious for your firm.

C. Andrew Head, Atlanta attorney with Holland & Knight LLP, makes the following suggestions to employers to preserve confidentiality and protect trade secrets:

1. Consider having employees sign a confidentiality agreement.
2. Use a lock or some other device to prevent unauthorized access to the home office and the telecommuter's computer terminal.
3. Use passwords and additional security measures when accessing the employer's computer system from home.[11]

Equipment Theft or Damage

Chapter 4 discusses theft and damaage and suggests products and software that can help secure the employer's and teleworkers' equipment from theft. Here, we suggest that you determine if your teleworkers have homeowners' policies. If not, you will want to check with your firm's insurance provider about coverage when employees work from remote locations.

In Denmark, an agreement is made between employer and employee that a computer and other equipment are made available to the employee by the employer, when the employee works at home. As the equipment belongs to the employer, the employee must return the equipment, essentially in the same condition, when the employee resigns or no longer performs outwork. The obligation to return the equipment often appears within the written agreement, but must be assumed to apply whether written or not. The employer assumes any risk for damage to the equipment, unless it arises because of the employee's acting "actionably," in which case the employer may require compensation from the employee.

Discrimination and Constructive Dismissal

In order to avoid discrimination charges of "favoritism" when offering telecommuting opportunities, employers should develop selection guidelines for telecommuting positions, just as they would for any other position posted within the company. Employees should be able to demonstrate the qualities and abilities listed in a telecommuting job description. Managers responsible for making telecommuting selection decisions should decide on the basis of definable, legitimate, nondiscriminatory factors.

Dr. Helen Solomons, adjunct professor in the graduate human resource program at Villanova University, says that companies are flirting with a legal problem when an employee who has been teleworking for some time has a new boss and therefore cannot work from home any longer. If this worker is a member of a minority group, for instance, discrimination accusations could result.

Dr. Solomons stresses that this type of informal program can leave the firm wide open to litigation. She notes that it is important to emphasize that these potential equity issues arise in the case of *informal* programs because the rationale for becoming a teleworker often depends solely on whether or not the supervisor is comfortable with the arrangement. In such cases, a person with a superior performance track record and job responsibilities appropriate to remote work may not receive approval from one supervisor, whereas someone else with poorer performance and tasks less suited to remote work may receive approval from a different supervisor.

Most employees view the opportunity to work out of their home as a benefit or perquisite; thus, an employee who has requested and been denied a telecommuting arrangement may allege that the employer discriminated in refusing to offer such an opportunity or refused the opportunity to the employee in retaliation for filing a discrimination complaint. In *Tarin v. County of Los Angeles,* plaintiff sued her employer for retaliation, alleging among other things that the employer refused to allow her to telecommute in the same manner as her coworkers because she had filed administrative claims under Title VII and other laws. The Ninth Circuit affirmed the award of summary judgment to the employer, holding that plaintiff failed to show a causal connection in support of her retaliation claim because the employer treated the plaintiff the same as her coworkers in providing its telecommuting arrangement. By recognizing that the record supported the employer's claim that plaintiff was allowed to telecommute in the same manner as her coworkers and that the employer has legitimate reasons for limiting telecommuting privileges among all of its workers, the Ninth Circuit implicitly held that denial of a request for telecommuting privileges may constitute an adverse employment action much like denial of a promotion.[12]

Constructive dismissal is also an area of concern with telecommuters, according to attorney Lauren Bernardi. She explains that constructive dismissal arises where the actions of an employer are such that they have, in effect, terminated an employee. This will occur where there is a significant change in the duties or remuneration of an employee. If you suddenly require an employee who has been working on site to work from home, the employee may be able to argue that he or she has been constructively dismissed. Conversely, unless you expressly reserve the right to have the employee return to the regular workplace should the arrangement be unsuccessful, the right to work at home may become a term of the employment relationship. This means that an employee who is forced to return to the regular work site could claim constructive dismissal.

Ms. Bernardi suggests that you require employees to voluntarily apply for telecommuting positions; that you make it clear to the employees that if telecommuting doesn't work out you can unilaterally require an employee to return to the regular work site; and that, in the initial stages, the telecommuting should be a part-time arrangement, set up on a pilot project basis, allowing both you and the employee to determine whether or not the arrangement will work.[13]

Confusion abounds in recent state court decisions in Florida and New York. Maxine Allen, a former technical specialist for the New York office of Reuters America, had worked out of her home in Florida. Allen was denied unemployment benefits in both states after her Reuters employment was discontinued. Ms. Allen, originally hired as a New York employee, requested and was given a telework opportunity when her husband's work took them both to Florida. Reuters paid for her phone line and computer at her Florida home office. In 1999 the employer decided to discontinue the telework arrangement, offering Ms. Allen a job back in New York. She declined, and applied for unemployment benefits. The State of Florida turned her down. She then applied in New York. In July of 2003 New York State also made the decision to deny her benefit claim.

While this situation appears to bring to light an as-yet unanswered question about unemployment benefits in a telework situation, it also emphasizes the need for formal telework policies (which, according to Kyle Arteaga, Director of Media Relations at Reuters America, the firm had in place at that time.)

The question may often turn out to be not, "Which state pays unemployment benefits?" but rather, "Is the employee eligible for unemployment benefits?" and even "Was the employee really dismissed?" If, as we have stated numerous times, you emphasize that telework is a privilege, not a right, and you state very clearly in your telework policy and individual agreement the method and time frame in which you, the employer, are free to cancel the telework arrangement your chances are far better of heading off this sort of thorny situation.

In responding to a reporter's question on the subject, telework guru Gil Gordon put it a little more colorfully, "I mentioned to the reporter that my advice for telecommuters themselves, and by extension to the employers, is to attempt to treat this problem like a marriage between a 20-year-old starlet and a 70-year-old dirty old man (well, I didn't use exactly those terms): if they get married presumably they intend for it to last, but they understand it may not—so they draw up a prenuptial agreement to spell out what happens if the marriage goes kaput. Same thing with telework, and especially with these multi-jurisdictional cases: it's in everyone's interest to spell out in advance how these matters will be treated if things should sour. A typical telecommuter's/teleworker's agreement should/does address some of these issues but not all of them."[14]

Katherine Schon states that in Denmark it is the employer's "general managerial right" to determine whether or not an employee may perform outwork. The employer's assessment shall, among other things, rely on whether the employer finds the said employee suited to performing outwork. However, if the employer in this assessment includes non-objective considerations, so that a trend emerges that the employer discriminates against employees of one sex, this will be in contravention of the Prohibition of Labour Market Discrimination Act. If the employer's decision to permit or refuse an employee to perform outwork is based on objective considerations, the employer's decision cannot be contested. In cases of dispute it is for the courts or the industrial system to make an assessment of the considerations that formed the basis of the employer's decision. Only in cases where it is clear that the employer was not objective can an employee claim damages.

Wages and Hour Issues

Attorney Kathleen Bray, in discussing the Fair Labor Standards Act as it relates to telecommuting arrangements, emphasizes that employers must be sensitive to criteria of exempt and non-exempt employees, as well as overtime issues with home-based employees. She advises that a specific agreement should be structured to address the keeping of time or hours, expectation of hours worked, and any prohibitions on working overtime or any hours over a certain maximum. The agreement, she says, should also address expectations of the employees' availability at home and by telephone or e-mail.

Attorney Darrell VanDeusen, partner in the law firm of Kollman and Sheehan and contributing columnist for HRLawForum.com, offers very specific advice for compliance with the Fair Labor Standards Act (FLSA). A problem facing employers today, he says, is ensuring that they comply with the FLSA for employees who telecommute. The regulations issued under the FLSA have long required employers to compensate employees for work performed off the work site, even if performed at the employee's home. In today's digital age, where telecommuting has become a more feasible and attractive option for both employees and employers, employers must be cautious of the risks attendant to allowing employees to work from home. For example, the recordkeeping requirements of the FLSA that facilitate proper payment of employees can become particularly problematic when an hourly employee works at home. Another potential problem is that a telecommuting employee may work an excessive number of overtime hours; in this case, the employer would be obligated to pay the employee for those hours.

To avoid some of the problems associated with telecommuting employees, VanDeusen suggests that employers create an accurate system for documenting the time worked by nonexempt employees, including overtime. For example, computer-generated reports that show login times and hours logged in could be effective for clerical workers, accounting staff, and word processors. He also explains that if an employer permits telecommuting, the employer is responsible for monitoring the telecommuters' hours and taking steps to restrict them if appropriate. The employer should develop a written agreement with the telecommuting employee that provides that the employee is not to work more than a certain number of hours per week without prior approval from her supervisor.

Another problem is that the employee's status could be jeopardized by the employer's system for monitoring the work of an exempt employee who telecommutes. To be exempt from the minimum wage and overtime requirements of the FLSA, an employee's salary must not be "subject to reduction because of variations in the quality or quantity of work performed." In addition, for most exempt classifications, the employee also must maintain a certain degree of independence and decision-making authority. If these tests are not met, the employee's exempt status may be compromised.

VanDeusen further states that an employer who allows employees to telecommute should:

- Ensure that it has an adequate system for monitoring the time for nonexempt employees work at home
- Limit the hours the employee may work without obtaining prior approval
- Ensure that it does not adopt policies for exempt employees that would compromise their exempt status under FLSA[15]

Attorney Kevin Fitzgerald concurs, stating that "The FLSA's wage and hour laws—and the related record keeping requirements—are per-

haps the most ticklish legal issues presented by telecommuting. . . .
Violations of these requirements can result in hefty fines and even land
your company in court." He suggests that employers should spell out
the recordkeeping rules so that telecommuters and their managers can
keep accurate time records, especially with nonexempt employees who
typically are paid by the hour and are eligible for overtime pay.[16]

In Denmark, as in much of Europe, wages are solely governed by
collective agreements and individual agreements, according to Attorney Katherine Schon. In records on outwork it is typically provided that
the collective agreement's provisions on working hours, overtime
work, and the like follow the general rules of the collective agreement.
If the employee herself determines the working hours, no overtime pay
is granted. Typically it will be part of the collective agreement that the
employee must register the time spent on work. In some records on
outwork, there are provisions stating the employee may demand outwork up to a maximum of 50 percent of his working hours, calculated
over a specific period. If the employee assesses that the benefit from the
outwork is not sufficient, the employer will typically revoke the
employee's right to perform outwork. With regard to insurance and
compensation, Danish law states that these rights are the same for
teleworking as for working in the principal workplace. (For an extensive look at telework taxation issues see Part 2 of "Framework Agreement for Employees in County Boroughs and Municipalities in
Denmark," found in Appendix A.)

Hiring the Disabled

The Americans with Disabilities Act (ADA) protects U.S employees
who have a qualifying disability by requiring employers to reasonably
accommodate the employee's disability, so long as it does not result in
substantial hardship to the employer. Kathleen Bray clarifies that generally no entity subject to the ADA shall discriminate against a qualified
individual with a disability, because of the disability, in regard to job
application procedures, the hiring, advancement, or discharge of employees, employee compensation, job training, and other terms, conditions, and privileges of employment [§ 42 USC 12112 (a)]. This analysis
is a very fact-specific evaluation, and one that somewhat varies from
state to state, in terms of the expected accommodations that must be
offered by an employer.

The issue of telecommuting as a reasonable accommodation has been
litigated, and Bray offers an example: In *Heaser v. The Toro Company*, an
April 26, 2001 decision of the Eighth Circuit Court of Appeals, the court
issued summary judgment in the employer's favor finding that the
employee's demand for telecommuting as an accommodation for her

disability was unreasonable, and the employee's claim under ADA failed.

In the Eighth Circuit decision, Heaser was a marketing services coordinator for Toro Company, responsible for taking orders by phone and processing the orders on carbonless paper and by computer. Over time, she had increasing problems with chemical sensitivities, fibromyalgia, and allergy-type conditions that she claimed were related to the air quality at Toro. Toro did not have a work-from-home policy, but periodically allowed her to leave the facility when she had flare-ups and work from home. However, she was not fully performing her job, by her own admission. After her short-term disability benefits were terminated, the employee requested as an accommodation that she be allowed to work from home.

Toro denied the request, but offered some other accommodations. The employee found it impossible to work around carbonless paper and copiers, among other things. Toro claimed it could not accommodate Heaser's restrictions. To do so, Toro would have had to change to a completely computerized system of order entry. The court, in agreeing that Heaser's demand was an unreasonable accommodation, held that "Toro was not required to make an overall change in its manner of conducting business to accommodate Heaser." Judge Lay dissented, claiming that the case should not have been disposed of on summary judgment, as there were sufficient factual disputes to proceed with the claim.

Ms. Bray explains that the case leaves open the issue of offering an employee a telecommuting arrangement as a reasonable accommodation if the employer has telecommuting as an already existing work alternative for some employees. As more home-based work sites are created, she comments, employers increasingly will need to consider the arrangement as an accommodation for disabled or injured workers. She mentions also that most jurisdictions are still hesitant to require employers to create new methods of doing business in order to facilitate the hiring or accommodation of a disabled individual.

Bray's practical pointer is that consistency is an employer's best protection; the more exceptions you make, the more likely you will trap yourself into a situation that could be construed as discriminatory. Create your policies, review them to ensure that they are nondiscriminatory, and then consistently use and apply them.

The European Union (EU) directive on equality of treatment as regards employment and occupation (2000/78/EC of November 27, 2000) has still not been implemented in Denmark. The implementing date expires on December 2, 2003. Katherine Schon, Copenhagen attorney, explains that the purpose of the directive is to "establish a general outline for the combat of discrimination as regards employment and occupation due to religion or beliefs, handicap, age or sexual orientation." Today, she explains, a Danish employer is not under an obligation to offer outwork to handicapped persons. It is not likely that this will change in connection with the implementation of the directive into Danish law.

Taxes

According to attorney Kevin Fitzgerald, "Generally speaking, a telecommuting program should have little effect on your company's taxes. You can fully deduct telecommuters' compensation and the cost of related equipment, such as modems, printers and hardware."

One potential wrinkle: a telecommuting program may indirectly increase your payroll taxes, depending on whether the value of working-condition fringes must be added to telecommuters' taxable income. Such fringes may include the cost of telephone service at telecommuters' homes—either paid or reimbursed by your company—and the value of computers and other equipment used by telecommuters. Although the Internal Revenue Service (IRS) has offered little guidance in this area, Internal Revenue Code Section 262(b) states that the value is not taxable if you can prove three things: that the working-condition fringe is needed to do the job, that the telecommuter uses it exclusively for work purposes, and that the equipment or other fringe is not offered as a reward for the employee's services.[17]

Finally, be sure to consult with your tax advisors about the issue of multi-state taxation in relation to telecommuting. The law in this area is only in its infancy, but some states may take the position that the employer or employee should pay taxes on an apportioned basis when telecommuting activities occur in those states, rather than in the employer's principal location.[18]

Attorney Charles F. Knapp, of the Minneapolis firm of Faegre and Benson, LLP, offers more specific advice and examples on this multi-state issue. In the ASK ITAC feature of the International Telework Association Web site, he states that employers whose only out-of-state workers are teleworking may "unknowingly expose their company to additional employment and tax law obligations."

He tells us that virtually every state has a number of employment law statutes that prohibit certain conduct and impose special obligations on employers, including but not limited to nondiscrimination statutes, leave laws, employee rights laws (e.g., drug testing, monitoring, and background investigations), and workers' compensation and unemployment compensation statutes. Whether these statutes apply to employers whose only contact with the state is that they have one or more employees telecommuting from residences in that state will depend on the specific statutory definitions. As a general rule, however, employers should assume that allowing an employee to telecommute from another state on a full-time basis would subject those employers to the employment law statutes of the other state with respect to the telecommuting employee. Therefore, an employee telecommuting from her home in Chevy Chase, Maryland, may have different leave of absence rights than her coworkers officing out of the employer's Arlington, Virginia, corporate headquarters.

In addition to statutory law, Knapp continues, states also have their own body of court-created law (or common law) that imposes varying rights and obligations regarding a variety of employment law issues, such as whether employees may be discharged "at will," whether employees have a right to privacy, and circumstances under which a noncompetition agreement will be legally enforceable. While not aware of any reported decisions directly addressing this issue, Knapp says that related case law suggests that courts will hold employers to the common law standards developed in the state in which an employee telecommutes on a full-time basis. Therefore, a Spokane, Washington, firm employing a home-based telecommuter from Helena, Montana, may be surprised to know that although Washington courts have adopted the doctrine of "at-will employment," Montana common law provides that employees are presumed hired for the length of term for which the employee's wages are calculated.

Mr. Knapp mentions another important issue—whether employing an out-of-state telecommuter will subject an employer to the corporate income tax of the telecommuter's home state. The answer to this question will depend, he says, on each state's tax code and regulations. While federal law places some restrictions on a state's ability to levy corporate income taxes on out-of-state businesses (e.g., states may not impose such taxes on businesses selling tangible personal property if the only activity of that business is the solicitation of orders by its salespersons), these restrictions do not prohibit states from imposing taxes on companies who employ production, administrative, or executive employees in another state. Most states will impose corporate income taxes on businesses that have sufficient "nexus" with that state. Whether the existence of telecommuting employees establishes sufficient nexus will depend on the statutory definitions of nexus and the specific work performed by the telecommuting employee(s).[19]

Telework expert Gil Gordon offers his thoughts on the telework tax issue:

> There is a . . . challenge to consider that has received relatively little attention, but it is growing in importance and deserves to be on the radar screens of both employers and government. It is the issue of "situs," or the

determination of the focal point of a business's operations when there is a difference between the physical centralization of the business offices and the actual location of the workers. In the old days, when a company's office was located in, say, New York City, it was fairly easy to determine who owed taxes to whom. Even with the complicated nature of New York City taxes, and those of adjoining states, and the commuting patterns from the three surrounding states, the rules were relatively clear. Both the employees and employer knew to whom taxes were owed and which payments to one jurisdiction would be credited against taxes due to another one.

Today things are different. Teleworkers who are employed by that same New York City employer may spend only one to three days a week working in Manhattan, and the rest of the time work at home in New Jersey, New York, or Connecticut—or perhaps farther away. The tax implications of this are not the same as for a sales representative employed by the same company but located in a territory in New Jersey; in that case, the sales rep probably does not have an office in Manhattan and spends virtually all of his/her working time in New Jersey—so the tax issues are clearer.[20]

As for the impact on the telecommuters themselves, state employees responsible for the tax decisions are still in the process of studying the issue.

The following paragraphs supply some general information on the tax implications of telework in Europe:

UK. "Benefits in kind" taxes on PCs provided to employees for home use by employers are being abolished, except where a company provides computers for use at home only to management-level employees and not to all workers.

Ireland. "Benefit in kind" taxes on PCs and communications equipment provided by employers for employees at home are still part of the country's tax laws but currently not collected. A proposal to abolish these taxes is awaiting legislative decision.

Germany. German employees who work out of their home over 50 precent of the time realize a tax deduction of 2,400 DM (approximately $1,800 U.S. dollars).

Holland. Since January 1, 1998, a company can give an amount of fl 800 (about 363 euros) per year or fl 4000 (1815 euros) once in five years as compensation for home office furniture. There should be a contract, and the minimum is one day working at home. . . . Furthermore, a company can also buy a computer for up to fl 5,000 for employees to use at home (or provide tax-free compensation for this amount).

Most Dutch companies buy furniture and equipment and make a loan agreement, so the employees can never be taxed. A second analog telephone line can be purchased and expensed by the company, but there is some confusion on ISDNs, which sometimes are taxed. An employee who works more than 70 percent of the time at home can claim up to 40 percent tax deductions for utilities and other telework-related expenses.

Denmark. As of June 1997 employers are no longer taxed on a computer supplied by an employer for private use in an employee's home. As a result, 75 percent of Danish employees' households received gifts of Pentium-level computers, often also including a printer, modem, and Internet subscription. In return, employees who had not learned to drive a vehicle were required by their employer to take a driving course, paid for by the employer, and were subsequently considered for telework.

The determination of the Union of Commercial and Clerical Employees in Denmark (referred to as HK) is that the establishment and installation of such work-at-home expenses as ISDN lines should not be taxable. According to their Executive Consultant Leif Limkilde Bloch, the existence of an ISDN line means that, as a rule, the employee will be liable for tax for the use of a free telephone away from the workplace regardless of whether a business phone is connected to the ISDN line or not. Even if the employee already has a private phone, the business phone will be treated as a "free telephone away from the workplace." By free is meant that the phone is either in the name of the employer or that the employer pays all or part of the costs for that telephone. He suggests the employer take note that for security reasons it is a good idea to set up the ISDN link as a closed net. If communications between teleworker, employer, and any other parties involved is "closed to the outside world," and it is impossible to make private calls, the ISDN link cannot be considered a free telephone, which means that it will not be liable to taxation.[21]

Belgium. Where a homeworking contract is signed, compliant with the 1996 law on homework, allowance for lighting, heating, and the like should be agreed upon with the employer. Without such an agreement, the employee has the right to claim 10 percent of the gross salary. These costs are considered businesses expenses for the employer, and no tax or social security applies.

Confidentiality

There are two sides to the confidentiality coin. One side, for the protection of the employer, requires a confidentiality agreement signed by the employee that basically requires the employee to secure from "prying eyes" the business-related correspondence, documents, and other materials of the employer while they reside in the teleworker's home office and on the teleworker's home computer system.

The other side, the rights of the employee, hinges on the issue of privacy. As much of the communication between teleworkers and their employer's home office will be by e-mail, an understanding of the law and the issues of privacy of electronic communications are crucial. Legislation is pending before the Senate Judiciary Committee that would severely impact an employer's right to monitor employees without prior notice. Entitled the Notice of Electronic Monitoring Act, this bill would require U.S. employers to notify employees of monitoring and would allow for monetary penalties for failure to do so. A House floor vote on the bill is expected soon.

Introduced in July 2000 by Senator Charles Schumer of New York and former representatives Charles Canady of Florida and Bob Barr of Georgia, the bill defines electronic monitoring as the collection of information concerning employee activities or communications by any means other than direct observation, including the use of a computer, telephone, wire, radio, camera, or electromagnetic, photoelectronic, or photo-optical system. It says that an employer may use electronic surveillance to collect any information as long as the information is collected at the employer's premises and confined to the employee's work. It lists an exception, however. The bill states that electronic monitoring, including security cameras, whose sole purpose and principal effect is to collect work-related information would not be prohibited even when it might unintentionally collect some information about employees not confined to the employee's work.

The legislation states that each employer who engages in any type of electronic monitoring shall provide prior written notice to all employees who may be affected. The notice must include the information that is to be collected, the means and times for collection, the location of the monitoring equipment, the use that will be made of the information gathered through monitoring, and the identify of the employees to be monitored.

There is an exception to this rule of notification. If and when an employer has reasonable grounds to believe that employees are engaged in conduct that violates the legal rights of the employer or the employer's employees and involves significant harm to that party and that electronic monitoring will produce evidence of this misconduct, the employer may conduct monitoring without giving notice.

The legislation also states that where an employer's monitoring program will include the employer's customer or members of the public, the employer shall provide notice to those affected. The notice, it says, "may take any form that is reasonably calculated to reach the affected parties."

There is also clarification of simultaneous notice, which states that employers that engage in random or periodic monitoring of employees' communications, such as telephone service observation or monitoring of electronic mail, shall inform the affected employees of the specific event being monitored at the time the monitoring takes place.

A very important exception in this legislation is that of quality control. The exception states that employers engaged in a bona fide quality control program need not provide simultaneous notice. A bona fide quality control program is defined as having five characteristics:

1. The information collected relates to the performance of a specific defined task.
2. The employer has a written standard for the performance of this task.
3. The purpose of the program is to compare the performance of employees performing the task to the standard.
4. Information is collected on a reasonably equal basis regarding performance of all employees performing to task.
5. The affected employees are given feedback on the employer's evaluation of their performance at a time when they can reasonably be expected to remember the events upon which their evaluation is based.

The bill further prohibits monitoring in private areas such as bathrooms, locker rooms, shower facilities, or other similar private areas. With passage of this legislation, any employer found in violation could be fined up to $500,000 for each violation.

As of this writing the bill remains in House and Senate committees with the possibility of a floor vote before recess. Originally scheduled for a vote in September 2002, the decision has been postponed in response to strenuous objections and lobbying by the HR Policy Association (former LPA, Inc., the public policy organization of senior human resource executives) and the Society for Human Resource Management (SHRM). Active proponents of the bill include the American Civil Liberties Union (ACLU) and numerous labor unions such as Communication Workers of America (CWA), American Federation of Labor-Congress of Industrial Organizations (AFL-CIO), and United Auto Workers (UAW).

The California Senate and Assembly have both passed the most recent legislation on this issue, the May 31, 2001 Electronic Monitoring in the Workplace Act. If it becomes law, employers would be obligated to inform their workers if they are reading employee e-mail or tracing

Internet sites visited by employees. The intent of the bill is to stop any secret monitoring of employees, not to stop the monitoring itself. A nearly identical bill was approved by the legislature in 1999 but vetoed by then-Governor Davis. The current act also languishes on the Governor's desk, and may do so for quite some time due to Governor Davis's recall and replacement in October 2003.

The only *federal* limit to employer surveillance comes from the Electronic Communications Privacy Act of 1986. The ECPA prohibits employers from deliberately eavesdropping on purely personal conversations that an employee may have at work. ECPA does not, however, prevent an employer from eavesdropping on business-related conversations or protect purely personal communications that occur through means other than the spoken word, such as e-mail. What this act does not clearly define is how telework would affect an employer's rights to these actions.[22]

Conversion of Property

When the employer terminates the telecommuting employee, the employer must repossess its equipment and files from the employee's home office. Unlike the office situation where the employee leaves and the files and equipment remain with the employer, the telecommuting employee stays and the contents of the home office must be retrieved.

In *Diamond v. T. Rowe Price Associates, Inc.*, the employer brought a counterclaim for conversion, breach of fiduciary duty, and violations of the Maryland Uniform Trade Secrets Acts arising out of the telecommuting employee's temporary refusal to return files after her termination. The court denied the employer's motion for summary judgment on the counterclaim because there was no showing that plaintiff ever misused the files or the information contained therein, that the firm suffered any damage from their temporary absence, or that any of the files contained trade secrets. The court reached this determination, however, by noting that the vast majority of these files had been maintained by plaintiff in her home office with the full knowledge and approval of her employer over the years. As to the employer's breach of fiduciary duty claim, the court noted that plaintiff's employer approved of her telecommuting arrangement, installing a computer in her house and messengering documents to her; therefore, no fair-minded jury could conclude that her possession of the documents in her home office was wrongful or a breach of her fiduciary duty to the company.[23]

The best protection an employer has is twofold. First, to protect business-related information the employer is wise to own the telework equipment, rather than trying to retrieve company-owned information from a teleworker's own PC. The second defense is inclusion in the telework policy and the signed telework agreement that such materials and information are solely the property of the employer and must be returned in a timely manner upon termination of a teleworker's affiliation with the firm.

Protected Communications

When allowing an employee to work at home, a U.S. employer must be careful not to restrict the employee's communications and other protected activities under the Labor Management Relations Act (LMRA). Generally, employees have the right to engage in concerted activities for the purpose of collective bargaining or other mutual aid or protection, and an employer must not interfere with the rights of covered employees.

The U.S. Supreme Court has held that employees may engage in protected concerted activity on company property during nonwork time, absent proof by the employer that restrictions are necessary to maintain production or discipline. Generally, distribution of written materials may be limited to nonwork areas such as parking lots and cafeterias, "because it carries the potential of littering the employer's premises which raises a hazard to production whether it occurs on working time or non-working time." The concerns that solicitation may be accidentally overheard or that distribution of materials presents a safety hazard and a danger of discovery by patrons are no longer relevant in the paperless communications of the telecommuter.

Moreover, where an employer allows its employees to use its property for both work and nonwork purposes, it may not prevent employees from using the property to the same extent for concerted activities under Section 7 of the LMRA. Therefore, an employer allowing its employees to telecommute must decide whether and to what extent its property (computer, fax machine, and phone lines at the employee's home office) may be used for Section 7 solicitation and other communications involving the telecommuting employee, either during or after work hours.

In *E.I Dupont de Nemours & Co.* 311 NLRB893 (1993), the National Labor Relations Board held that the employer discriminated against bargaining-unit employees in violation of their Section 7 rights by prohibiting them from using e-mail to distribute union communications while allowing employees to send frivolous and non-union messages over the employer's e-mail system. The board's decision required only that union access be equal to the access granted to other employees, leaving open the possibility that the employer may forbid all nonwork uses of its e-mail system without violating the LMRA. While this prohibition may be appropriate for employees who can meet in person, such an outright ban on all nonwork use of e-mail would prevent telecommuting employees from exercising their Section 7 rights to concerted action and would therefore violate the LMRA.[24]

Noncompete Covenants

Commonplace practice before the prevalence of e-mail and telework, the noncompete covenant constrained the employee from employment with, and thus from sharing of employer information with, a competitive firm within a specified time period and geographic area after leaving the first firm's employ. Firms attempting to expand these covenants to nationwide limitation have not met with success. In Georgia, for instance, courts have refused to enforce noncompete or nonsolicitation provisions with a nationwide limitation unless the agreement is limited to contact with those customers whom the employee actually contacted during her employment.[25]

Katherine Schon explains that under Danish law a noncompetition clause may be imposed on salaried employees who hold a "special position of trust" or who enter into an agreement with the employer regarding the use of an invention made by the salaried employee. She believes that employees who telework may just as well be considered as salaried employees, as they too fill a special position of trust.

Ms. Schon affirms, "The global market does—in my opinion—not affect the question whether there is in the individual employment relationship a need for a non-competition clause. Non-competition clauses which are assessed to be excessive may be disregarded completely or partly by the courts of law."

One interesting piece of legislation, mentioned by Katherine Schon, is the Treaty of Rome, to which Denmark accedes. The Treaty applies to contractual obligations in all situations where a choice must be made between the laws in different countries. The basis of the Treaty of Rome, is that the parties are free to agree which country's legislation will apply to a contractual relationship.

The basis is, however, modified significantly in the treaty that pertains to employment. The main principle regarding choice of employment law is that the law of the country in which the employee usually performs his work shall apply. This main principle may, however, be departed from by agreement between employer and employee. The employee will, however, with reference to the Treaty of Rome, be able to claim the rights that are accorded to him or her in pursuance of mandatory rules in that country's legislation that according to the main principle would apply in the general country of work. Should a dispute arise between an employee and employer both of who reside in countries recognizing the Treaty of Rome, it should not be a problem to establish the legal position between the parties.[26]

NOTES

1. Congress amended the Clean Air Act in 1990 to address, in part, the persistent failure of urban areas around the United States to attain the health-based national ambient air quality standard (NAAQS) for ozone. It was recognized that relatively steady increases in rates of vehicle miles of travel (VMT) were counteracting reductions in the rates of motor vehicle emissions from engine improvements. Consequently, the CAAA set provisions to rectify the delay in NAAQS attainment and reduce mobile source emissions, specifically requiring:

- Time frames to attain standards on the severity of pollution
- Quantifiable emissions reductions consistent with the attainment time frames in a state's air quality improvement plan (state implementation plan or SIP)
- Conformity of federal actions with the SIP based on a comparative test between an action's emissions and the SIP emission reductions
- Sanctions for noncompliance

With regard to NEPA compliance for projects funded by FHWA (Federal Highway Administration), an important determination is the projects' conformity with the appropriate SIP. Section 1768 of the CAAA states that "no department, agency, or instrumentality of the Federal Government shall engage in, support in any way *or provide financial assistance for,* license or permit or approve, any activity which does not conform to an implementation plan after it has been approved or promulgated under section 110." Section 176(c) (4) of the CAAA requires that the EPA establish the criteria and procedures for determining that transportation plans, programs, and projects funded or approved under the Federal Transit Act conform with state or federal air quality implementation plans. The EPA issued its conformity rule on November 24, 1993.

The basic purpose of the conformity rule is to ensure that emissions from the transportation system conform to SIP emissions budgets for attaining/maintaining health-based air quality standards. Specifically, transportation plans, transportation improvement plans (TIPS) and projects cannot

- Create new air quality standard violations
- Increase the frequency or severity of air quality standard violations
- Delay attainment of air quality standards

If transportation plans, TIPs and projects do not conform to the emissions projections of the SIP, then they cannot be approved or funded. The conformity rule also requires that FHWA projects not cause or contribute to any new localized CO or PM violations or increase the severity of any existing CO or PM violations in CO and PM non-attainment and maintenance areas.

2. Donald L. Moseley, Secretary of Administration, Commonwealth of Virginia, Office of the Governor.

3. Jack Heacock, presenter and ITAC president, 1999 ITAC Awards Luncheon, Sixth Annual International Conference, *Telework: A Virtual Revolution,* Seattle, Wash., October 5, 1999.

4. The bill notes: "Existing law authorizes local air quality management districts to impose an annual vehicle registration fee surcharge of up to $4 to ensure that the districts have the necessary funds to carry out their responsibilities for implementing the California Clean Air Act of 1988. Revenues from the fees must be used solely to reduce air pollution from motor vehicles and for related planning, monitoring, enforcement and technical studies necessary for the implementation of the Act."

The bill's proposed revision would:

• Authorize expenditures for zero emission vehicle programs
• Authorize expenditures for telecommuting activities
• Repeal the January 1, 2000 sunset date on the authorization for bicycle facility improvement projects, allowing the program to continue indefinitely
• Authorize expenditures for an incentive program to encourage local governments to adopt "smart growth" strategies

5. Kathleen Bray is a shareholder in the Duluth, Minnesota law firm of Hanft Pride, P.A., practicing primarily in the areas of employment and lab or law, and workers' compensation defense, as well as general civil litigation. She represents insured and self-insured employers on matters involving both workers' compensation and employment law issues, including ADA, FMLA, and Minnesota Human Rights Act disputes. Additionally, Ms. Bray is a frequent writer and presenter for seminars on employment law and workers' compensation issues.

6. OSHA press release, statement by Secretary Herman, January 5, 2000.

7. Excerpted from Statement of Charles N. Jeffress, Assistant Secretary for OSH, U.S. Department of Labor, before the Subcommittee on Employment, Safety and Training, Senate Committee on Health, Education, Labor, and Pensions, January 25, 2000.

8. Transportation Management Association Group, *TeleManagers Handbook,* September 1997, page 9. TMA Group describes itself as "partnering with the public and private sectors to implement transportation and mobility options to ensure a better quality of life for Williamson County." Its member firms and organizations are the Williamson County Economic Development Council, Williamson Square Development, Crescent Resources, Inc., Williamson County, Nations Bank, First Tennessee Bank, Hampton Inn & Suites, and Trace Realty.

9. Jack Nilles, "Oh, Oh, OSHA," Jala International, [database online] http://www.jala.com.

10. UK Online, "Working Anywhere: Exploring Telework for Individuals and Organizations." For further information see the Health and Safety Executive site www.hse.gov.uk.

11. Andrew C. Head, "Telecommuting: Panacea or Pandora's Box?" [database online September 1, 1999.] http://www.hklaw.com, Sept. 1, 1999

12. Ibid.

13. Lauren Bernardi, "Telecommuting: Legal and Management Issues," *Canadian Manager,* Canadian Institute of Management 23 (3) (Fall 1998): 18 [database online reprint] at http://www.hr.com/Hrcom/index.cfm/97/6EB1745-A-ID58-11D4-8DE1009027E0248F.

14. Gil Gordon, "Media Mini-uproar over Latest Telecommuter Legal Case" [database online July 2003] http://www.gilgordon.com/review/july_10_03.htm.

15. Darrell VanDeusen, "Maryland Wage and Hour Law Pitfalls," HR.Com [database online, June 2001], http://www.HRLawForum.com.

16. Kevin Fitzgerald, "Telecommuting and the Law," *Small Business Reports* 20 (9) (1994): 14 [database online reprint], http://www.hr.com/HR.com/index.cfm/18/85a26aa1-2DC6-11D4-8jDE7009027E0248F. Consider the examples of clerical workers or word processors working from home. The recordkeeping for these will include:

1. The regular rate of pay for any workweek, whether it's per hour, per day, etc., and the amount of pay excluded from the regular rate. What that means is that you must explain when the employee is eligible for premium pay, such as overtime and holiday pay.

2. The total hours worked each workday and workweek, using FLSA-mandated definitions of each.

3. Separate tallies of straight-time earnings per workday or workweek and premium pay for overtime hours.

4. Total additions or deductions from wages for each pay period—FICA, taxes, health plan deductions, 401(k) contributions, pay advances, car mileage reimbursements, etc.

You can't average the number of hours an employee works during two or more weeks to avoid paying overtime for any one of the weeks. Your company's telecommuting policy also should prohibit unauthorized work on Sundays and holidays by non-exempt staffers. Although the law is somewhat cloudy regarding this issue, you may be required to pay overtime for these hours, even if employees work of their own accord. To hedge against such unintentional liability, outline disciplinary measures for telecommuters who violate your work hour restrictions, such as verbal or written warnings. If your telecommuters are exempt—executive, administrative, or professional capacities, for instance—the special recordkeeping requirements don't apply. Therefore, you needn't worry about whether they are working nights or weekends because they're not eligible for overtime pay. In fact, the FLSA recordkeeping requirements for exempt telecommuters generally are the same as for exempt employees who work on site. Basically, you must keep track of the day and time their workweek begins, along with the total wages and date of payment for each pay period

17. Suppose, for example, that you cover the cost of basic telephone service at a telecommuter's home. This amount may be taxable unless the employee has more than one telephone line. The reason: the IRS considers reimbursements to be a benefit if the employee would incur the expenses anyway. The same might be true of computers and other equipment. If employees use their own equipment and you reimburse them for all or a portion of the purchase price, you may have to include that amount in their income. *By contrast, if you own the equipment and supply it to telecommuters to do their jobs, the value most likely can be excluded.* This is generally the best way to go, since your company can deduct the cost of the equipment, just as you do for on-site use.

18. Fitzgerald, "Telecommuting and the Law."

19. For example: Wisconsin law provides that the following will constitute sufficient nexus to subject an out-of-state corporation to Wisconsin corporate tax:

1. Maintenance of a business location in Wisconsin, including any kind of office.

2. Usual or frequent activity in Wisconsin by employees . . . soliciting orders with authority to accept them.

3. Usual or frequent activity in Wisconsin by employees . . . engaged in purchasing activity or in the performance of services.

4. Miscellaneous other activities by employees . . . in Wisconsin such as credit investigations, collection of delinquent accounts, conducting training classes or seminars for customer personnel in the operation, repair and maintenance of the business' products.

5. Leasing of tangible property and licensing of intangible rights for use in Wisconsin.

Based on this statutory provision, it is easy to conceive of telecommuting scenarios that may subject a Minnesota employer with an employee telecommuting in Wisconsin-to-Wisconsin corporate income tax. It is possible that the Wisconsin Department of Revenue may consider a home office used by a full-time telecommuter as "any kind of office" maintained in the state of Wisconsin.

20. Gil Gordon, "Employer Scheduling, Staffing and Work Location Issues," presented at Labor Telework and the New Workplace of the 21st Century, New Orleans, La., 2000.

21. Leif Limkilde Bloch, "National Reports Denmark," HK/Danmark [database online, July 2000], http://www.telework-mirti.org/dbdocs/national.doc.

22. American Civil Liberties Union, "Workplace Rights," ACLU [database online], http://www..aclu.org/issuesworker/legkit2.html.

23. Head, "Telecommuting: Panacea or Pandora's Box?"

24. Ibid.

25. Ibid.

26. The "Treaty of Rome," signed March 25, 1957, was a collaboration of the leaders of the countries of Belgium, France, Germany, Italy, Luxembourg, and the Netherlands, establishing the European Economic Community, stating their mission thus: "Determined to lay the foundations of an ever closer union among the peoples of Europe, Resolved to ensure the economic and social progress of their countries by common action to eliminate the barriers which divide Europe, Affirming as the essential objective of their efforts the constant improvement of the living and working conditions of their peoples, Recognizing that the removal of existing obstacles calls for concerted action in order to guarantee steady expansion, balanced trade and fair competition, Anxious to strengthen the unity of their economies and to ensure their harmonious development by reducing the differences existing between the various regions and the backwardness of the less favored regions, Desiring to contribute, by means of a common commercial policy, to the progressive abolition of restrictions on international trade, Intending to confirm the solidarity which binds Europe and the overseas countries and desiring to ensure the development of their prosperity, in accordance with the principles of the Charter of the United Nations, Resolved by thus pooling their resources to preserve and strengthen peace and liberty, and calling upon the other peoples of Europe who share their ideal to join in their efforts."

Feeling Safe and Secure

A safe, secure home work environment involves more than just protecting your teleworker's computer from invasion by viruses. Not only may the computer become a target for unwelcome guests, but the worker himself may be in danger from health problems brought on by ergonomically poor furniture or lighting decisions, by unsafe electrical or other setups, or by less than secure practices—nosy neighbors, prying eyes, and so on—that might, of course, also lead to litigious or financial problems for your firm.

KEEPING YOUR TELEWORKER SAFE AND HEALTHY

While home inspections, either periodic or by one initial home visit (which may include technical support and set-up assistance) are the preferred method of ensuring employee safety and thus reduction of employer liability concerns, there are times and situations where this might not be feasible. If teleworkers do not live in a reasonable proximity to one of your office locations, you may need to rely on the homeworkers' signatures on the agreement form indicating their compliance with your home set-up requirements. You can also ask that they provide photos of their home offices.

In Region 8 of the Environmental Protection Agency, based in Denver, Colorado, employees fill out a checklist to ensure that their home offices are safe. The U.S. Forest Service also requires employees to fill out safety self-certification forms, as does the National Institutes of Health for all its divisions. The issues these public sector agencies address include the following:

- Is the workspace free of asbestos-containing materials?

- Is the space free of indoor air quality problems?
- Is there a drinkable water supply?
- Are file cabinets and storage closets arranged so drawers and doors do not open into walkways?
- Are bathrooms available with hot and cold running water?
- Is all electrical equipment free of recognized hazards that would cause physical harm (frayed wires, bare conductors, loose wires, flexible wires running through walls, exposed wires fixed to the ceiling)?

In EPA Region 9, if an employee answers three or more of the 22 questions on the self-certification checklist negatively, then the employee and her or his frontline supervisor meet to discuss safety concerns. If necessary, the region's health and safety staff can go to an employee's home for an inspection, though that has yet to happen. "What we generally find is that home work stations are often nicer than what you might find in the gray cubicle at the workplace," states Director Kris Jensen.[1]

The U.S. Forest Service Region 5 telecommuting agreement mandates that employees allow the agency to inspect home work stations for safety standards, as long as the agency gives employees 24-hour notice.

The state of Florida, in its "Checklist for the Home Office" offers several other potentially hazardous features to assess:

- Are all the stairs with four or more steps equipped with handrails?
- Are all circuit breakers and fuses in the electrical panel labeled as to intended service? Do they clearly indicate open and closed positions?
- Are electrical outlets three-pronged (grounded)?
- Is the computer connected to a surge protector?
- Are aisles, doorways, and corners free of obstructions to permit movement?
- Is the space crowded with furniture?
- Are the phone lines, electrical cords, and extension wires secured under a desk or alongside a baseboard?
- Are floor surfaces clean, dry, level, and free of worn or frayed seams?
- Is there a fire extinguisher in the home, easily accessible from the office space?
- Is there a working smoke detector detectable from the workspace?[2]

FYI . . .

Initially Merrill Lynch conducted home inspections prior to the start of any telework, sending one male and one female inspector to avoid any issue of impropriety. As the volume of teleworkers and their distance from the office increased, the inspections became unworkable. The company now requires each candidate to provide pictures of the home office, demonstrating a safe, comfortable, ergonomically correct environment and furnishings.

For a sample home inspection form see that offered by the Midwest Institute for Telecommuting Education (MITE) in Appendix B. MITE is a consultant group that provides expertise in strategic planning, manager/employee training, and policy development for telework implementation. The organization is the creation of more than 50 business and government leaders who contribute their time and expertise to develop telework curricula, seminars, and implementation manuals. Do peruse their site and publications. They also offer an online "Ask the Experts" form, free of charge, that allows you to ask telecommuting-related questions of their varied telework professionals. Visit them at www.mite.org.

An excellent, easily understood, and visually appealing ergonomic training resource, which offers teleworkers free training in keyboard and workstation ergonomics, is found at www.ergonome.org. Each teleworker should be directed to take the Key Moves Training Program. It walks them through everything they need to know about setting up their computer workstation and preventing discomfort or injury due to improperly designed or arranged desks, chairs, computers, or keyboards.

The ideal home-security situation would be a room solely dedicated to work-at-home, with a lock on the door and the file cabinets, and whose computer is used only by the teleworker. While you can't, of course, build an addition on a teleworker's home, you can best assure home security by providing the computer and other equipment and thus secure the right to demand a signed agreement that its use be solely for work-at-home by your employee.

PC SECURITY

The security gurus at Tech Target's searchsecurity.com (do sign up for their free e-mail security newsletter) warn that the only way to make your computer completely hackerproof is to turn it off or disconnect it from the Internet. The real issue, they say, is how to make your computer 99 percent hackerproof. Let's see if we can't teach you how to do that.

Most, if not all, telework experts advise the need for remote workers to have broadband access, as opposed to dial-up access if they need

Internet access. Not all teleworkers need such access. Broadband does, however, create a security issue not found with dial-up modems. The broadband Internet connection, with its static address, is easily hacked into because of its always-on status. Most 56k dial-up modems use a new IP address each time the worker logs on; the hacker, unless using a Trojan horse, will find it much more difficult to find the telecommuter's computer and hack into the system.

The basic security products and methods we discuss in this chapter are:

- Personal firewall
- Anti-virus software regularly updated
- Strong passwords
- VPN
- E-mail and hardware encryption
- Software to permanently erase files from the hard drive
- System backup
- Software patches, regularly applied to detect viruses and bugs
- Hardening the "box" (the operating system)
- Regularly scheduled operating system and application maintenance
- File and print sharing
- Anti-theft devices
- Security-conscious employees

Personal Firewalls

Steve Gibson, security consultant and founder of Gibson Research Corporation, talks about work-at-home computer security: "A personal firewall is so important," he says. "It is like wheels to the car." He affirms that, in the near future, firewalls will automatically be included on computers.

One of the simple and friendliest places to access firewall information is found on HR.com. Former staffer Connie Liu, in her "Firewalls—A General Overview," offers a general understanding of how firewalls can assist with security.

"Simply put," she explains, "A firewall is a software or hardware device that filters information coming through the Internet connection into your private network or computer workstation." She differentiates between hardware and software firewalls.

Hardware types are physical pieces of equipment that are usually connected to a whole system of computer networks . . . software firewalls, on the contrary, can be installed or downloaded into our individual computers or our home/office computer network.

FYI . . .

Helen Birkmann, certified network engineer, is co-owner of Bainbridge NY's MKL.NET, (www.mkl.com), providing a myriad of services including solutions to problems incurred by connecting to the Internet. Birkmann explains that the ideal firewall includes both hardware and software.

> Firewalls are able to offer a chance to monitor and track Internet usage. They can be programmed to deny users from accessing certain websites based on their domain name or IP address, thus preventing users from accessing websites unrelated to business needs. They can also deny access to websites by being instructed to look for keywords that have been designated as forbidden.

(For more information on these firewall "production filters," see the "E-mail and Hardware Encryption" portion of this chapter.)

When selecting a personal firewall, according to Home PC Firewall Guide, you should consider whether you want one that controls outbound communication with the Internet. The advantage is that you are alerted the first time any program tries to call out to establish a connection to the Internet, and you are given the option of deciding whether to allow it one time, always, or never. The disadvantage is that you may have no idea what the program trying to call out is or what it does. New releases of Norton, Zonealarm, and other firewall products make it easier to set up outbound communication rules and understand what is going on.[3]

Tech Target's recommendations for business payware firewall security products are Norton Personal Firewall 2002 and ZoneAlarm Pro 2.6 with networking and mail safe features. MKL.Net's Helen Birkmann concurs.

Norton also offers Norton Internet Security 2002, a complete remote worker-security package including personal firewall, anti-virus, ad blocker, cookie manager, privacy, and parental control features.

Anti-Virus Software

With an estimated 50,000 known viruses and with new, more resistant ones being created daily, protection from viruses is a vital security issue. Two inexpensive anti-virus products are McAfee VirusScan 7.0, and Norton Anti-Virus 2003.

From *Smart Computing* magazine we gleaned this anti-virus tip:

> Don't immediately upgrade to the latest versions of software, particularly Web browsers, e-mail applications, operating systems, and office

applications. Most viruses work only when you have a specific combination of software, and many take advantage of previously unseen security holes associated with new software versions. Nearly every time Microsoft rolls out a new version of Internet Explorer, for example, the hacking community probes it for weaknesses and exploits any sloppiness. It's usually better to wait until the first patch or service pack is available before upgrading from older, more secure versions. Once you upgrade, check the manufacturer's Web site frequently for security alerts.[4]

Marcia Branco, lead network engineer for DecisionOne Corporation, independent provider of multivendor computer maintenance services, adds her caution:

> Many make the mistake of thinking that the anti-virus program they installed three months ago will continue to protect them, even though new computer viruses are developed daily. Applied regularly, anti-virus software "patches" and signature file updates can serve as added armor against these troublesome bugs. Signature file updates, keeping your anti-virus software itself current, play a similar role in assuring that data remains contaminant-free.

Helen Birkmann and other security experts recommend you check your anti-virus vendor's Web site weekly to check for and download upgrades. Birkmann also clarifies the issue of Microsoft security, stating that the security concerns are primarily with Outlook and most especially Outlook Express. Her recommendations for e-mail are the less virus-susceptible Eudora and Netscape.

Strong Passwords

Neal O'Farrell, founder and CEO of the security education firm Hackademia, emphasizes that poor password habits are a big problem, pointing out that a hacker running a password-cracking program on a 433 mhz PC could try 250,000 login/password combinations in less than 60 seconds.

Jack Nilles, in *Managing Telework,* suggests three password-related security features in the typical situation where the sensitive information is kept on the company mainframe or LAN, and the teleworker accesses by modem:

- Using "smart cards" that display a password that changes every 30 seconds or so, in synchronism with a password identifier in the computer being called (the teleworker pulls out her smart card, dials up the company machine, and enters the password appearing on the card at the moment).

- Using a "call-back system"—assuming all the password routines are completed correctly (many notebook computers have them built into the communications software, which is why they are desirable theft objects), the central computer dials the teleworker's home or other prearranged phone number.
- Requiring a positive identification of the caller, such as retinal scan, fingerprint, or hand-shaped detector.[5]

The MKL.NET network engineering team of Helen Birkmann and Tim Barbeisch discussed the issue of passwords. Birkmann explained the callback system. "Let's say, for instance, I was home trying to access the office network and we had a call-back system in place. The computer would recognize what is allegedly my computer, hear me call, hang up on me and call back to be sure it's really me."

She clarified that call-backs, retinal scans, fingerprints, and the like are a very high-end security function—very high-tech and generally used for sites such as the that of the CIA. "Remember the movie *Air Force One*?' she asks, "when the terrorists boarded the plane as reporters? If you recall they did that by cutting off the fingers of the real reporters. The government had a fingerprint scan in place there."

Tim Barbeisch recommends a password of 15 or more characters, with both upper- and lower-case letters and numbers, and points out that too many people use obvious things like their birthday. Birkmann suggests that your teleworkers use something familiar to them but not obvious—maybe a place they traveled to, or the name of a deceased pet. They clarified, however, that, while many ISPs allow their clients to choose their own passwords, MKL assigns random passwords, making them more secure because the code has no relevance to the user.

There are additional ways to strengthen passwords assigned by your firm or the individual teleworker, though these further complicate the issue of recall. For this, LanWrights, Inc.'s James Michael Stewart, in his contributing article for Tech Target's Search Security.com e-mail newsletter, offers a uniquely workable solution. He lists the elements of a strong password:

1. Six or more characters
2. Changed every 30–60 days
3. Restriction of changing password in less than 2–7 days (i.e., a minimum required age)
4. Prevention of re-using 6–24 previous passwords (i.e., managing password history)
5. Use of at least three different character types: upper case, lower case, numerals, keyboard symbols

6. Prevention of use of any part of your real name, e-mail address, computer name, phone number, social security number, or any other personal ID number, name, or phrase
7. Prevention of common dictionary words, slang, or industry acronyms

Sounds imposing, right? Stewart explains why it doesn't have to be intimidating. He says, "Seeing these restrictions often leads one to think that users must select a password that is so complex that they often can't remember it, such as oA16l8aCCp." He assures us that oA16l8aCCP is easy to remember if you know one simple fact: "As humans, we can remember activities, events, people and occurrences," he explains. "We especially remember things that happen to us or near us that are either exciting, dangerous or at least out of the ordinary. . . . Using this fact, I suggest to users to think of an event that they can easily remember."

Stewart goes on to suggest that once you recall the event you think of a simple sentence to describe that event. He offers these examples: "Hey, Bob, I just saw the weirdest thing during lunch," and "Amanda, I just went hang gliding in the Virgin Islands!" His next instruction is that you add a date to the event: "On July 5, I saw a weird thing during lunch," is Stewart's example. "You then take the first letter of every word, and keep any numbers: OJ5Isawtdl," explains Stewart. He also mentions that you can elect to drop common articles—"a," "an," and "the"—alternate capitalization, replace common letters or words—3 for e/E, or 8 for ate. "In my first example," he clarifies, oA16l8aCCp is created from the sentence "on April 16 I ate a Chucky Cheese pizza."

VIRTUAL PRIVATE NETWORKS

A Virtual Private Network (VPN) is an intelligent pipe that uses "tunneling" to encrypt data at the IP level and send it securely from one network to another over the Internet. In other words, the home office network uses a VPN to secure communications from the home office to satellite offices, telework centers, and teleworkers' systems. It encrypts at the sender end and decrypts at the receiver end. In a telework situation, a firewall would be used at the employee's home and the VPN would be in place and managed at the employer's main site, with its counterpart VPN installed on the homeworker's computer. The primary culprits your office is protecting itself from, according to Tim Barbeisch, systems administrator for MKL.NET, are "script kiddies." Barbeisch explains who they are. "The average script kiddie," he says, "is 13–18 years old. They only download other's exploits. They do it just to be able to say they've done it." Barbeisch explains that most grow out of it.

The speed of your system will partly be determined by what you spend on a VPN router. You can probably acquire one for under $1,000, but keep in mind that you will need a pair at least, one at each end.

E-mail and Hardware Encryption

Most of us already know the importance of not opening unsolicited e-mail attachments. E-mails are most often the source for hackers, viruses, and Trojan horses. Then there's the issue of what your employees are doing; can their use of e-mail, in-house or remote, put you at risk of litigation? Besides the anti-virus software already discussed, you can minimize the risks of libel or harassment litigation through content control packages that filter certain types of e-mail while allowing others. They can also be configured to filter e-mail messages based on keyword searches; for example, you could filter out messages with bad language or abusive or discriminatory content. Content control can be used to block attachments of certain types.

MKL's Internet Control Filter (ICF), what coowner Helen Birkmann refers to as their "porn filter," blocks access to over 95 percent of all Web sites, e-mail, chat rooms, and newsgroups in the categories of pornography, drugs, cults, hate groups, and anarchy. A dedicated MKL research staff continually searches the Internet, identifies objectionable sites, and updates their server at least once daily.

They also offer a check e-mail feature for their clients, a service you will want to inquire about with your own and your teleworkers' Internet Provider. They recommend their clients check their e-mail from the MKL site before downloading to their own home computer. "Attacks do a lot more damage than they used to," cautions Helen Birkmann. "Now attackers have DDOS, Distributed Denial of Service (an attempt to "flood" a network, preventing legitimate communication), which is coming from thousands of hosts and can't be blocked.

Viruses use address books or previously received mail to distribute themselves to all those contacts, using their names. Let's assume, for instance, a teleworker gets an e-mail from her friend, Hbirkmann. If she received mail again from Hbirkmann, she would open it. But it could be a virus. The old adage of not opening attachments or e-mails from people you don't know, while still good advice, doesn't solve the problem."

Birkmann goes on to clarify that Trojan horses, the viruses that "call out," can look very innocuous. She has found some herself, named command.exe and word.exe. Tim Barbeisch concurs, explaining that hackers have their systems working on autopilot; and once a Trojan horse is installed, a "victim" computer can then start scanning too.

MKL.NET's ICC for business has Internet filtering solutions designed especially for businesses large and small, monitoring up to 10,000 computers or more and minimizing the time employees, including teleworkers, spend on nonbusiness sites, avoiding costly legal liabilities. This also preserves network bandwidth against downloading movies or photographs, which can slow the network to a crawl.

(This is one more reason to provide computers and Internet connections for your at-home workers, rather than relying on their own purchases. If the product is yours, you have the right to control its use.)

You may also wish to block any MP3 (audio) attachments to e-mail messages. With very few exceptions, telecommuting employees do not need musical e-mails to accomplish their work tasks. Content control can be used to filter chain letters and spam from your e-mail traffic. This software can be configured to attach legal disclaimers to outbound e-mail. It can also be used to filter for potentially abusive or inappropriate words in inbound and outbound e-mail. You also need to encrypt your sensitive e-mail, ensuring first, however, that the recipient's system has the key that allows it to be decrypted. Tim Barbeisch states that not all e-mails offer this decryption service. Both ZoneAlarm and Norton Internet Security 2002 do.

Software to Permanently Erase Files from the Hard Drive

The idea that you can empty your recycle bin or erase your file and the contents will be gone is a fallacy. As Tim Barbeisch explains, when you erase a disk you are just preparing that disk for reuse, but what you erased is still there, available to be found by others unless overwritten.

One example of the seriousness of this issue is the collapsed energy giant Enron Corporation, once the seventh largest company in the United States, and its now-jeopardized accounting firm, Arthur Anderson. Anderson, one of the "big five" accounting firms in the nation, is being investigated for hiding huge Enron debts from its client's books. Now comes the task of finding evidence that Anderson employees, at the advice of their lawyers, removed the truth of the Enron financial plight by deleting e-mails and files. Ian Hopper, AP technology writer, in a Foster's online article talked with a representative of the "computer sleuth" firm Internet Crimes Group in Princeton, N.J. Internet Crimes, charged with the job of retrieving evidence of Anderson complicity, has been able to recover Lotus Notes e-mail messages that were deleted up to eight months earlier.[6]

Numerous software products are available to assist your teleworkers with permanent deletion. We will look at two.

White Canyon Software's Clean Drive permanently erases your data by overwriting it. It is sold (licensed) by user, for an unlimited number of uses. They also offer a Secure Clean product that purges files and manages your Internet browser cookies and cache. Both offer a free try. Their site is www.whitecanyon.com.

Another product, Webroot Software's Window Washer, is the recommendation of PC Internet editor Graham Wing.[7] (See www.pcin.net to sign up for their free e-newsletter.) "For as long as I've been helping people," Wing says, "one of the most common questions is, How can I permanently erase xxxx file on my computer?" Clarifying that generally the question pertains to Internet files, he affirms that Window Washer is the answer.

Wing explains that the software erases browser cache, browser cookies, browser history, mail trash, recycle bin, recent files, temp folder, document histories (last file opened list), registry streams, windows run and find histories, MS Office 97 and 2000 Tracks, Windows Temporary Files Directory, and ScanDisk.CHK files. The employer can set up the program to run every time the teleworkers start and shut down their computers, or employees can run it whenever they or the employer chooses to. Users can also choose to specify which cookies not to erase, if there are some that telecommuters need or wish to keep.

"What really sets Window Washer apart," says King, "is that it doesn't just erase files, you also have the option to 'shred' the files. If you just erase a file," he clarifies, "an experienced user can use a simple utility to bring it back. Erasing a file just wipes the file entry away from the FAT (like a hard drive's table of contents), but leaves the data on the hard drive." To explain the importance of this, King tell us that the National Security Agency (NSA) has set a standard that the location of a file needs to be erased and rewritten and erased again seven times before it is officially destroyed.

Window Washer also lets you add custom options to the program, with free plugins from the WebRoot Software site that allow you to delete the tracks left by other popular programs. At the time of King's review, there were 28 plugins and more were being added regularly.

System Backup

Besides the obvious issue of having duplication in case of damage, theft, or destruction, for purposes of securing sensitive information, telework pioneer Jack Nilles recommends removable hard disks or Zip disks (which hold 100 mb) to allow the information to be kept separate from the computer. Teleworkers can keep disks locked up at home or carry them along as they travel between home and telework center or the principal office.[8]

Helen Birkmann emphasizes that backing up is the responsibility of the end-user, not technical support: "We have clients come in to us when their computers crash, upset that we have to reformat the hard drive and they are going to lose what is on it. If the information is that important they should have been backing up all along."

Both the need for the teleworkers to be responsible for this back-up and the minimum schedule requirement should be noted in your telework policy and signed by each teleworker.

Hardening the Box (the Operating System)

Network engineers Helen Birkmann and Tim Barbeisch, the Internet support/ISP team at MKL.NET, explained that hardening the box best done prior to the computer's first use, consists of shutting off what you don't need and downloading patches. They emphasized that the procedure is especially important in UNIX, a system vulnerable to file sharing.

Operating System and Application Maintenance

Decision One's Marcia Branco emphasizes that it is vitally important for remote workers to have clear guidelines on what to do when technical problems arise or they feel security has been breached. "Help desk support needs to be in place for remote workers," she insists. "This way most technical problems can be expertly diagnosed and hopefully fixed."

Steve Mencik, science advisor for IIT Research Institute, points out that one big problem with remote-worker security is the failure to use the tools provided. He warns that "users may be provided with file or disk encryption tools for their remote computers, but either find them too cumbersome to use, or simply can't be bothered. Thus, their data is left unprotected."[9] While this may seem a cumbersome task for the employer, it should be noted that the latest outside attack on Microsoft was accomplished through a teleworker's home computers.

Absent regular home visits, and as noted with previous security issues, the need for teleworkers to follow agreed-upon security and maintenance procedures and minimal schedules should be written in your telework policy and signed by each telecommuter prior to their starting telework.

File and Print Sharing

Security guru Leo LaPorte, host of TechTV's "The Screen Savers," offers the advice that teleworkers should turn off Windows file sharing by opening the remote computer's network control panel and turning off "file and print sharing."[10] (Not necessarily a bad thing to have it open—if, for instance, a printer is hooked up to the back of one computer, another networked computer can print from it—but...when Windows 95 first came out, it was set up with a default of file and print sharing enabled and all those who had Road Runner, for instance, could access each other's files and printers. Clearly a security problem!)

LaPorte's software recommendation is twofold. The first product he suggests is ShieldsUp. This Gibson Research Corporation product, designed by founder Steve Gibson, is a free download from their site, www.gsc.com.[11] You may wish to direct your teleworkers to take advantage of this free opportunity to check their computer's security when connected to the Internet. Not only does it pinpoint open ports but it also gives "friendly" repair instructions and explanations. This may also be something you would want your technical support people to accomplish with the initial home inspection.

LaPorte also recommends ZoneAlarm. The suggested process would be to have the home worker use Shields Up, determining the unsecured computer ports, to then install ZoneAlarm, returning afterwards to Shields Up to discover how much more secure the computer has now become. The ZoneAlarm or ZoneAlarm Pro, free to personal users, can be purchased for businesses and offers such protection as e-mail attachment protection, automatic network detection, customizable security controls, hacker tracker, ability to block specific Web addresses, password protection, and restricted zones. To download ZoneAlarm for a free 60-day trial, go to www.zonealarm.com.

Anti-Theft and Recovery

According to the SANS Institute, in their 2000 survey of 643 major U.S. corporations, 60 percent of the surveyed firms had experienced laptop thefts. According to the insurance firm Safeware, in the year 2000 there were 387,000 incidents of notebook theft and 16,000 of desktop theft in the United States alone. Safeware insures computers against damages caused by accidents, power surges, theft, lightning, vandalism, water damage, and natural disasters. The three primary causes of computer damage or loss, they point out, are (1) accidental damage, (2) theft, and (3) power surges.

Their coverage includes complete repair or replacement of your computer system with no deduction for depreciation, replacement of purchased software, 30-day trial period *except in the state of Texas,* and coverage for computers in transit up to $10,000. For the purchase of additional coverage they offer computer rental electronic equipment, and *protection against computer fraud by employees and others.*

Their site, www.safeware.com, offers an online quote. While we do not recommend purchase of Safeware's services, we mention their firm as an example of the type of computer insurance coverage available.

There are some innovative programs and devices to protect your teleworkers' computers from theft or aid in their recovery. Here are some we found, listed not as recommendations but as examples of the types of products and services coming to the forefront to meet our growing computer security needs.

CyberAngel®, by Computer Sentry Software: This unique software, the dream child of recently deceased actor Robert Urich, is designed to locate and protect the information on desktops and laptops alike in case of theft. The security process is threefold: alert, lock, and locate in the event of unauthorized access of a computer.

Using a secure password entry system, the CyberAngel will *alert* the registered user of any unauthorized access of that protected computer, *lock* the communication ports to prevent the unauthorized user from using any dial-up networking software or utility to access the Internet, an on-line banking account, or more important, remote access to a corporate server. It can also lock the data stored on that computer with its 448-bit encryption module.

When you notify CSS's Security Monitoring Center that a registered computer has been stolen, they can then *locate* the computer when it reports an unauthorized access. The software currently works on Windows 95, Windows 98, and Windows ME platforms. CSS can also provide the CyberAngel without encryption for Windows NT 4.0 and Windows 2000. Peruse their site, www.sentryinc.com, for further details.

CompuClamp, a newly patented, portable security clamp, is engineered to protect desktop computers, towers, servers, printers, fax machines, scanners, laptops, medical and lab equipment, cash registers, TVs, and VCRs from theft. Its use provides a discount on your Safeware computer insurance. It has a vise-like grip and allows your teleworking employee's equipment to be attached to a hard surface such as a table or desk, is fully removable and portable, and does not harm the desk's surface. For further information, see the company's site, www.compuclamp.com.

Kensington offers two security products: Its *Notebook MicroSaver Security Cable* is a six-foot steel cable that loops around an immovable object and can be custom-keyed. Its *CompuTrace*, hidden, nondisruptive, tamper-resistant and easy to use, tracks and recovers stolen PCs.

Lucira Technologies, Inc., has created *MobileSecure 2002*. This software-based service allow firms to protect and control their laptop and desktop populations from loss or theft by tracking and recovering, safeguarding, and retrieving data and viewing comprehensive information about the hardware and software assets of the entire enterprise IT fleet. Its recovery feature locates the IP address and telephone number leading to the physical location of the hardware, collecting all the data needed for law enforcement to obtain the necessary warrants.

MobileSecure 2002 allows you to retrieve, encrypt, or delete the data on your machine before a thief reads it. You can also remotely view the data on the machine and make choices about which files to delete, retrieve, and/or encrypt. If you choose to subscribe to the asset-management feature you can receive reports containing information on the various machines in your fleet. This information includes, but is not limited to, hardware configuration, software configuration, and network configuration. It also offers, for no additional charge, an auto-upgrade feature. These can be deployed to the machines of your remote workers seamlessly and unobtrusively.

MobileSecure 2002 thus allows you to easily determine whether or not your teleworkers are complying with organization-wide security policies or are capable of upgrading their systems with new software. The information provided would include baseboard, CD ROM, display card, floppy, hard disk, printer, processor, RAM, BIOS, keyboard, modem, monitor, mouse, network card, operating system, system specifications, miscellaneous hardware, and all software installed on the machine.

MobileSecure's Data Protection Suite also allows the administrator to retrieve data from an employee's machine if you are worried about the loss of such data. The retrieval functionality allows end users to view their files online and allows firms to specify their own file storage location. Recovery can be done via Internet or phone. One of its installation mechanisms, designed to go unnoticed by the end user, allows management to combat any internal theft problems.

Security-Conscious Teleworkers

One component of security that must not be overlooked is your employees themselves. Jack Nilles, in his *Managing Telework*, emphasizes that the fundamental security rule is the same for everyone: "Hire the best employees, motivate them, train them, give them the best tools, and keep them informed of security issues."

Neal O'Farrell, Hackademia CEO, states, "There's a growing consensus in both the hacking and the security community that your biggest vulnerability, and best defense, has nothing to do with technology at all and may, in fact, already be on your payroll." He affirms that employees' willingness to help telephone callers makes them especially vulnerable to social engineering by hackers posing as legitimate employees.

O'Farrell states unequivocally that security can no longer be seen as a task, chore, or set of rules, but as a culture. He advises that as a culture, security will strive to make all employees think about security all the time, with every decision and before every action. "When security is as second nature as being polite to customers," he says, "it should kick in automatically without regular training and constant reminders."[12]

Decision One's Marcia Branco concurs that employees are crucial to security. Branco warns that the belief that a network is as secure as its weakest link *must* be extended to teleworkers. In her "Telework Security" white paper she suggests teleworker security should be enhanced by ongoing training and awareness programs and teleworkers should be made aware that their use of company technology will be monitored.[13]

Marcia recommends instituting a documented process and procedure for remote workers to regularly download and properly install anti-virus software and update signature files. She adds, "For optimum protection, it may be necessary to change default configuration settings, depending on your network requirements. A thorough understanding of your system's security capabilities as it relates to your needs is paramount."

Although requiring a little more technical know-how, the SANS Institute, creator of the Center for Internet Security, offers a list of the 20 most critical Internet security vulnerabilities, as well as details on countering or preventing the problems and detailed explanations of the issues. See http://www.sans.org/top20.htm.

Another source for user-friendly computer security advice and news is ZDNet's Anchordesk.com. They also offer downloads and purchases of software products such as the aforementioned ZoneAlarm, complete with online user testimonials.

NOTES

1. Brian Freil, "Agencies Responsible for Work-at-Home Safety," *Government Executive Magazine* [database online, January 6, 2000] http://www.govexec. com/dailyfed/0100/010600b1.htm.

2. Florida Department of Management Services, "State Employee Telecommuting Program Checklist for the Home Office," [database online], http://fcn.state.fl.us/dms/hrm/telecom/tcklist.html.

3. Home PC Firewall Guide [database online, 2002], http://www.firewallguide.com/index.htm.

4. Mark Anderson, "Potential Threats to Your PC's Security," *Smart Computing Magazine*, February 2001, pages 38–43. Reprinted with permission from Smart Computing Magazine. Subscription information 800-733-3809, www.smartcomputing.com.

5. Jack Nilles, *Managing Telework*, (New York, N.Y., John Wiley & Sons, 2000 reprint of 1998 book), chapter 4, page 12.

6. D. Ian Hopper, "Computer Sleuths Take on Challenge of Finding Deleted Enron E-mails," *Foster's Daily Democrat* [database online], www.fosters.com/special_sections/online/articles2002/tech0118b_02.htm.

7. Graham Wing is the editor of *PC Improvement News* (PCIN). His desire to help others get more from their computing experience led to PCIN. The first issue of the newsletter went out to seven people and now goes out to thousands in countries all over the world. PCIN currently consists of PC industry news, weekly polls, a help forum, and tips and links. [database online 2002] http://www.pcin.net/help/software/windowwasher.shtml.

8. Jack Nilles, *Managing Telework* (New York, N.Y., John Wiley & Sons, 2000 reprint of 1998), Chapter 4, p. 12.

9. Crystal I. Ferraro, assistant editor at SearchSecurity, "Facing Remote Security Challenges" [database online, 23 October 2001], http://searchsecurity.techtarget.com/originalContent/0,289142,sid14_gci777404,00.html.

10. Leo LaPorte, TV Tech "Screen Savers" presentation, May 16, 2002. Software designer and technology consultant LaPorte is co-author of *101 Computer Answers You Need to Know* and author of *Poor Leo's 2002 Computer Almanac*.

11. Now president and founder of Gibson Research and contributing editor for *InfoWorld* magazine, Steve is a respected software designer, consultant and columnist, whose career began in high school while employed by Stanford University's Artificial Research Laboratory. During these same high school years he actually conceived, implemented, and taught two years of computer science curriculum. An electrical engineering and computer sciences graduate of UC Berkeley, Gibson's former positions include vice president of systems development for Advanced Information Design; vice president of marketing, Operations and Product Design and Development for Palo Alto's Minicomputer Technology; and director of engineering for Hovik Corporation.

12. Neal O'Farrell, Hackademia, "Security Training: A Call to Arms, " Tech Target's Search Security [database online December 14, 2001] www.searchsecurity.com.

13. Marcia Branco, "Telework Security: Why It Matters and What You Should Know," Decision One white paper [database online Jan. 2, 2002], http://www.decisionone.com./d1m/news/wh.../white_paper_05.shtm. Decision One's telework services include planning, broadband provisioning and installation, remote connectivity, help desk services, and other support in partnership with Kinetic Workplace and Equis Corporation.

Home Away from Home

While most telecommuting is accomplished from home, another option is the use of a *telework center,* an alternate worksite generally, and most effectively, set up in geographically convenient locations and leased by employers for the use of the telecommuters in their various organizations. Unlike satellite offices owned or leased by one firm for the use of that firm's employees, telework centers are established by cooperative ventures or partnerships, government entities, or private sector organizations.

It should be noted that in our research into telework centers, those provided by nonprofits or government entities (other than the federal Washington-area telecenters) are few and far between. Most of those started have not succeeded, nor do many others seem to be emerging. In follow-up research to the U.C. Davis/CalTrans September 1997 report *Telecommuting Centers in California, 1991–1997,* for instance, we found only one of the twenty-eight then-active telework centers still open, this one housed at a community college in Ventura.

Not that the federal telework centers aren't struggling also. As mentioned in Chapter 1, these centers are the result of the federal government's General Services Administration (GSA) Telecommuting Center Pilot Project—a response to traffic congestion issues in and around Washington, D.C. Between fiscal years 1993 and 1997, Congress made available $11.25 million for GSA to establish, operate, and equip these telecenters. The centers' objectives were and are to assist in supporting and promoting telework for all federal workers as part of family-friendly work initiatives endorsed by the federal government.

Under this pilot project, GSA and its private and university affiliates opened 14 telecenters in the greater metropolitan Washington area. As of this writing there are 16 telework centers—seven in Maryland, eight in Virginia, and one in West Virginia—all 20–70 miles from downtown. At the close of 2001, 362 federal employees representing 17 executive branch agencies were using 339 fully equipped workstations.

The real estate advisory services firm of AEW Capital Management completed an independent study in February 2001, recommending closure of all but the Frederick, Maryland, location because of the centers' failures to become financially successful. The authors cited Frederick's extensive private sector marketing and resulting private sector use as the reason for its financial success. (It should be noted, however, that it was not until fiscal 1997 that the telecenters were even allowed by legislation to be available to other than federal agency employees.)

The report pointed to low utilization and, as with the Washington State executives, to federal agency manager complaints that they had to pay double overhead for teleworking employees. (This double overhead case may, however, point not to problems with the telework center idea but to an agency's failure to reduce real estate or lease expense by reassigning agency office workstation use to more than one person when one of those persons is a telecommuter.)

Our tours of two federal telework centers were very positive experiences. In visiting both the Fredericksburg and Fairfax centers, we found comfortable, ergonomically correct, well-equipped sites with easy highway access and success-oriented administrators avidly marketing their centers. We viewed numerous users hard at work.

Jennifer Alcott, director of the Fredericksburg (Spotsylvania), Woodbridge, and Stafford centers, an avowed telework supporter, enthused that telecommuters "love the centers." She said she has witnessed a "good cross pollenization of idea sharing." Federal telecommuters from numerous agencies, she explained, meet each other and end up casually brainstorming issues that they would never have approached together had they not met at the center. The Fredericksburg site is primarily used by federal employees—98 percent, she said— many of whom are Department of Agriculture staffers. Its general utilization is 70 percent, Woodbridge's is 55 percent, and Stafford's is 50 percent. These centers are managed by Radco.

Alcott also explained that most workers saved at least three hours each day in commute time. She pointed out that another car commute alternative, van pooling, is viable unless you miss the van. "They don't wait," she said, "and then you're stuck in D.C." She also shared that some teleworkers have actually been able to join their children for lunch at their child care centers—an impossibility if working at their agency's D.C. office.

In touring the center we saw privacy cubicles, much like a large phone booth with retractable, see-through, sound-absorbing privacy doors; open desk space, copiers, fax, and scanner; reception area with receptionist and technical support; kitchen with microwave, refrigerator, table, and chairs; and a conference room. The center is in an easily accessible shopping plaza, with retail outlet stores, restaurants, and even a Comfort Inn. There is plenty of free parking.

Each of the three centers that Alcott manages offers the same amenities: workstations, networked PC and phone with voice mail, Internet access, and modem. A printer with dial-up modem is available to resolve firewall and incompatibility issues that require employees to access their agency office intranet from their own laptops. The center is very secure, requiring key entry at all times.

Keith Segerson, who describes his job title as "Guy in Charge," talked with us about the Mason Enterprise Center. This federal Fairfax, Virginia, agency serves as a business incubator, offering small business development services and low-cost office space to small new businesses.

Mason also houses and manages the Fairfax telework center. Segerson and Russell Miller, the center's business manager for entrepreneurial services, showed us around their center. Much like Fredericksburg, with workstations, puppies (no one seems to know how they got their name but these are stubby little rolling metal file cabinets that lock), privacy cubicles, DSL, and 56k modems, the Fairfax location also offers a classroom. Equipped with overhead, dry erase board, PCs, and workspaces, this training room is often used by local private firms and agencies.

Fairfax also provides videoconferencing and, unlike Fredericksburg, is highly utilized by the private sector. The city of Fairfax, for instance, contributes a $30,000 grant for 28 evening and weekend hours of use by the local residents. Miller mentions that the use is very high at tax time and around Christmas when residents prepare taxes and shop online. He explained that the center's marketing includes a monthly open house, print ads, public service announcements (PSAs), and Web page links. Its utilization is 61 percent.

Open-house marketing is not exclusive to Fairfax, however. As of 2002 they have partnered with the Herndon, Sterling, and Manassas locations to alternate open houses the third Friday of each month and advertise this online at info@nocommute.org.

We spoke with Dee Christensen, telework project manager for Washington State University about telework centers' struggle to succeed. She explained that the first telework centers were all government grants, "but once the grant money ran out they had not figured out how to be self-supporting."

Speaking of WSU, she said: "We had one of the first telework centers ourselves, and state workers loved it because it was in Seattle, and with Olympia the state capitol they saved an hour commute each way." She went on to explain that managers did not support it because they maintained the pre-telework real estate costs at their agency site and, like the federal agencies, were effectively paying double overhead. (We discuss the solution to this problem later in the chapter when we talk about hoteling.) The first year, the year of the grant, there was only a nominal charge to agencies. Once the grant year ended and the center approached the agencies with the "real cost," the state agencies declined, and the telework center was closed.

Christensen affirms that a few telework centers still exist that have learned to expand their services, offering videoconferencing, for instance, and finding a core tenant.

Tony Whitehurst, former Merced County, California, Supervisor, now vice president of National Telecenters Inc. and former director of the disbanded Los Banos California Telecenter, concurs that management resistance is an impediment to telework and telework centers. His firm is now finding success offering telemedicine services only. "If telework centers worked anywhere, they should have worked here in Los Banos," he stated.

A low-cost-of-living bedroom community for the nearby Silicon Valley/San Diego area, Los Banos telework center's death knell, like others, was tolled by Silicon Valley managers whose Los Banos residents wanted to work from the center. "They preferred butts in chairs," he bluntly affirmed, talking about managerial resistance to management by performance.

Janet Jones, owner of Jones Works consultancy group and former member of the team that created and marketed the Washington State University Rural Telework Projects, has extensively researched the success and failure of a number of telework centers. Jones found that the center failures were often due to lack of patience. "Some administrators," she explained, "simply gave up too soon." Jones describes the key to telework center success as "sheer tenacity," clarifying that generally telework centers need three to five years to become established.

She also discovered that some center administrators spent funds on creating their facility, with little or nothing left over for marketing and promotion. Other reasons for telecenter failures, she tell us, are poor site selection, sites not well used, inadequate marketing and recruitment, employer resistance to telecommuting, incomplete definition of target markets, inadequate staffing, consolidation due to inadequate demand to justify multiple sites, start-up funding that expired, start-up phase too short, poor business planning, lack of a compelling purpose, or lack of complementary services.

Jones's consultation services were instrumental in the creation and success of the one continuing California CalTrans telecenter in Ventura. Located in a rural community on the fringe of Los Angeles, this center is in the heart of a densely populated area and attracts numerous teleworkers, including state employees who wish to avoid the lengthy and costly commute into Los Angeles. The center, born in January of 1995 with a CalTrans grant, is housed in a modular building on the community college campus, on an arterial street with spacious grounds and convenient parking. Operated as a program separate from the college budget, the Ventura center must create its own revenue to support its services.

The center is aggressively marketed to county and city governments and even the federal government, direct marketed by mailings to local businesses, campus brochures, bulletin board announcements, student surveys, advertisements in the *Los Angeles Times*, and television public service announcements. Ventura's center offers two private offices, two conference rooms equipped with whiteboards and meeting tables equipped with pop-ups for laptop connections, and workstations that can be rented by the hour, day, or month.

The center, with 24-hour access, seems to be providing what telecommuters need: an attractive street-front with easy parking, a reception desk and waiting area, telephones, voicemail, laser printers, fax machines, copiers, and conference rooms with videoconference equipment and a kitchen. Workspaces have natural light and many windows. Its campus location offers proximity to other valuable amenities as well: a library, bookstore, postal and Fed Ex service, and UPS on request. Banks and restaurants are nearby.

Its marketing approach, focusing on relieving stress, is working. A typical promotion reads:

Why go to work when you can go back to school? Remember how relaxed things were on campus? Why not turn in your work from there again? Try telecommuting from the Ventura Community College Telecenter for a change. It's easy. It's fun. You'll cut down on your drive. Save gas. Save the air. Save wear and tear on your psyche. Besides, your campus office is perfect. With floor-to-ceiling windows overlooking campus you'll enjoy a serene place to work. So, you'll be as relaxed as you are productive.[1]

An offshoot of the typical telecenter is the more recent innovation known as a telecommunity center, designed as part of a rural economic development program. Janet Jones shared her experiences implementing telecommunity centers in Clackamas County, Oregon. The first Clackamas center, in the downtown area of the small rural town of Canby, Oregon, opened April 1, 2000, funded largely by a Mount Hood Economic Alliance Grant and a 2-year rental donation of 1,000 square feet of office space by DirectLink of Oregon.

Unlike failed telework centers, the project managers for the Canby center planned their marketing strategy well, as did the administrators

According to consultant Janet Jones
A SUCCESSFUL TELEWORK CENTER NEEDS:

• A project champion
• Community involvement
• A clear, compelling purpose
• A business plan
• Community and outside grant funding
• Partnerships for diverse programs (college, coffee shop, etc.)
• Planning with the customer in mind

for their other two locations. In Clackamas these centers are part of the county's brand positioning as an excellent location for technology and telecommunications. A distinctive telecommunity center logo, shared by all of the centers, reinforces their identity as a countywide resource.

The center is used by the city, Clackamas Community College, freelance and self-employed residents, and telecommuting employees of various firms. Its services include access to technology, distance learning, and training; the center serves as a magnet for teleconferences, community information, and business services. While residents clearly enjoy the Clackamas country lifestyle, they are also employed and have an average 50-mile round trip to work. Sixty percent of Clackamas County residents commute outside the county for work, the highest rate among all counties in Oregon.

Clackamas County soon followed the Canby center with another in nearby Molalla. Midway between Portland, the largest metropolitan area in the state, and Salem, the state capitol, Molalla is a rural community with a population of 5,700 residents. Long relying on farming and forestry as the foundation of its local economy, the community has recently struggled to replace job losses in these declining resource-based industries. Designated by the state as an economically distressed area, Molalla's economic base has eroded. Many residents have sought job opportunities outside the local area. Their situation may be comparable to that of many other communities, such as the long-suffering Mid-Atlantic areas whose industry-based economies are also eroding.

We spoke with Renate Mengelberg, project manager of the Clackamas County Telecommunity Project, who advised us that construction has begun on a third county center, in Estacada, which will serve as the community center also, housing a senior center as well as the county sheriff's office downstairs from the telework center.

Mengelberg shared some frustration about the length of time it was taking to see fruition of their hopes of ongoing telecommuter activity in the centers, stating that only two regular telecommuting employees

MOLALLA TELECOMMUNITY CENTER
(Clackamas County OR)

KEYS TO SUCCESS
(Courtesy of Janet Jones)

- **Convenience**—Provide a convenient, welcoming office/training experience.
- **High-speed Internet connection**—Provide the fastest available connectivity.
- **Right pricing**—Price services attractively for the value received.
- **Software availability**—Upgrade software and hardware to keep current with the cutting edge. Prospective telecommuters are looking for a variety of specific, technical quality software used in their jobs. They are interested in software that ensures a secure connection to their office networks.
- **Employer willingness**—Cultivate employer support. Telecommuters need to persuade their employers that a telecommunity center work site is a viable alternative to telecommuting from home and commuting to the office. Whether the employer or employee pays to rent a workstation depends on the situation.
- **A businesslike, collegial environment**—Provide an atmosphere that is attractive, friendly and conducive to work. Teleworkers want to find other telecommuters and business people there, and not experience the distractions or loneliness commonly found in a home office setting.
- **An integral part of library services**—Create a cohesive community learning center by making the technology center part of the library. The library provides financial strength, attracts customers and reduces risk.
- **Partnerships between the business community and the library**— Tap and integrate expertise from within the local business community.

were using the Molalla Center. She did, however, admit that the center had not been as proactively marketed as she might have liked. She cautioned anyone interested in creating a telecommunity center: "It takes a long-term commitment. Each area has different needs, and you have to be flexible."

Molalla's target customers continue to be teleworkers and their employers, small and emerging businesses and home office workers, entrepreneurs, individuals engaged in distance learning activities, continuing education, and job training, traveling government agency field personnel and other visiting professionals, and others who need access to information technology resources.

Molalla's mission is to facilitate telework and technology access for the greater Molalla community of telecommuters and small and emerging businesses. It is their stated belief that this will contribute to achieving a stronger local economy, higher quality of life, and reduced traffic congestion. Janet Jones, who administered the program and wrote the business plan for all three centers, cautioned that success and motivators can differ from one center to the other and research prior to implementation is an absolute must.

We toured Oneonta, New York's telecenter, a joint venture of Hartwick College and Wilber Bank. Its mission is to develop economic opportunities for area residents, whether supporting new business ideas or providing technical training to someone looking for work. This center's telecommunity focus is slightly different in that it serves as both an incubator enterprise and a local telework center.

Created in 1995 by key community leaders, its tenants are small new businesses who make month-to-month or lease commitments for small telecondos. Tenant services include low-cost rent, fax, 100 free photocopies per month, basic digital phone service with local calls and voice mail, unlimited Internet access, free Hartwick College technical support, desk, chair, and filing cabinet. The center provides day use work space for teleworkers, as well as two conference rooms and a fully equipped computer training facility providing training in Quick Books, graphics, Word, Excel, Power Point, grant writing, business development, customer service and fundraising.

TELECOTTAGES

The United States has not cornered the market on telecommunity centers. In fact, the European "telecottage" is actually a predecessor and in most cases provides a greater array of services that include community relations.

In England, for instance, the Megavissey Telecottage in Cornwall provides office services such as photocopying, fax, computer, and telecommunications. Users can train on computers, drop in and work, or have the telecottage staff do the work for them. Users of telecottages may be small businesses, community groups, or individuals who work from home. In rural areas, telecottages are a focus of community and commercial activity, providing a place where people can meet and share work and ideas. Mevagissey, for instance, offers video conferencing, Internet consultancy, photocopying, fax, printing, scanning, data backup and recovery services, and even tourist information. Warwickshire Rural Enterprise Network (WREN), a UK project of the National Rural Enterprise Center, established its first telecottage in 1991 as support to local business and residents. The telecottage provides training, a computerized workspace, childcare, incubator services, IT support, social events, and networking opportunities.

The Hungarian Telecottage movement, a product of a 1993 community development program, has given birth to over 150 telecottages. Hungary has a large number of very small villages, of which approximately 4,300 have fewer than 3,000 residents each. These communities, with poor access to state and public service delivery, educational institutions, retail and business services, and job opportunities, are the locales for most Hungarian telecottages. Telecottages bordering neighboring states such as Romania and Serbia have been promoting and assisting in the development of telecottages in those countries.

Although each Hungarian cottage is an independent entity, its assets are normally owned by a local nongovernmental organization (NGO); the local government, largely through contracting out of public services, contributes its office space, personnel, and financial resources. In some cases, the telecottage is based in a local library, school, or community center. Often used for training purposes, especially when the local schools are not adequately equipped, they also offer an impressive array of other services, such as community space and public forum, communications technology, Internet and e-mail access, local advertising, news and office services, computer and multimedia use, alarm monitoring, babysitting, bookkeeping, copying services, desktop publishing, employment training, grant-writing assistance, photo, video and postal services, media services, newspaper reading room, second-hand book sales, snack bar, call center operations, telephone answering services, tourism, videoconferencing, and word processing.

PRIVATE SECTOR ALTERNATIVES

Executive suites, the private sector alternative to telework centers, while undoubtedly pricier, offer many appealing services and amenities and many more locations. While differing from one city or office to another, all executive suites provide certain basic services including a receptionist, phone with voice mail, postal service, equipment, and meeting rooms.

As of this writing there are approximately 4,000 U.S. office suite facilities, rented by hour, week, month, or longer to sole practitioners, small companies, start-ups, or corporations. These suites, with private offices, common area, and cubicles, almost always offer maintenance and security and may include a concierge service to order supplies and arrange conferences and training.

We will take a look at two executive suite firms to give you an idea of the services available. For a hefty list of the various executive suite firms, locations, and products and services available, see www.esuite. com.

Regus, Inc., offers a global network of business offices and meeting rooms to rent by hour, day, week, month, or year. Each of their 400+ locations provides videoconferencing, as well as administrative and secretarial support, phone, IT and audio visual equipment, meeting rooms, training rooms, cybercafes with free Internet access, and so on.

Marketing manager Sherry Aponte is proud of Regus' contribution to telework: "We help employers outreach to a talent pool previously beyond their geographic reach, and if they're wanting to do a pilot program we are a more cost-effective way of doing that. We can offer a commitment as small as three months, as opposed to the conventional three-year lease of conventional rentals." She also shared that they have helped such firms as Intel introduce their telework programs, setting up remote locations that saved their employees a two-hour commute. Their newest telecommute project is a partnership with Nokia to provide remote workstations for a quarter of its employees. For more information or online booking, see their site at www.regus.com. Regus also offers a "contingency telework package" of services, which we will discuss in depth in Chapter 7, "Preparing for Disaster."

HQ Global Workplaces has been in the executive suite business for 30 years and offers what may be the world's largest videoconferencing public room network with over 3,000 videoconferencing and 400+ executive suite locations, including metro D.C., 30 U.S. states, Puerto Rico, and the countries of Argentina, Australia, Belgium, Brazil, Canada, Chile, China, Colombia, England, France, Indonesia, Jakarta, Japan, Malaysia, Mexico, New Zealand, Philippines, Singapore, South Africa, Spain, Switzerland, Thailand, UAE, and Venezuela. They also, in conjunction with a firm called Teleportec, are beginning to update their videoconferencing to a state-of-the-art 3-D effect. Currently Teleportec is only available in New York City, Dallas, and San Francisco.

HQ takes care of thousands of teleworking clients every day, from road warriors, to entrepreneurs, to local representatives of big corporations." In response to the World Trade Center disaster in 2001, calls to their videoconferencing reservation center increased from a pre-terrorist attack total of 2,500 each day to a whopping post-attack of over 8,000, as companies investigated videoconferencing as an alternative to airline travel.

We toured one of HQ's three metropolitan Atlanta locations, a site used primarily by national and international firms whose local sales representatives require an area office presence. Housed in a modern, attractive high-rise, complete with a garden courtyard with fountain and free covered parking, this office is easily accessible to three major highways. It is also surrounded by shopping centers that offer everything from Kinko's to Home Depot to hotels.

There are several different HQ purchase options available to meet your firm's specific needs. Their "full program" includes a prestigious business address, furnished private office, suite or team room, fully featured telephone system and voice messaging, reception area and receptionist, kitchen break area, client service area with essential office equipment, 24/7 building access, building directory listing, and mail handling. Additional services could include administrative support, meeting and training rooms, audiovisual equipment, videoconferencing, high-speed Internet connectivity, and LAN configurations.

A scaled-down agreement, called "Business Access Program" offers prestigious business address, personalized call answering during business hours, 24/7 integrated voice messaging with call forwarding options, building directory listing (where available), and private offices and meeting rooms as needed.

Another source for videoconferencing and a corporate "friend of telework" is the Mountain View, California, firm of Placeware, Inc. Placeware is lauded by publications such as *PC Week* and *Info World* as offering the most comprehensive services, including dial-up, security, post-meeting service, and training, and as one of the first products that doesn't require users to download and install a browser plug-in or client applet. We attended a three-part Placeware videoconference on telework, sponsored by ITAC.

Placeware conference speaker Janice Miholics, vice president of Global Work Life Strategies for Merrill Lynch, affirms that Placeware is very easy to use, although she admits it did take her some time to get used to not being able to view participants. Placeware offers a daily demonstration of its product and services conveniently timed for Web attendance from the United States, Europe, and Australia, as well as archived access to two telework conferences on "HR and Legal Issues in Telework Implementation" and "Facilities Planning Issues in Telework Implementation." Their site address is www.placeware.com.

Office Quest, an online executive-suite reservation system, offers reservations within 24 hours for over 500 international cities, with your choice of private office, meeting room, workstation, team room, training room, videoconferencing, virtual office, or workspace. Their site also provides a reservation management system called "MyOffice-Quest," which allows users to view and edit existing reservations, update account information, and create reports on Office Quest activity. Other than the rental fee charged by the center itself, there is no charge to the Office Quest user. Their revenue is generated by retaining 10 percent of the center's reservation revenue. In a sample search we found 40 New York City and 20 Chicago workstation locations, 20 training room facilities in Dallas, 15 private office sites in San Francisco, 15 Boston locations offering videoconferencing, and facilities available in such international locations as Kiev, Ukraine; 10 cities in Switzerland; Istanbul, Turkey; Hanoi, Viet Nam; Dubai, UAE; Montreal, Toronto, Vancouver, and Ottawa, Canada; and numerous locations in France and Germany. Access their site at www.officequest.com.

HOTELING

Our telework center information would not be complete without an understanding of the hoteling concept. As the name implies, hoteling is about reservations. A teleworker makes a reservation, by phone or online, for daily use of a workstation, conference room, and office or training room space. A part-time teleworker may even be reserving workstation space in the central office of her own employer. Hoteling is one vital key to the real estate savings inherent in successful telework. A firm that offers part-time telework but fails to offer hoteling will experience the "double overhead" catastrophe that doomed some public sector telework centers.

Let's translate this telework/hoteling concept into monetary savings. The estimated costs of a workstation range from $7,000 for a public sector job to $10,000–$15,000 for the private sector. When each employee's workstation is not utilized 100 percent of the time, the company is able to reduce the number of stations by combining those of telecommuters. For every workstation that is eliminated, the organization can realize annual savings of at least $3,500–$5,000. Of course, the greater the percentage of teleworkers your firm has, the greater the savings.[2]

Hoteling reservation systems, typically online, allow the teleworker to schedule at the last minute or several days or weeks in advance, and also to locate other teleworking employees using the same facilities. One reservation system, Richmond Virginia's Agilquest, also offers phone switching. No matter where your teleworkers are—workstation, conference room, or office—the Agilquest system will route your phone calls there. The company's founder and CEO is John Vivadelli, also a board member of ITAC, the International Telework Association and Council. Vivadelli emphasizes the advantage of reservations in a contingency telework (disaster) situation, noting that a reservation system can find desk or meeting room availability elsewhere and locate each employee. Yvette Lucio, Telework Manager for i2 Technologies, raves about Agilquest, noting that for her firm phone switching is a must.

Another reservation systems product, offering a work-at-home forwarding feature as well, is PRM, Inc.'s Deskflex. President Art Goes explains that his firm's Deskflex software for hoteling is accessed directly from the client's intranet and allows the teleworker, whether road warrior or part-time work-at-home employee, to reserve a desk at the primary office location by day or week. Its phone system provides voice mail and message lamp (to notify the teleworker when he has messages waiting). "We have one client who saved $1 million in rent by reducing floor space through hoteling and our Deskflex system," he enthuses.

Timothy Kane, president of ITAC and head of Deloitte Consulting's virtual work practices, emphasizes that hoteling is crucial to a firm's financial success with telework.

In speaking about telecommuting employees who work from home some days and at the office others, he says it is imperative that the company set up hoteling and not leave the employee's desk space vacant on the work-at-home days. He explains: "We [Kinetic Workplace] recommend the firm pay for the technology and connectivity and provide ergonomic guidelines for work at home. But we only recommend this if they are combining telework with hoteling, so the cost of the equipment, etc. is offset by the real estate savings."

John Vivadelli concurs. He responds to employee complaints about giving up "their own desk" by explaining that saving money does not need to be a 2:1 employee desk ratio. It can be 1.3 or 1.5 to 1 and still reduce costs. "So," he explains, "to those that say, 'but I want my own desk,' a manager can say, 'Yes, but if you give that up we can offer you a little more space when you do come into the office.' "

The U.S. Department of Commerce's Trademark Office launched its highly successful telework program in 1997 and now almost half of its 250 attorneys work form home three days a week. In November 1991 the agency launched a hoteling pilot in which 20 attorneys work mostly from home. When the attorneys do commute to the Trademark Office's Arlington, Virginia, facility they reserve their office space in advance. The hoteling pilot becomes a permanent program in November 2003, and all teleworkers will then be hoteling. The Trademark Office projects a ratio of five teleworkers to each desk with an annual real estate savings of $900,000–$1.3 millon.[3]

In summation, seeking any of these options in or around your area of interest, you may find helpful esuite.com for executive-suite information and direct contact with the executive-suite firms, officequest.com for executive suite reservations, prminc.com or agilquest.com for hoteling reservation systems software, placeware.com for your firm's on-site videoconferencing, or hq.com for information on their videoconferencing sites and reservations. As is the case throughout the book, these for-profit resources are not mentioned as a recommendation by the authors but rather as a starting point in your information-gathering process.

NOTES

1. Provided courtesy of Janet Jones, owner of Janet Jones Works, whose consulting business specializes in marketing, communications, research, and strategic market planning for businesses, nonprofits, and communities. For more information on Clackamas County Telecommunity Centers see www.no-commute.net/ or www.oregontelcom.org/cctp/jj01.ppt.

2. Jennifer Dumbrow, "Electronic Communications and the Law: Help or Hindrance to Telecommuting?" Indiana University, Bloomington, School of Law [database online, May 6, 2001], http://www.law.indiana.edu/fclj/pubs/v50/no3/dombrow.html.

3. Toni Kistner, "Telework Thrives at Trademark Office" [database online December 9, 2002], http://www.nwfusion.com/net.worker/news/2002/1209netlead.html.

An Organized Response

We're now going to take a look at numerous labor union organization attitudes, policies and telework contracts and agreements. It is not our intention to suggest that these union attitudes and the various stipulations in the contracts and agreements are ideal for successful telework. In some cases, we disagree with the union attitude.

This chapter's primary purpose is to advise you, the employer, of the stumbling blocks to telework implementation that you may encounter when your employees are labor union members.

Debbie Goldman, corporate media representative for Communication Workers of America shared with us that while CWA does not have any telecommuting trials, they have implemented telecommuting language into past contracts. "We had a telecommuting trial with a major local telephone exchange carrier in the mid 1990s in two locations that involved credit rep work," she said. According to Ms. Goldman, "The company did not extend the trials because of internal reorganization and unwillingness to invest in upgrading home-based hardware and software."

She also explained that CWA has contract language that allows telecommuting trials with another local carrier but there are none involving occupational employees. She adds, "We had a two-month telecommuting trial with a major long-distance carrier around the Atlanta Olympics, but that was driven by the Olympics-induced traffic problems." (Contract language examples were provided by Debbie to clarify CWA's views on telecommuting as shown in Appendix A.)

"I would sum up CWA experience this way," she concludes. "Inbound call center work is not conducive to telecommuting. I wonder if most of the telecommuting is professional work where managers are more willing to be flexible, give up some control over work process, and where the investment per higher-paid employee seems more worth it."

In January of 2003 the U.S. Department of Commerce's Patent and Trademark Office (USPTO) and the Patent Office Professional Association (POPA) finalized a telework program agreement after extensive negotiations. This agreement exemplifies a labor union contract concern that did not exist prior to telework, i.e., what power labor unions should have in determining which employees are allowed to telework.

The stumbling block in contract negotiations seems to have been that Patent Office management, concerned about the confidential nature of the department's work, wished to reserve the right to exclude from telework those employees with ongoing performance or conduct issues. The labor union objected.

Toni Kistner, managing editor of Network World's Net.Worker section and editor of Fusion's SMB Network's site has followed the conflict from its inception. In her online article "Of Mysteries and Bargaining Chips," she shares her concern: "But what place labor unions should have in deciding who teleworks is a sticky issue that could prompt a fair number of stalemates like this one, and hopefully some strong advances."[1] The final USPTO/POPA agreement (available in its entirety in Appendix A) offers one-day-a-week telework to 700 of its 3500 patent examiners. These 700 represent 60% of the agency's top-level examiners. The contract stipulates that eligible participants must be performing at the fully successful level and be in full compliance with all of the agency's ethical, conduct and confidentiality standards."[2] The Service Employees International Union Local 660 negotiated a contract for its members, employees of Los Angeles (CA) County. Their stipulated telecommuting standards are that telework is always voluntary, with some days each week spent at the office. Teleworkers receive all benefits, including overtime and vacation, and are eligible for workers' compensation for job-related accidents.

The International Brotherhood of Electrical Workers (IBEW) locals 827 and 1944 bargained with Bell Systems for a telecommuting arrangement allowing clerical staff to work from home. Bell pays for phone lines and other necessary equipment and compensates the employees for 30 minutes each month to attend union meetings. Bell also provides voice mail to allow the union to communicate with its teleworking members.

The UAW (United Auto Workers) and Michigan Blue Cross–Blue Shield agreed to a telework pilot program. Customer service representatives are allowed to work from home on a voluntary basis with no change to wages, benefits, or contract terms. Employer and union together maintain joint oversight of the pilot program.

The state of California's Telework Advisory Group stresses to its employees that agency management should involve their labor relations office in the planning and development stages of the program to ensure that the program will not be in conflict with the provisions of collective bargaining agreements. "Prior to implementing a telecommuting program" they advise, " the Labor Relations Division of the Department of Personnel Administration should be notified. Additionally, employee unions should be given the opportunity to discuss the proposed program and its impact on unit employees."[3]

In Europe, where workforce procedures are commonly regulated by collective agreement rather than by legislation, examples abound of union telework position papers and labor contracts.

The Swedish Confederation of Professional Employees (TCO) represents 1.2 million workers in 18 various unions, including occupations such as civil service, teaching, agriculture, art, media, music, and health services. The confederation's telework agreement typifies European labor union agreements, including a requirement that telework be voluntary, that the employer cover home workspace equipment and work-related telephone and electricity costs, and that each individual agreement be renewed annually.[4]

In Denmark more than one million employees have telework guidelines stipulated in their collective agreement. The most prominent example is the country's largest trade union, Union of Commercial and Clerical Employees (HK), representing 377,000 Danish workers.[5]

The Netherlands firm Koninklijke PPP Nederland (KPN) has contracted with various labor unions to make telework available to its 30,000 organized employees.[6]

In Italy labor union agreements support the telework of the country's 300,000 telecommunications workers, all banking sector and government employees, and numerous other firms such as international software designer Bull (Bull Italia employs 1000+), and Florence-based "Answers," Italy's first virtual call center, employer of 1000.[7]

Union Network International (UNI), in its *Organizing in the Network Economy*, talks extensively about the need for retraining of union employees in the global trend towards Internet-related employment and telework jobs. UNI represents over 15 million workers in 900 unions from 140 countries worldwide. Philip Jennings, general secretary, in discussing the new E-commerce economy, clearly states, "Unions have to acknowledge these developments and we have to change ourselves— that's what UNI is all about." He goes on to affirm, "We want to make union members global players and make sure that their voice is heard in the new, global economy."[8]

Unions have been using the Internet as an organizing tool and a new online means of communication to talk directly to call center staff. In New Zealand, the financial sector union FinSec has a dedicated Web home page for call center staff, which includes pay comparisons and health and safety information (http://www.finsec.org.nz/campaigns.html). FinSec promotes itself as "Your call centre union." FNV Bondgenoten in Holland also makes use of the Web, to provide a series of pages of information for call center workers, regardless of whether or not they are FNV members (www.callcenters.fnv.nl).[9]

In March 2001, UNI-Europa and EuroCommerce, recognized by EU as social partners for commerce, drafted a *European Agreement on Guidelines on Telework in Commerce*. This agreement offers telework as a potentially good solution for employer or worker and discusses issues such as employment conditions, holidays, absences, tasks, confidentiality, venue, equipment, and teleworkers' union participation.

The agreement stresses that measures should be taken to ensure that social contact is not lost, and advocates part time telework where possible. It also advocates for workers to be allowed to return to the office when they request it and stresses that the employer should be responsible for purchase and maintenance of work-at-home equipment.

While it emphasizes that a teleworker should have every right to privacy that the law allows, the agreement does also state that the employer should be allowed to inspect the work-at-home premises for safety reasons as long as the teleworker is given advance notice. The agreement further says:

> The teleworker must have the same right as other employees in the company to participate in any trade union or other personnel activities, which take place in the company or at company premises. However, participation in union activities and communications between the teleworkers and their trade union representatives should not lead to unreasonable costs for the company, in comparison with those resulting from similar activities on the part of other personnel working at the premises of the employer.[10]

MSF (Manufacturing, Science, and Finance) refers to itself as "the union for skilled and professional people . . . a modern campaigning union that fights for its members whenever and wherever appropriate. And . . . one of the largest unions in Britain or Ireland." MSF members come from all facets of manufacturing (engineering, electronics, aerospace, cars, chemicals, pharmaceuticals, tobacco, food and drink), insurance and finance, craftspeople, technicians, scientists, doctors, nurses and other health service employees, university and nonprofit staff, as well as other business services.

Peter Skyte, national secretary for MSF's Information Technology Professionals Association, in his *Teleworking: A Trade Union Perspective* offered MSF's ideal *code of practice for employees.* "According to various studies," Mr. Skyte begins, "Teleworking is expanding. Quite clearly the technology is now available to make this an attractive option for employers. It can also have advantages for employees including a more flexible working life enabling people to combine work with other responsibilities which they could not do at the traditional workplace." He adds the following warning: "But there are disadvantages too, including the feeling of isolation from the employer and from fellow employees."

The following teleworking guidelines, adopted by numerous labor organizations, were written by MSF representatives "to address the problems teleworkers might face and to ensure that they are treated in the same way as other employees."

- Teleworkers should be employees of an enterprise and not deemed self-employed. (Having heard this issue of "employee, rather than self-employed" concern voiced by several labor unions, we inquired of Willow CSN, whose workers are independent contractors, whether they have had labor union problems. CEO Asim Saber offered that one resistant union became a Willow supporter after seeing that Willow's CSRs, available for overflow calls during the client's peak time, eliminated their client employees' forced-overtime problem.)
- To avoid isolation, contracts of employment should require home workers to periodically attend the office;
- There should be a separate room available at home for teleworking, a separate telephone, and payment for additional costs such as heating and lighting.
- There should be regular meetings between teleworkers and the provision of electronic mail and telephone links with other teleworkers, all to be provided at employer expense.
- There should be weekly liaison discussions between a teleworker and his or her supervisor/manager.
- Teleworkers should enjoy the same rates of pay and employment benefits as office-based workers, including childcare provision and family leave. There should be a defined number of working hours. They should be included in career development and appraisal schemes, including training opportunities.
- All computer equipment should be provided, paid for, and serviced by the employer, who will be responsible for installation, maintenance, insurance, and compliance with health and safety requirements. The employer should also accept legal responsibility for any accident or injury.

- Teleworkers should have access to trade union representatives and be able to attend meetings within working hours. Health and safety advisors and trade union representatives should be able to visit teleworkers.
- Teleworking should be voluntary with a right to return to working from the office.[11]

One of the most progressive, and most cooperative, organized labor responses is seen in the European Commission's March 2000 summit meeting of European heads of state. Held in Lisbon, Portugal, this conference's participants drafted a cooperative "Joint Statement for the Lisbon Summit," a culmination of cooperative efforts of government, employer firms, and trade unions. The essence of the statement by the employers and unions contributing to the report includes the following commitments:

- Work together in order to promote the use of Internet-based ICT training within the sector, leading to certified and *portable* qualifications for all employees.
- Work together during the current and coming year (2000 and 2001) in order to develop a set of voluntary Europe-wide guidelines for telework."

Partnering employers and trade unions affirmed their belief in telework:

> A new paradigm of work is developing with opportunities to create new and higher quality jobs *which are less dependent on location*. New technologies, global competition, rapid economic changes and speed and volume of information call for flexible and adaptable work relationships and organization. Telework constitutes a new form of work organisation, which is particularly important for the sector. Its increasing use is a clear sign of a necessary trend towards a more flexible and mobile workplace. . . . European guidelines will contribute to the removal of obstacles to telework provoked by the absence of an adequate framework at European level.

Contributing European employers were Belgacom, British Telecommunications, Europa Telecom, Deutsche Telekom, Eircom, France Telecom, KPN, OTE, Portugal Telecom P&T Luxembourg, Sonera, Telefonica, Tele Danmark, Telia, Telecom Italia, and Telekom Austria.[12]

The Public Service Alliance of Canada (PSAC), in its 1994 telework policy #33, expressed some of the same concerns mentioned by HK. One of Canada's largest unions, with membership coast to coast and international in embassies and consulates, PSAC represents 150,0000 workers who traditionally perform tasks such as issuing pension and employment insurance checks, forecasting the weather, operating airports, and inspecting meat plants. Their newer members may work in women's shelters, casinos, or universities.

Expressing their mission as the "best protection and working conditions for members that it represents" and "cognizant of the accelerating changes in work patterns," PSAC policy indicates they strive to achieve flexibility for workers. They recognize telework as one method of achieving this flexibility.

In conducting extensive research into the history of work-at-home they concluded that "over the past century, homework has resulted in a female-dominated work ghetto." They exemplify this with textile workers in Canada, non-unionized white-collar claims processors in Toronto, and non-unionized textile, electronic data processing, and assembly workers in the United States, some of whom lost their right to unionization by working in the home.

They commented, "For the most part, PSAC members have worked at home because there isn't enough time at work to complete the heavy workload during the regular workday." They also feared that "members will assume current employer-paid costs—furniture, hydro, telephone." Their research led them to conclude: "Working at home is often an individual coping mechanism to solve larger social policy problems."

PSAC very reluctantly made the decision to support telework. Their reasoning:

> The Alliance does not support telework as an individual response to larger social policy issues. Having taken that position, the Alliance recognizes that for some members, those who would be unable to work other than from their home, telework offers the only alternative of paid labour. Therefore, the PSAC does not stand in the way of telework as a means of maintaining a job.

Calling telework "a low-wage, low-capital cost employer initiative that serves the employer agenda of 'more for less,' but does little to provide a healthy alternative to workers' individual needs for flexibility and more leisure time," the alliance nevertheless recognized that some members would derive individual benefits from telework and wrote the following guidelines:

- Telework must be voluntary.
- Telework arrangements must not contravene the existing collective agreements and teleworkers must remain members of their respective bargaining units.

- Offering telework must not replace the employer's legal and social obligations to promote employment equity within the workplace.
- With few exceptions, telework must not be done on a full-time basis. However, the Alliance recognizes that telework may provide a short-term solution for members with disabilities or chemical sensitivities.
- Telework must not be used by management to avoid its responsibility of providing and maintaining a quality, safe and healthy workplace.
- Telework arrangements must not result in piece rates being introduced as a method of payment.
- Productivity level increases must not be a condition for teleworkers.
- Training for teleworkers must be provided to clarify the implications of working away from the central office. These implications must include an awareness of consequences where, in the employer's opinion, security is breached. Training for managers must be provided from the point of view of learning how to supervise teleworkers who work away from the central office.
- All overtime work must be authorized in advance, and remuneration provided as outlined in the collective agreement.

The PSAC action plan for telework has included the creation of what they call Local Tech Change Committees, created by each union local, for the purpose of developing a plan of action to investigate, coordinate, and "take action against adverse effects of technological change." They survey members, monitor and track the acquisition and installation of new technology, strategize maintaining contact with teleworkers, meet with management to monitor telework arrangements, and disseminate a *Local Tech Change Handbook.*

PSAC's Health and Safety position is that they will "push the employer to pay for ergonomic furniture for all teleworkers and, in the event of any occupational injury, will press Workers' Compensation Boards to cover teleworkers in the same manner as those who work in central offices." Stating their intention to press the employer into providing a workplace accessible to all workers, PSAC's policy states: "The Alliance will not accept work at home where the sole result is to marginalize and exclude members with disabilities from the office environment." PSAC has created an electronic bulletin board that allows teleworkers to electronically access the union for general information.

For an excellent review of several Canadian collective agreements with various labor unions, see "Work and Family Provisions in Canadian Collective Agreements." The study was conducted by the Canadian government's Human Resources Development Canada.

NOTES

1. Toni Kistner, "Of Mysteries and Bargaining chips" [database online June 8, 2002], www.nwfusion.com/net.worker/columnists/2002/0708kistner.html.

2. Brigid Quinn, U.S. Patent Office, "Agreement Reached on Patent Telework Program" [database online January 30, 2003], http://www.uspto.gov/web/offices/com/speeches/03-02.htm.

3. State of California Telecommuting Advisory Group, "Telecommuting Work Option," June 1992 [database online], http://www.dpa.ca.gov/telework/guidelines/tele2036.shtm#E11E10.

4. Euro-Telework, "TCO Union, Sweden model" [database online July 10, 2001], http://www.telework-mirti.org/agreements/docs/con-tco.htm.

5. HK/Denmark [database online], http://hk-pro32.hk.dk/hkwww/omhk.nsf?OpenDatabase&unid-5F2F7EE5539D1437C125675500477CDA.

6. Euro-Telework, "Collective Agreement KPN 2000" [database online].

7. Euro-Telework, "National Reports Italy" [database online February 21, 2003], http://www.telework-mirti.org.

8. Philip Jennings, "Organizing the Network Economy," UNI [database online June 2, 2001], http://www.union-network.org/Unisite/Events/Conferences/ Organising-e.doc.

9. First UNI World Congress, "Organizing in the Changing Global Economy" [database online, April 10, 2001], http://www.union-network.org/uniibits.nsf/c642ee014caad5a6c12568110025fa6a/012a737165dfc8a2c1256adb0038a59b ?EditDocument.

10. UNI-Europa and EuroCommerce, "EuroCommerce and UNI-Europa European Agreement on Guidelines on Telework in Commerce" [database online April 3, 2001], http://www.union-network.org/unisite/sectors/commerce/ Social%20dialogue%20agreements/Telework_English.htm.

11. Peter Skyte, National Secretary, MSF Information Technology Professionals Association [database online], http://www.eto.org.uk/faq/faq01.htm.

12. European Commission, eWork 2000, *Status Report on New Ways to Work in the Information Society,* annex 1: Joint Statement for the Lisbon Summit," page 150.

Preparing for Disaster

Whether your firm makes a determination to implement a formal telework program or not, you should always be prepared for the eventuality of contingency telework—an emergency implementation in response to unforeseen events or circumstances such as flood, earthquake, fire, or terrorism.

Jeff Zbar, in his book *Safe@Home*, walks his readers through virtually every aspect of work-at-home safety, from protection from computer hackers to thieves intent on home invasion. He explains his attitude towards disaster preparedness:

> As a storm is approaching is no time to prepare for a hasty exit. Parents might recall the advice given to them before the birth of their first child: Prepare your personal belongings *before* the mother goes into labor. Once labor begins, the mad dash to head for the hospital is no time to fetch and pack the camera, toiletries, clothes and anything else desired for the hospital stay.

We begin our contingency telework instruction with guidance provided by a government agency that had to implement telework literally at a moment's notice. The 1989 Loma Prieta (San Francisco Bay area) earthquake, a devastating 7.1 level event, destroyed the Environmental Protection Agency's (EPA) San Francisco (Region 9) office. EPA, and its 800 Bay area employees, responded to this unexpected catastrophe by forced implementation of telework, followed by two written evaluations of this contingent telecommute situation. The first, *Report on State Agency Responses to Work-At-Home in Region 9*, gleaned several tips from personnel of other states' agencies who conduct business with the EPA office. In their comments, respondents indicated that the ease or difficulty of making routine contact with Region 9 employees in this post-earthquake time period had a strong influence on productivity during the work-at-home trial. As one complained, "Each project officer had different schedules and instructions concerning our communications with them."

You should keep in mind that the earthquake and these resulting reports occurred well in advance of commonplace use of such technological advances as intranet, Internet, e-mail, and instant messaging. Although some of the suggested procedures could now be altered to include these advances, the reports still contain valuable insight and suggested procedures. Their tips:

- Equip employees at home with computers including printers, modems, and fax machines; with answering machines or voice mail; and with call waiting.
- Establish a central telephone directory/locator service to provide phone numbers where employees can be reached away from the regional office and a separate directory of phone numbers and work schedules of teleworkers for distribution to state [coworker] contacts.
- Require a regular schedule of part-time office hours for telecommuting employees and require employees to call the office for messages on a regular basis.
- Expedite the routing of correspondence and assure regular mail deliveries to the home address of telecommuting employees.
- Cross train office-based personnel to better cover the absence of telecommuting employees. Inform in-office employees of the names of telecommuting staff and their schedules and assign an in-house counterpart to support telecommuting staff.
- Require at-home employees to contact their supervisors regularly for the purpose of resolving problems that require supervisory attention or approval.[1]

In a second survey, *A Qualitative Evaluation of EPA Region 9's Work-at-Home Experiences,* many of the Region 9 employees themselves, primarily the professional staff, stated their belief that they became efficient and productive only after they had PCs or laptops at home. Over and over, they stressed the need to make computers available as one important lesson from the earthquake experience, simply because they felt they were not nearly as productive without them.

Many of the staff members who insisted that computers were a key to productivity used their computers only as word processors. The advantages of writing with a computer, instead of a typewriter or a pen, were perceived as very great. Those who had become accustomed to word processing appeared to find it nearly impossible to write effectively in any other way.

They also stated their conviction that work-at-home experience after an earthquake is not a direct indication of how a work-at-home program might function under more normal, planned conditions

If there was an area in which supervisors felt that the work situation made it impossible for them to do their job satisfactorily, it was in working with employees who joined the agency just prior to or after the earthquake. These employees missed the individual attention from supervisors they would normally have received. Furthermore, they missed almost entirely the informal learning and impromptu tutoring from coworkers that is usually part of a new employee's orientation and socialization on the job.

Many participants reported that one of the lessons about how to implement work-at-home following a disruption or disaster is to obtain office space to serve as a base as soon as possible. As one participant put it, if there is a conflict between getting "good" space and getting space quickly, speed is probably more important.

To many employees, the most negative thing that happened was the long delay in obtaining enough office space even to serve as an adequate administrative base and staging area for those working at home. What made matters worse was the succession of dates announced on which more space was supposed to be available, and the disappointment as each date passed with an announcement of difficulty and another postponement. One participant commented, "Productivity increased exponentially once there was an infrastructure . . . some secretarial support, a way to schedule meetings."

Other staff observations and tips:

- The policy of talking to staff members daily, and meeting weekly, was seen as beneficial.
- Staff members and supervisors dwelled at length on the importance of communication, with such services as mail distribution, voice mail, long-distance calls billed to the employer, answering machines, electronic mail, and telephone upgrades such as call waiting.
- Problems encountered were lack of access to copiers, faxes and other services, lack of access to files and work materials, carrying large amounts of heavy papers back and forth, finding places to meet, and signature concurrences (documents requiring supervisory signatures to implement procedures).
- Participants applauded upper management's immediate design of efficient procedures to cover crucial administrative functions. Surveyed staff reported what they considered a crucial success: everyone was paid on time, travel vouchers were paid almost as quickly as in normal circumstances, and there was no disruption in pro-

cessing such actions as promotion and leave. There was appreciation of the management effort to keep such services on track right from the beginning.

- Some workers attached special significance to the recorded telephone announcement through which news was disseminated in the first days of the crisis. For some staff, the importance of this recorded message transcended the value of the information it contained. It was a tangible sign that an EPA structure existed, that management was functioning, and most of all, that EPA had a "center," as one of the participants put it. The fact that there was a telephone recording and that it was changed daily meant that there was a place where things were happening. "A real feeling of assurance that there was a center. Until then it was like an overturned ant hill."

- The all-hands meetings, especially the first one, were regarded as very important psychologically. Personnel were reassured of the safety and well-being of their friends and coworkers. The meeting and the way it was conducted was sometimes seen as a demonstration that upper management cared about staff and wanted to support them. The meeting also demonstrated that upper management was working to make progress toward restoring the organization's work and functioning. Workers began forging the relationships and creating the arrangements that would serve them during the months ahead. Psychologically the meeting signified the vitality of EPA and reinforced the workers in believing that the organization had not been completely crippled. It perhaps marked the end of a brief period in which the organization seemed to be in chaos, and the beginning of reconstruction.

- There appears to have been no fear or anxiety that supervisors would be second-guessed by their superiors as new rules for work were invented. Most supervisors seemed able to act vigorously in inventing responses to the new realities. Had supervisors not felt they enjoyed the trust and support of those above them, self-preservation might have inclined many of them toward more conservative responses, or even to inaction.

- There were complaints by a few that the sensitivity of upper management to the adverse working conditions diminished as the months passed. In one example, staff that worked at home, asked to brief a senior manager, made the trip to the region's temporary office on the appointed day only to be told that someone forgot to inform them that the manager had been called away. What the staff saw as carelessness cost them each a half-day's work. Under normal circumstances, when everyone was in the office anyway, such a cancellation would have been a very minor inconvenience. The senior manager seemed to have thought that such was the case here.

- Many supervisors and staff members indicated that one lesson from the earthquake was to get the mail going as soon as possible; the early establishment of mail delivery was seen as important for whatever progress was made at that time.
- Naturally, there were individual differences in how well individuals tolerated the messiness of work spread out in a home. "The people it worked for [were those who] could set aside a room."
- Some of the clerical staff and some of the supervisors felt it might have been appropriate to temporarily sever the lines between clerical personnel and individual groups and supervisors, and assign all the clerical personnel to a single pool. That would have freed the supervisors from worrying about the difficult task of providing work for a clerical person at home, and it would possibly have provided more fairness in work assignments if all clericals were under a single line of authority. A clerical staff member: "If it had been well thought out, they would have conglomerated all the clericals and had them report to one person who distributed the work. But supervisors wouldn't give up their control of their clerical staff."[2]

FYI . . .

At the Minneapolis, Minnesota office of international software giant Sopheon, severe winter weather is an ongoing concern. Sopheon executives have installed emergency evacuation procedures that, while not designed with very strict guidelines, do assign tasks to teleworking employees that will offer at least minimal services to clients when the staff is unable to get to the office.

The disaster most prominent on almost everyone's mind is the September 11, 2001, terrorist attack that killed hundreds, felled the New York City World Trade Center, and destroyed parts of the Pentagon. A partnership of the General Services Administration and Office of Personnel Management created a recovery Web site, encouraging federal agencies and managers to "make optimum use of personnel flexibilities such as telework and alternative work schedules to help relieve traffic congestions in these areas." They also stated "telework can assist employees who have been displaced because their federal building has been destroyed."[3]

These agencies pointed out that teleworking could help employee trauma recovery by alleviating the stress of the lengthy commute, and would give the employee more time with loved ones. They did caution, however, that it is usually not a good idea to separate anyone for long periods of time from a place where they have experienced a traumatic event, or to isolate employees from fellow employees who shared the event with them. By discussing their shared experiences, the report advised, they can help each other to resolve the event and recover from it. Their suggestion, therefore, was that generally a part-time, perhaps a two-day-a-week, telework schedule might be best. They also suggested that working at a telework center might resolve both the commute and isolation issues.

As mentioned in the Chapter 1 discussion of the financial incentives for telework, the move to telework-preparedness in the aftermath of that disaster may not only be for purposes of disaster response. It may, in fact, be a near necessity. To continue workers' compensation insurance coverage, or at least to avoid a rate increase of up to 50 percent, you may need to relocate some of your staff so that fewer than 50 employees work at any given location.

FYI . . .

In direct response to the terrorism of September 11, 2001, the U.S. Department of Health and Human Services issued its Departmental Telecommuting Program Policy on November 19, 2001. Stressing the need to actively promote telecommuting as a legitimate flexibility for managers and their employees, HHS executives emphasized their wish to promote the agency as an employer of choice and to enhance the Department's efforts to employ and accommodate people with disabilities. The complete policy, a collaborative effort by labor, labor union and management, can be viewed online at http://www.os. dhhs.gov/ohr/telework/policy.html.[4]

From the "Telework Guys" come the following additional tips:

- Plan now by applying the military strategy of asset dispersal (specifically, data, files, and staff) to distributed locations— teleworkers' home offices.
- Have no doubt that home is often the best place to work during shutdowns and transportation difficulties, when getting to the workplace may be impractical or impossible.
- Build a "telework kit" for yourself and your employees. Include basic telework guidelines, lists of important phone numbers, email addresses, passwords, and procedures for backing up key data.
- Invest in laptops for your employees, and don't forget extra batteries and a battery backup power source.

- Remember that even pen and paper can allow the work to continue, so identify ahead of time what tasks can be teleworked, and make sure that your staff takes relevant files home.
- Think, "If I'm not covered by a contingency plan, maybe my competition is."[4]

About.Com's Catherine Roseberry adds her advice:

- Make two lists—what equipment is absolutely necessary for temporary work-at-home, and what equipment would be "nice" to have.
- Make a list of what each of your employees already has—type of computer equipment, Internet connections, cell phones, pagers, etc.
- Find out if there are a few employees in close proximity to each other who could share resources.
- Make note of what materials or additional resources may be required by each employee to carry out their positions. Can these items be duplicated in order for employees to have a copy at their home office?
- Run tests to ensure that employees can connect to company systems and that it is possible to send emails.
- Find out if your employees would be able to make the connection to your company system (if fulfilling their job tasks would require it) and that the communications provider can support them.
- Find out if employees with direct lines at the office can call in from home and switch the line to call forward.
- Make sure that there is always someone that an employee is able to call upon with questions or for other assistance, including technical support.
- Create specific teams, which would include management and technical support as well as subordinates.[6]

Marcia Branco, lead network engineer for Decision One, offers her thoughts on your computer system's disaster readiness. She recommends a disaster recovery plan whereby each teleworker would know to whom they report. "Quick and effective response to a security breach," she says, "is key to minimizing damage." She adds,

I also think there may be a little confusion with what happens during and after an incident. A Disaster Recovery Plan provides clear procedures for all to follow after a security disaster. This plan helps a company get back to at least essential computing functions after a disaster in a timely manner.

Incident handling procedures determine what steps employees should follow during a cybercrime or computer security incident. Workers would know to whom they report what type of information. Such procedures afford a quick and effective response to a security breach. This is key to minimizing damage.

Regus, Inc., which lost its World Trade Center location and all staff members during the disaster, not only understands firsthand the impact of such an event but has also packaged an offer to assist firms with their need to get up and running in an alternative location after such a tragic loss. Regus, a global outsource office provider, offers a business continuity program, which provides back-up office space and professional resources. Companies impacted by disaster can access these locations and services immediately in the event their space is rendered unusable.

"Many of Regus' clients were tasked by their CEOs to update their existing disaster recovery programs to include a contingency office space plan," said Bob Gaudreau, executive vice president. "In order to meet the demands of our clients, we created a variety of cost-effective and flexible packages to accommodate any business needs should their staff be displaced."

Regus' three business-continuity options are designed to facilitate the process of securing back-up office space prior to a disaster and enable companies to resume operations within hours of being affected. While not necessarily the sole provider of some of the following services, their listing does offer firms and their managers a glimpse of what's out there to assist them:

- *Guaranteed Office Space Program*—Business can predetermine the location and configuration of their back-up office space from within Regus' global network. Companies can preselect fully furnished and equipped offices and/or team rooms designed to their specifications. The space is available upon client demand and includes dedicated phone and fax lines, prewired high-speed Internet connections, and a direct communications link to a company's existing business continuity site to ensure a seamless transition from one location to the Regus center. The space is also prewired for a local area network so that PCs and servers can be pre-installed.
- *Guaranteed Hot-Desk Space Program*—Companies can secure non-dedicated workstations within their preferred Regus center or region that are available to use on a just-in-time basis. The hot desks come equipped with a telephone, handset, phone, and fax number, as well as power and secure Internet connections. The package also includes local area network capabilities. A direct link to a company's business continuity IT site can be pre-installed as an option.
- *Continuity Link Program*—Companies affected by disaster can stay in touch with clients and employees. Regus will establish a dedi-

cated direct-dial telephone number for each employee. Priority access to workstations will be made available to businesses. The package includes all fax and phone handling as well as mail-forwarding service.

For more general information about Regus' and other outsource and executive-suite vendors and services, see the executive-suite section of Chapter 5, "Home Away from Home."

NOTES

1. Nancy Carlisle, *Report on State Agency Responses to Work-At-Home in Region 9*, Office of Policy and Management Planning and Analysis Section, April 1991.

2. National Analysts, A Division of Booz-Allen & Hamilton, Inc., *A Qualitative Evaluation of EPA Region 9's Work-At-Home Experience*, January 1991.

3. GSA, OPM, "Telework and Recovery Needs of Federal Employees" [database online, October 2001], http://www.telework.gov/recovery.htm.

4. U.S. Department of Health and Human Services [database online, January 14, 2002], http://www.os.dhhs.gov.

5. The Telework Guys are: Bob Fortier, Ottawa-based CEO of InnoVisions Canada, president of the Canadian Telework Association, also one of the "Remote Rascals" and director of the International Telework Association and Council; and John Edwards, Virginia-based CEO of Telework Analytics International. Both sit on the ITAC board.

6. *Contingency Telework Plans* by Catherine Roseberry (http://telecommuting. about.com/), licensed to About.Com Inc, which can be found on the Web at www.about.com. All rights reserved.

The Implementation Process

Once your firm is prepared for an unexpected crisis, you have a safety net. You can now carefully study your decision to include telework in the array of work options. You can take advantage of the software, expertise, and publications (such as this one) that will assist you in making a good decision and, if the decision is to implement telework, to formalize the process.

The state of California, in its *Guidelines for Implementing a Telecommuting Program,* stresses that potential problems with telecommuting can be mitigated by careful planning and design of the telework program. "Successful telecommuting," points out the state's Telecommuting Advisory Group, "requires thorough orientation, support of top management, a controlled pilot, careful selection of managers/supervisor and telecommuters, focused training for participants and their peers, and ongoing monitoring and evaluation."[1]

FYI ...

Janice Miholics, vice president of Global Work Life Strategies for Merrill Lynch, explains that the firm began its telework with a small pilot program of 36 employees, who were asked to telework but were given no training, direction, or structure. As a result of the non-voluntary aspect and the lack of direction, they lost 18 of those 36 employees.

SEVEN-STEP IMPLEMENTATION

This presentation is a compilation of advice from various managers and experts, with much input from the human resources offices of

California, Arizona, and Oregon, the telework consulting firm In-teleWorks, and human resource software expert Auxillium West.

Step 1. Determining Corporate Goals

Corporate goals establish the organization's expectations for the program—why you are considering it and what you hope to get out of it. This will determine both the desirability of implementation and the criteria you will use to evaluate continued improvement. The key here, according to AuxiliumWest, is that "the organizations select the criteria against which their decision will be made and against which the program will be evaluated on an on-going basis."

You will want to make a list and prioritize the issues. Ask yourself why your firm is thinking about telework.

1. *Are your employees asking for it?*

   This has happened with most firms that implement telework. If this is the case with *your* company, you will want to know *why* your employees are asking to telework—what issues they need resolved for themselves that are not being resolved in the current situation.

   You should also assume there are others not as vocal who might also like to take part in telework. It could even be that they have been considering a move from your firm because of un-addressed issues, such as commute times, transportation costs, time away from family, or stress.

   A survey, delivered on your intranet or in a newsletter or by supervisors, or a meeting to gauge interest is appropriate. If you offer exit interviews you may find discontent of former employees that could have been resolved by telework. It might even be possible to bring someone back into the firm with an offer of telework.

2. *Is your turnover rate unacceptable?*

   Are you losing folks to firms offering flexible options such as telework?

3. *Are you having difficulty recruiting employees?*

   Is it because the local labor pool has a shortage of qualified candidates? Is it because you are not setting yourself up as the employer of choice?

4. *Is productivity and/or production lower than it should be or needs to be?*

   Do you need to get more from the employees you have?

5. *Is absenteeism a problem*?

6. *Are you in a financial crunch*?

   Do you need to implement some cost-cutting measures? Are you considering telework as a way to reduce real estate or rental

costs? Or as a way of improving productivity, to eliminate positions or leave others unfilled?

7. *Do you need to expand?*

    Do you find that you're prohibited from doing so because of
    the high cost or lack of availability of real estate or rental space?

8. *Are you in a congested or smog-ridden area?*

    Do government mandates require that you get employees off
    the roads during peak periods? Are employees complaining
    about the commute?

9. *Are you having trouble complying with ADA or EOE/Affirmative
    Action regulations?*

10. *Are you concerned about the environment, or just desire to be a respon-
    sible part of the community?*

    (After all, goodwill has bottom-line benefits, too.)

11. *Are you running out of parking space?*

12. *Do you have employees who might still produce work during temporary
    leave if they were able to work at home?*

    Examples might be maternity, paternity, or temporary disabil-
    ity leave.

13. *Any other reasons?*

You will want to quantify the issues as much as possible. For instance,
assume a turnover rate in your industry of 20 percent, while yours is 40
percent. You might set your goal as reducing turnover by 20 percent. To
put a money figure on this goal you would simply multiply the turnover
of one of these positions by the figure that represents 20 percent of your
employees.

While not every issue can be easily converted to a money figure, most
if not all can be quantified. Benchmarking and/or networking can help
with some of this. For example, if, in your industry on average, in firms
of your size, 3 percent are disabled and your disabled workforce is 2
percent of the total, you have room for improvement. In a firm of 4,000
you may set a goal of bringing 40 more disabled employees on board.

Not until you know the reasons you are considering telework and
document these reasons and the statistics involved, will you be able to
go back over the results of your pilot program. *It is not until you recognize
and quantify the problems that you will be able to understand if you arrived
at the solution.*

FYI...

For software assistance with this portion of the process, and the
cost analysis and assessment of telework's implementation, you may
want to take a look at two software packages—Telework Audits and

Telework Analysys, products of the firm Telework Analytics International, Inc. TeleworkAudits is a 24-"page" Window-based point-and-click program that collects the data required to work out the costs and all the benefits to your firm of offering Teleworking. TeleworkAnalysys reads the data recorded by TeleworkAudits and downloads it to Excel® 5, 7, or 8 workbooks. These workbooks are then analyzed in Excel using TeleworkAnalysys for Excel. You may choose between individual, departmental, and/or corporate analyses, which are automatically generated. Analyses include executive summary, costs/benefits, capital needs budget, environmental analysis, and supporting charts and graphs.

Step 2. Assigning the Overseers

The next step in the process is appointing a telework "champion," a coordinator who will report directly to top management, whose responsibility will be to put together an advisory group and to liaise with management about the discovered pros and cons of telework implementation. Most probably a management-level employee, the two most important attributes of the telework champion should be having the ear of senior executives and being an avid believer in telework.

The advisory group, ideally composed of a cross-section of organization representatives from human resources, technical support, finance, public relations, and the firm's legal department, will, if the decision is made to implement telecommuting, develop the written guidelines and policies, establish the training program, and oversee the company-wide implementation plan.

Input from key customers and suppliers with whom the telecommuters may be interfacing could be important to the decision-making process also.

If your employees are organized, do ask for the input of a labor union representative in the process. This can be the key to avoiding problems later. See Chapter 6, "An Organized Response," for guidance on what unions want to see from your telework plan.

The questions to be resolved by this group will be:

- What equipment, supplies, connectivity, and furnishings will they require to work at home? (You will want the input of immediate supervisors. Each teleworker will have varying needs depending on the tasks of the particular positions.)
- Who will pay for the teleworkers' home equipment, supplies, furnishings, and connectivity?
- How will these be installed, chosen, and delivered?

- How do teleworkers maintain interpersonal business relationships with their supervisors and coworkers while teleworking?
- How can teleworkers use interactive tools like videoconferencing and instant messaging in the most effective way?
- How can teleworkers stay in the loop? How do they access HR information, including medical and other benefits? How do they acquire regular company newsletters, memos, and so on?
- Whom should they call when software stops cooperating or equipment fails?
- How will software and hardware be updated or replaced?
- How will the teleworkers keep track of equipment upgrades and service activity?
- Who will order telephone service, and where should the bill be sent?
- What is the procedure should a teleworker switch locations (move to a new home)?
- May the teleworker use company software on her personal computer?
- How and when is mail routed to the remote worker? Is overnight shipment necessary, or will weekly delivery suffice?
- Is a courier service in place for timely pick-up from remote workers?
- What is the procedure for requesting and procuring office supplies?
- Where does equipment go when it's no longer needed?
- Do the employees identify themselves as remote workers during business calls? Are they even allowed to make business calls to clients from their home locations?[2]

Once the telework program is implemented, the group will continue to monitor it against the established evaluation criteria. It will be their responsibility to provide continuous feedback, which will drive the recommendations for change and improvement to the program. The coordinator will have direct responsibility for completion of guidelines and policies and for ensuring that telecommuter agreements are completed and filed.

FYI . . .

Sopheon's permanent telework program includes a Telecommute Task Force composed of five employees, only two of whom are management level. Two employees are from IS, one a manager; the HR representative is a manager; the other two task-force members are non-managerial teleworkers. While the immediate supervisor of the telework candidate goes through an extensive 10-point review process to determine the candidate's suitability for telework, the task force then has the job of okaying the manager-recommended candidate. The final decision is made by the head of finance, who looks at the cost of offering telework to this specific candidate.

Step 3. Perusing the Resources

The feasibility assessment is based on information obtained from a literature review and employee survey. The information to review can include:

- The Clean Air Act Amendment, the Americans with Disabilities Act, and other pertinent legislation
- Government initiatives to encourage telecommuting—tax incentives, etc.
- The attitude of employees toward telecommuting—surveys, meetings, forums

What is crucial here is not only that you talk to those interested in telework, but that once you have determined who's uninterested or not participating because they were not chosen, you go back and find out *their* concerns. Those in sales will understand the concept that you need to probe for the objection in order to answer the objection and then close the sale.

Appendix B offers an excellent sample survey (see "State of Colorado Co-Worker Survey—Before"). Not only will you acquire good information but you also will assure these employees that you value their input and their opinion.

- The effects of telecommuting on employees and organizations. Go online and peruse the various telework associations recommended throughout this book. Periodicals such as *Workforce Magazine,* sites such as HR.com, and news sites such as CNN.com also address this issue quite often.
- Practical application of telecommuting, including competitors' experience. Network with HR professionals now offering telework. Call them, e-mail them, participate in such organizations as SHRM. Bookmark and regularly visit the following sites: www. gilgordon.com, www.ivc.ca, www.telecommute.org, www.langhoff. com, www.mite. org, http://www.att.com/telework, www. matac.org.
- Methods to ensure the successful implementation of a telecommuting program. Read our book and follow its guidelines.

The initial Step 3 functions (other than the employee survey) can be completed by following the instructions and resources in this book.

Other resources mentioned should be visited on an ongoing basis to keep abreast of legislation changes, new software, and so on.

Step 4. Choosing Teleworkers

Expert after expert emphasize beginning a formal telework program with a pilot (trial run) program of six months to one year—long enough to assess the feasibility of telecommuting and determine both the positive and negative impacts. They stress the importance of including in this pilot not only a telework champion but also managers who are already sold on telework and the most self-directed, knowledgeable employees.

Part of the decision about who can telework is determining, what, if any, positions cannot be accomplished during telework. In general, knowledge- and information-based positions with finite tasks are ideally suited for telework, while those requiring face-to-face contact or continual office/main work site presence—such as maintenance, construction, and reception—are not. This would seem fairly obvious were we talking about full-time telecommuting.

Most telework, however, involves work away from the office two–three days each week, and some employees may work from home as seldom as one day each week or for occasional projects. For this reason it might be said that no position should be eliminated from telework consideration, if only for specific well-defined, discrete projects and tasks.

The question that often arises is whether the managers themselves can telework. Helen Solomons, president of the human resource consulting firm Harrison Associates, is a former human resource director for Kulicke and Soffa and SCT (Systems and Computer Technology). She often hears managers say, "I am very much in favor of telework but I don't think *managers* can do it." She then asks them if they travel, to which the inevitable reply is yes. She then asks how they manage to do that and still supervise. "That gets them thinking," Solomon states.

FYI . . .

Clayton University does not exclude any position from telecommuting except custodial, and even in that department maintenance and grounds crew *supervisors* can be considered for telework.

We are providing as a guide the following list from the experts at MATAC.[3] While certainly not all-encompassing, this list does show the variety of areas in which these managers have witnessed successful telecommuting:

Accountant • Advertising Staff • Applications Programmer • Architect •
Attorney • Auditor • Bookkeeper • CAD/CAM Engineer • Civil Engineer
• Clerk Typist • Collections Staff • Community Relations • Copywriter •
Creative Staff • Data Entry Clerk • Design Engineer • Economist •
Environment Manager • Executive Support Staff • Financial Analyst •
Graphic Artist • Human Resources Manager • Industrial Engineer •
Information Services Staff • Insurance Broker • Journalist • Editor • Labor
Relations Staff • Lobbyist • Market Analyst • Marketing Staff • Product
Manager • Public Relations Liaison • Purchasing Staff • Quality Staff •
Research Staff • Sales Person and Support Staff • Sales Manager • Soft-
ware Engineer • Statistician • Strategic Planning Staff • Supplier Relations
Staff • Systems Programmer • Technical Writer • Telemarketer • Tele-
phone Operator • Web Designer

FYI . . .

The state of Florida's general rule is that if someone can close his
office door for eight hours, without the need for face-to-face contact,
then the job should be considered for telecommuting. If someone can
"cluster" her work into eight hours not requiring face-to-face contact,
her position is also a candidate for telecommuting.

There are three different documents you can use to choose
teleworkers. Unlike the permanent telework program, this pilot phase
must include your most self-directed employees—those already sold
on telework and those whose oral and written communication skills
are up to the task of giving reliable feedback. You will need their
continued input for decision-making on implementing and improving
the program.

Each manager will probably have valuable input on who might be
the best candidates. Employees themselves may have already stepped
forward to be included.

You will want to design applications with self-assessment aspects or
allow the candidates to apply and then offer self-assessments subsequently. These applications and/or self-assessments should be directed
to the telework champion. (See Appendix B for sample forms.)

The first step in choosing teleworkers is their submission of an application. In addition to the obvious elements—name, position, supervisor, location, and date—you will want each telework candidate to tell
you the following:

- What their job duties entail
- Which of these tasks could be done from home and why they
  believe so
- What days and hours they wish to telework

- Why they wish to telework
- What their home workspace is like
- What they will need at home to accomplish the work-at-home tasks
- Where they live (how many miles from work)

(Three sample telework applications are available in Appendix B.)

A self-assessment, or a self-assessment portion of the application itself, can be a highly effective and employee-empowering tool for choosing teleworkers. Not only does it allow workers to determine whether they are right for telework but it also helps allay negativity toward the manager decision maker when candidates are not chosen.

Bob Fortier, president of Innovisions Canada and the Canadian Telework Association, emphasizes the value of these self-assessments, calling them "a practical and palatable way to gather information necessary for management and decision-making."[4] He believes that completing the questionnaire will give most candidates a good idea of their suitability and their chances of success and will also show these employees that their organization trusts their judgment.

TMA Group of Tennessee also suggests involving employees in the determination of selection criteria for the jobs and employee types best suited for telework.[5] They point out that the development of selection policies includes the protection from possible equity and discrimination issues. They mention that allowable selection criteria include past performance, home workspace, commute distance, and supervisor approval.[6]

There are numerous sample self-assessments available. Some use true or false questions, and some offer multiple choices, while others ask open-ended questions requiring introspection. (For examples of telework self-assessments, applications, guidelines, and agreements, see Appendix B.)

The following self-assessment questions have been recommended by numerous experts or experienced managers, with special thanks for their extensive contribution to Oregon Office of Energy,[7] ALL-earnatives,[8] and AT&T.[9]

- Are you self-motivated, self-disciplined; can you complete projects on time with minimal supervision and feedback; are you productive when no one is checking on you or watching you work?
- Do you enjoy working independently?
- Do you like to think through and resolve problems yourself?
- Are you a procrastinator?
- Can you balance attention to major objectives and small details?
- Can you pace yourself to avoid both overworking and wasting time?

- Can you resist a refrigerator that is only a few steps away?
- Do you have strong organizational and time management skills; are you results oriented; will you remain focused on your work while at home, and not be distracted by television, housework, or visiting neighbors?
- Do you manage your time and workload well, solve many of your own problems and find satisfaction in completing tasks on your own; are you comfortable setting priorities and deadlines; and do you keep your sights on results?
- Are you knowledgeable about your organization's procedures and policies; have you been on the job long enough to know how to do your job in accordance with your organization's procedures and policies; do you have well-established work, communication, and social patterns at the central office?
- Are you adaptable to changing routines and environments, with a demonstrated ability to be flexible about work routines and environments; and are you willing to come into the central office on a regularly scheduled telework day if your supervisor, coworkers, or customers need you there?
- Are you an effective communicator and team player, able to express needs objectively and develop solutions; with developed ways to communicate regularly with supervisor and coworkers during telework?
- Are you successful in your current position; do you know your job well; and do you have a track record of performance?
- Do you have the right job for telework—responsibilities that can be arranged so that there is no difference in the level of service to the customer; minimal requirements for direct supervision or customer contact; low face-to-face communication requirements; the ability to arrange days when communication can be handled by telephone or e-mail; minimal requirements for special equipment; ability to define tasks and work products with measurable work activities and objectives; the ability to control and schedule work flow?
- Does your job have tasks that can be quantified, measured, and monitored?
- Do you have an appropriate home work environment—safe, comfortable work space where it is easy to concentrate on work; the level of security required by your employer; the necessary office equipment and software (if your employer is not providing it); household members who will not disturb you?
- Does your home office space have adequate lighting, sufficient ventilation, a safe number of electrical circuits, no zoning or lease restrictions that preclude telecommuting, and adequate insurance

coverage to protect business equipment? Is it a pleasant and comfortable space you would enjoy working in?
- Is your home office a reasonable distance from any needed business services?
- Is your family supportive of your desire to telecommute?
- Do you have the technology literacy level and ability to work with technology where there is not a technical support person on site?

The self-assessment may result in the weeding out of some candidates. Once the applications and self-assessments are in, your committee is ready to make its decision on candidates.

Colin Tierney, independent organizational consultant, emphasizes that selecting the right people is a crucial factor in successful implementation of teleworking projects. "Many projects were flawed in execution," he warns, "because selection criteria were loose or inappropriate, for example:

- Volunteers often come forward for reasons which are personally compelling, but may harm their capacity to telework, e.g., caring for aged or sick family
- People chosen solely on the criteria that they were best at the job as it was currently organized
- People chosen for organizational convenience, e.g., they were most distant from the workplace
- People chosen for their IT experience alone."[10]

Who's the ideal teleworker? There are numerous authorities on the subject, and a compilation of several views brought us to the following list:

- Is a self-starter—independent, self-motivated, not needing constant supervision
- Is results-oriented
- Is flexible
- Is well organized
- Has low affiliation needs—not needing continual social interaction with coworkers
- Has strong job knowledge. While some firms hire brand new employees to telework from day one, this is not the norm. Teleworkers generally work more effectively and stand a better chance of success with telework if they are already familiar with their work, their organizational culture, and their coworkers. Both coworkers and teleworkers can be reluctant to make contact when they don't know each other.
- Has a strong understanding of organization objectives

- Has a measurable product, with an informational component. Advances in remote technology have allowed the performance of many job tasks to be completed and monitored remotely.
- Is able to balance work and family life. Child or elder care and telework do not mix.
- Has a home environment conducive to teleworking—safe, hazard-free, ergonomically sound, uncluttered, quiet, free from distraction; ideally with separate lockable office space.
- Has excellent communication skills. Working remotely, without face-to-face contact, eliminates the use of several senses for communication. A teleworker needs clear, succinct, organized thought processes to be able to communicate effectively by phone, fax, e-mail, and mail. He also needs good spelling skills or a good spell checker.
- Is comfortable with emerging technologies. While numerous telework positions are not high-tech, they are increasingly reliant on software, hardware, e-mail, fax, computer, printer, scanner, and ISDN lines, which not only require a teleworker's proficiency or at least familiarity with the products but the ability to do some initial troubleshooting via personal knowledge, online or printed manuals, or technical support not available on site.
- Is a team player. (There is more on coworker resentment and what to do about it in Chapter 9, "Clearing the Hurdles.")
- Typically holds a knowledge-based position
- Does not need to rely exclusively on using resources accessible only at the home office location
- Has strong time and priority management skills
- Recognizes that telework is a privilege, not a right
- Is able to schedule face-to-face contacts in advance. Positions that require spur-of-the-moment meetings at the client's site—service and sales calls and the like—where those clients are nearer the primary work office than the employee's home, are not well suited to telework.
- Demonstrates exceptional work commitment. As one manager put it, "There are some folks to whom you can give an assignment and just walk away."
- Is able to produce work where or whenever possible
- Has a good working relationship with supervisors
- Has available equipment. While not necessarily a requirement that the teleworker already own a computer, fax, or second phone line, if the employer is not committing to buying or reimbursing for the purchase, the available hardware and software must be compatible with that of the primary office.

Telework guru Gil Gordon offers his list of do's and don'ts in the teleworker selection process:

- Do be clear about how you make your selection decisions.
- Do discuss those decisions with employees individually, not in groups.
- Do let employees know exactly why they were, or were not, selected.
- Don't rely on vague descriptions of performance to justify your decision.
- Don't pass up the opportunity to coach and counsel those not selected.
- Don't give the impression that telecommuting is a perk or benefit.[11]

Two important points that should always be made prior to the selection process of your pilot program or the subsequent permanent telework program is that telework is a privilege, not a right, and that the selection process is based not only on the determination of the candidate's ability to succeed in telework but also on the office or department's equipment or budget limits and the limits on the number of workers that can be spared from the office for telework.

As an example, let's look at a department staffed with ten workers. We'll assume there are eight fine telework candidates—self-motivated, flexible, long term, with great job knowledge and work records. Let's also assume this office needs a minimum on-site staff of seven to answer phones, provide clerical support, and assist walk-in customers. Let's also assume that Monday payroll and advertising deadlines require all ten workers to be on-site. If each of the eight teleworker candidates wishes to work from home two days each week, accommodating every telework request would leave you, the manager, with a staff of six on Tuesdays through Fridays. This is not a workable plan. Someone is going to have to be disappointed.

Another factor might be your firm's or your department's budget. If your firm has committed to provide the home equipment, and some of your employees are not already equipped with home computers, faxes, and the like, your budget may not allow for purchase, lease, or rental for all who wish to telework. You may have to choose those who already own some of this equipment.

The point here is that to allay resentment and jealousy the sharing of this specific information—the clarification early on of the reasons for deciding who is chosen—can assuage much disappointment. In the case of those not picked to telecommute, it may be possible to assure them that they can be considered in the future, especially if you have made the determination to limit the length of time a worker can telecommute before returning to the primary office location.

It may also be that some people are not chosen because they have not held their positions long enough. If they are showing the kinds of job skills needed for telecommuting, telework guru Gil Gordon points out that the manager could suggest—not promise—that telecommuting might be a possibility after more time has passed and as long as the skills are maintained or improved.

Mr. Gordon offers the specifics of "how to deliver the news." In cases where an applicant is denied telework for performance issues, he stresses, the manager must be clear about the reasons for not selecting the person to work at home. "This should be done with descriptive language and not just labels or summary judgments," he states. Saying "I was concerned that your projects or reports are often late or incomplete" is far preferable to "you're not conscientious enough," he explains.

Gordon also points out that this is a golden opportunity to give performance feedback where the opportunity may not have already arisen. "The employee who wants to telecommute will want to know why she hasn't been selected—even though it might be painful or upsetting to hear," he advises. He points out that you, the employer, now have the person's attention and can do some performance coaching. Gordon warns, however, that a manager not "do or say anything to promise the employee that he will be allowed to telecommute once these performance problems have been corrected. The message that must be conveyed is, "I'm not guaranteeing that you'll be able to telecommute once you improve in these areas—that will depend on lots of factors. *However, I can guarantee that I won't be comfortable with you telecommuting as long as these problems remain.*"[12]

Michael Dziak, in his firm InteleWork's booklet, *The Techniques of Really Smart Telemanagers,* answers a question frequently asked by skeptical managers: "How will I keep marginal employees from wanting to telework?" While he points out that your firm must start out with publicized and enforced selection criteria, he also says, "If a marginal performer with potential wishes to telework, consider a 90-day trial with some very specific work deliverables."[13] While he is referring to the permanent telework program and not the pilot (remember, your most self-directed employees are the *only* ones chosen for the pilot program), what you can say to applicants for the pilot program is another version of this, such as: "Although you will need to work on such and such, and are not ready to be a part of the telework pilot, let's take a look at your progress when we're starting our permanent telework option. Then it might be possible to offer you a 90-day telework trial."

Dr. Helen Solomons of Harrison Associates clarifies her belief that with the right level of motivation and training, and appropriate management and support, most people who really want to telework and who are in jobs all or part of which can be done off-site, can be successful teleworkers.

If you wish online or on-site professional guidance in choosing teleworkers, there is help out there. Several firms have emerged in the last few years to offer consultation and their software. One such consulting company, Kinetic Workplace, has designed a PAST software program, used as part of their Kinetic Assessment service, described by founder and president Timothy Kane as a "Meyer Briggs for telework ability."

Yvette Lucio, telework product manager for i2 Technologies, a Kinetic Workplace client, acknowledges that KW was instrumental in their 1999 telework implementation. "I most definitely recommend them," she says.

While programs such as PAST offer organized documentation and outside expertise in the choosing of teleworkers, their secondary virtue is their ability to take the liability and exposure away from the manager. This alleviates much of the resentment and demotivation of the employee not chosen for telework. Kinetic Workplace has devised a list of the abilities and qualifications crucial to telework success but emphasizes that managerial input on the key areas of the individual firm still plays an important part.

Nor does the manager abdicate his right to decide or lose the opportunity to counsel. Once the PAST results are in, the manager can sit down with the candidate not chosen and discuss the results, with a positive look to the future: "you scored low in . . . but, if you did such and such in the next . . . months, we may then be able to allow you to telework."

Helen Solomons says that her telework consultancy includes a very elaborate selection process, starting with the application. She studies the applications and completes a report with recommendations to the manager. The manager has the final say, but she encourages the manager to explain any disagreements.

With a large implementation—several applicants with numerous managers—she brings all managers together and lets them hear each others' comments. She said they learn from each other; one might voice an objection that another had but did not bring up. She said this process gets objections answered.

The following examples show how other firms choose teleworkers:

- Employees of Sopheon Resource Network Corporation are selected for the telework program based on the suitability of their positions for teleworking, the length of their commute, and their past and present work performance.
  To be eligible they must be self-motivated and conscientious and have good organizational skills, a high degree of job knowledge and skill, advanced computer hardware/software knowledge and

the skill and ability to make decisions independently. They also must meet with a member of the IS team one time prior to telework to assess and hone their computer troubleshooting skills.

- While managers at Merrill Lynch have the final say-so on who may telework, Vice President of Global Work/Life Strategies Janice Miholics stresses that the human resources department does, and must, take the lead. While they allow managers latitude, they also continually review and analyze telework in terms of demographics, compensation, mobility, and retention. They watch who is applying and who is denied. They determine selection and performance criteria—assessing positions, defining performance attributes, developing decision-making framework, and defining expectations tailored to the individual and performance measurements.

- Bell South has developed an internal course to help telecommuters develop the necessary skills.

- Washington Mutual makes a site visit to approve the homework space. The bank's district offices encourage appraisers to become teleworkers unless they do not have suitable home environments, do not have separate spaces available for home offices, are new staff, have performance issues, or for other reasons perform best in an office environment. Teleworkers are encouraged to set standard business hours but have a large degree of flexibility in when they accomplish their tasks.

- BT gives the line manager "ultimate sanction," providing education and training for individuals and managers to recognize and develop key core competencies.

- Surrey County Council leaves this judgment call to the manager. They look for an ability to be organized and self-disciplined, with good IT skills, good communications skills, and an ability to cope with the potential isolation of working remotely. More important, they stress, is how the team adapts to having telework as one of the work options.

- Other than those hired directly for telework, Auto Desk employees must be in the office six months, and each manager decides if a candidate is suited for telework. The candidate can assess her own suitability by completing a self-assessment questionnaire on Auto Desk's Web site, as well as reading on line ergonomic information for the home office.

- Prudential is one of the few firms that will hire with the prospect of telework as long as the employee has a proven history of productivity and self-reliance.

- The state of Utah's Division of Information Technology Services allows employees to telecommute after appropriate training and integration into ITS and their work group. Management determines when employees are able to work effectively without constant, direct supervision. Employees who are the subject of corrective or disciplinary action are not considered. Documented declines in performance during telework may be grounds for canceling the telecommuting arrangement, disciplinary action, or both.

- Pearson Education does hire some new employees with the intention of allowing them to telework immediately if they have proof that they have succeeded in a telework environment elsewhere. All teleworkers go through a three-month evaluation period of being managed by completed tasks.

- Willow CSN, which hires independent contractor CyberAgents for their virtual call center, has an extensive selection process. CEO Asim Saber admits that only 35 percent of applicants make it through the process and become CyberAgents.

  The first step is a 1.5-hour orientation process at the Willow office in Fort Lauderdale, Florida. Each candidate then pays $25 to take a PC skills test. The second step is a 50-question psychological profile each candidate completes from home. Subsequent to this is a phone interview in which the applicant's ability to "think on his feet" is evaluated.

  Candidates who make it through these steps then attend a 40-hour CyberAgent 101 class, back at the Florida office. They learn small business success tips, taxes, handling irate calls, and the actual process for assisting the client's customers.

- TManage has a profiler to help determine the better telework candidates. Project management, communications, motivation, and a stay-on-task work ethic are the big four that Glenn Lovelace recommends as primary characteristics of a successful teleworker.

  If needed, TManage provides social adaptation through training, as they believe that is the primary aspect of teleworking that can be trained. An employee cannot be considered for telework until on board six months, and each teleworking "newbie" goes through a 30-day trial period.

- The state of Florida has designed a very formalized selection process, complete with Internet access for telework candidates. Candidates can peruse the information, which lists not only the typical attributes for successful teleworkers but also the home office safety, security, and ergonomic needs, as well as tips for succeeding in work-at-home.

  The state has chosen categories suitable for telework, as well as positions (i.e., "accountant" would be a category, "accountant in purchasing" would be a position). They have a formalized orientation program, introducing candidates and their supervisors to telecommuting. Employees in the selected positions who wish to participate, after an orientation session, complete an employee survey. Managers can then use the survey as a guide for the potential success of an employee in the program.

Managers and direct supervisors of potential telecommuters select the participants. Chosen employees and their supervisors then complete and sign a written agreement.[14]

- InterWorks of Portugal asks these (and other) questions of its telework candidates: are you a self-starter? Are you able to effectively manage your time and work? Are you able to work alone? Would you react to an unforeseen problem or difficulty by panicking, seeking help from others, or working through it yourself? Has your spouse or partner the psychological ability to accept the situation?

- Nortel Networks provides an "optional" online assessment questionnaire. An employee wants to determine if she or he is suitable, can answer the questionnaire, and get a grade from the responses, indicating suitability. The grades are purely optional and for the information of the employee only. The candidate cannot be rejected from telecommuting by a bad score.

  The questionnaire highlights such things as whether office social interaction, like going out to lunch, for example, is highly important. It highlights challenges of telecommuting that the employee might not have thought about. Nortel also offers an employee network online, so that employees can talk to other telecommuters, discussing their experiences. Once telecommuting, they can also hook in for telework support or guidance. There is a managers' network as well.

- Health Alliance of Cincinnati has a formal decision-making program in place and a contract. The direct supervisor, Sherry Doggett (director of corporate medical transcriptions), and the quality training manager make the decision.

  Health Alliance does not direct hire for telework because there is so much to learn. To qualify for telework generally requires in-house employment for a minimum of three months, with the average nine months to one year.

- Art & Logic hires employees with the understanding that they will work at home full time. Their interview process is lengthy, beginning with the candidates' study of their Web site, followed by a 20–30-hour programming test, which they must do at home online. A candidate who studies the Web site and can follow through and successfully pass this programming test has already indicated she can produce adequate work at home.

Step 5. Beginning the Pilot Program

The pilot study serves to test hypotheses and possible options to be included in the program. An important aspect of the pilot program is an assessment by both subordinates and managers to determine the success of the study in terms of the goals set by management and, in particular, productivity. (Again, see appendix B for sample assessments.)

You will need to write a "definition" of your pilot study, including your teleworker selection criteria and methods—that is, step one is application, step two is self-assessment, such and such member of the committee will assess. You need to determine if the whole committee together will make a decision on each candidate, or if the duties and names are to be divided up.

You should also define the start and stop dates of the pilot, what equipment and services will be provided, and if allowing for individualized decisions, determine who will be the decision maker. For instance, would a candidate's immediate supervisor decide whether the telework candidate's job tasks require that she have a second dedicated phone line in her home?

Once the pilot study is completed and you are considering implementing a permanent telework program, you would bring together those managers who may not have been proponents, may have even been adamantly opposed, and those employees who have expressed concerns about allowing others to telework (perhaps these employees applied and were not initially chosen, or they do not wish to do so and resent others teleworking).

With the positive results of your pilot program in hand you will have a better chance of winning them over, and indeed you may already have done so if the pilot program has been visibly successful.

Remember, success should *always* be visible by way of testimonials, bulletin boards, intranet, meetings, memos, and e-mails.

Nor does visibility have to be retained within your organization. There may be times when telework can be a public relations bonus for your organization. Perhaps you are in a rural, remote, or economically deprived area that is struggling to retain its residents. Perhaps your telework shows other struggling employers in the community how to expand their geographic reach. Perhaps you are the first in the area to offer telework. Perhaps you are the first in the industry to offer telework. Or perhaps your telework pilot has been so successful, your employees such telework proponents, that it shows you to the public as the employer of choice. Any of these circumstances—and you can probably come up with others—might indicate something of interest to the media.

By now you will have determined your problems—the issues you need resolved—have set their resolution as your goals and have quantified those goals. You have chosen the administrator for your project (the telework champion) and the managers involved. You have brought together your implementation team. You know the legal issues and union concerns and have decided on what hardware, software, equipment and services you are going to supply and maintain for each teleworker. You have chosen the pilot program's teleworkers.

Here is what you need to do before you start:

1. *Prepare a Budget:* Include the expenses involved in implementation, from additional IT support including their travel for home implementation or home inspection, installation and purchases, employee down-time while meeting, discussing, applying and training, and so on.

2. *Submit a Proposal to Management:* Explain the problems, how telework will contribute to the solution, anticipated savings, managerial and subordinate participants, and evaluation criteria.

3. *Write a Telework Policy:* The basic difference between a company telework policy and the specific telework agreement is that the policy addresses the issues and regulations that pertain to *every* telework arrangement the company allows, while the agreement addresses those issues and decisions pertinent to the specific teleworker, or any issue or circumstance that the company policy states may be altered by individual agreement. There can, therefore, be an overlap on the issues addressed. We also sometimes see that what one employer considers the auspices of the policy another addresses in the agreement. What is crucial is not so much where the issue is addressed but that it is in fact addressed.

   Telework policies vary considerably; depending on the consulting company or employer, some list in the *agreement* what others list in the *policy*. In general, however, the experts recommend the following elements:

   • Company telework mission statement—the commitment to pursue telework and the benefits of doing so
   • Statement that the policy applies to all employees
   • Clarification that telework may not be suitable for all employees, or all positions
   • Statement that telework should be voluntary, unless specifically stated as a condition of employment
   • Statement that telework can be suspended due to operational needs of the employer

- Definitions—telework, telework site, central work site, remote access, telework agreement, telework application, telework self-assessment, and so on.
- Guidelines for determining who can telework—work habits, workability of position. Also will state that decision to telework must enhance the issues bringing the firm to telework—that is, air quality, commute time, enhanced productivity, and so on.
- You may need to include a statement that teleworkers must reside in your state, or set other predetermined geographic boundaries, depending on legislation issues.
- Statement that in case of injury, theft, loss, or tort liability the teleworker must allow agents of the organization to investigate and inspect the telework site as needed
- Statement that employee shall sign and abide by telework agreement
- Statement that the telework agreement will by reviewed by the supervisor and teleworker during performance review and revised as necessary
- Clarification that the teleworker's condition of employment shall remain the same as nonteleworking employees
- Statement that organization policies, rules, and practices shall apply at the telework site and that failure to follow these may result in termination of the telework arrangement and disciplinary action
- Notification that the teleworker will not be paid for time involved in travel between the telework site and central work site, nor will travel expense be reimbursed (Numerous firms do state in their policies that on any given day a teleworker's first trip to and from the office would not be paid, but that subsequent trips *on that same day* would be reimbursed.)
- Clarification that the number of work hours will not change because of telework, although for some positions more flexibility in work hours and days may be feasible
- Statement that the teleworker must determine federal, state, and local tax implications resulting from working at home and satisfy their personal tax obligations
- Requirement for teleworker to comply with applicable state and local zoning ordinances
- Statement that the teleworker must get his supervisor's advance written approval before working overtime
- Statement that telework must not adversely affect customer service delivery, employee productivity, or the progress of an individual or team assignment

- Notification that in approving the telework schedule, the employee's supervisor will take into consideration the overall impact of the teleworker's total time out of the central work site
- You may decide to require the teleworker to attend job-related meetings, training sessions, and conferences, as requested by the manager. In addition, the teleworker may be requested to attend "short-notice" meetings. If so, this needs to be stated in the policy.
- Statement that the teleworker must establish work practices that make telework arrangement transparent to customers, ensuring that customers are not inconvenienced in their dealing with employee or company
- Statement that while teleworking, the employee must be reachable by telephone, fax, pager, or e-mail during agreed-upon work hours or specific core hours, and that teleworker and manager will agree on how to handle telephone messages and determine who in the office is to have the employee's home number
- Arrangement for long-distance work-related calls from teleworker's home office—limits on the calls, how they are supposed to be accomplished—calling card, reimbursement
- Notification that teleworker will not act as primary caregiver for dependents during the agreed-upon work hours
- Clarification whether the teleworker is permitted to hold business meetings with clients or customers, the public, or professional colleagues at his residence
- Teleworker's accessibility to restricted-access materials
- Security issues—Where the employer-owned laptop and PC can be used, who is liable in case of its theft, details of the type (brand) of virus and surge protection, software licensing provisions, duplication of organization-owned or licensed software, requirements for work-related data backup, accessibility to files and passwords, requirements for firewall, VPN, and programs providing the data encryption
- A statement that the employer is not responsible for loss, damage, or wear of teleworker-owned equipment
- A statement that the employer may pursue recovery from the teleworker for organization property that is deliberately, or through negligence, damaged, destroyed, or lost while in teleworker's care, custody, or control; that the repair and replacement costs and liability for privately owned equipment and furniture used during telework is the responsibility of the teleworker

- A statement that the repair and replacement costs and liability for organization-owned equipment used during telework is the responsibility of the organization
- Telework application and implementation procedure, including contact names, and any training requirements
- Process for rescinding telework agreement
- Procedure to appeal denial of telework, if your firm decides to offer an appeal process
- Monitoring and evaluation procedures

Several companies have divided their written policies into categories of responsibility—those of the manager/direct supervisor, the employee, and the company itself (usually the human resources staff). You may decide that this is helpful for your company.

4. *Publicize the program:* Communicate with all staff. You will have already done this once, when inviting teleworkers applications but this is a step that should continue throughout the pilot program.

As Smart Valley executives put it, "Sell the program constantly." Start with briefings to management; follow with a memo or article in your firm's newsletter or on your intranet; and then hold orientations for all interested parties.

Keep the news coming throughout the trial, conduct focus groups throughout, and encourage teleworkers to share their experiences with non-teleworking employees. Publish personal testimonials—by intranet, bulletin board, newsletter, and the like.

Make it clear that you are always open to suggestions and to ideas on problems and solutions. Set up a process for managers and employees to offer feedback to a designated person or committee member by e-mail, phone, or written memo, or perhaps to a telework pilot program suggestion box.

5. *Orientation and training:* Schedule and design an orientation for all managers and prospective telecommuters, followed by formal training for participants (managers, supervisors, and selected telecommuters). This phase should include identification of telecommutable work tasks, work hours and attendance reporting, security issues and resolution, equipment and ownership, maintenance and use, communications and other technology needs, health and safety, agreement on what constitutes successful performance of job or task, and identification of and solutions to potential problems.

Your managers need to be trained in monitoring, supervising, and measuring and evaluating performance.

Your teleworkers will need direction on supplies, furniture and equipment needs and how they will be met, ergonomics, computer security, technical support procedures and contacts, other contacts, distraction issues, time management, home safety, isolation, suggested reading, and Internet sites.

And don't forget the non-telecommuting coworkers. They will need to know the availability and contact information for teleworkers and the expectations for any job responsibility changes in the absence of coworkers.

(For extensive information on the training and telemanagement process, see Chapter 9, "Clearing the Hurdles.")

6. *Telecommuting agreements should now be designed and signed.* (See sample agreements in Appendix B.) Each telework agreement needs to be signed and dated by the agreeing parties—typically teleworker and immediate supervisor—prior to the telework effective date. A copy of the agreement should be retained in the teleworker's personnel file.

Contributing attorney Kathleen Bray offers legal insight into the design of a telecommuting agreement. She believes that a telecommuting agreement, reviewed by the employer's legal counsel, is an essential document in creating and regulating the home-based worksite. Issues that she indicates should be addressed by the agreement, along with other general provisions, are:

- *Insurance.* The agreement should address what the employer provides and any requirements for what must be provided by the employee, including proof of insurance. In evaluating these issues, consider automobile insurance, property insurance, liability insurance, and workers' compensation insurance.
- *Employer access and employee privacy.* The agreement should address rights of access by the employer to the telecommuting property and work product, either electronically, physically, or both. Provisions may include notifying the employee that employer has full right to review the contents of the computer, reminder of the lack of privacy with e-mail or online usage, and the employer's right to review and right to physically inspect the home-based worksite upon reasonable notice.
- *Confidentiality concerns.* Consider and address the exclusivity of and restrictions on property use. In order to preserve confidentiality and minimize corruption of data or intermingling of information, an employer may want to consider restricting use of telecommuting equipment to business purposes only. The agreement also should address issues of unauthorized access through providing for password protection, keyed lock access, and the like.

- *Rights upon termination.* The agreement should include provisions relating to the return or retrieval of company property and data upon the employee's termination or separation from employment.
- *Employee availability and wage and hour issues.* As discussed earlier, address the expectations regarding the employee's hours worked, availability for communications, and documentation regarding time, projects, and/or hours worked. Also, any expectations regarding what work must be performed from the employer's worksite, or meetings that must be attended at the employer's place of business, should be discussed.
- *Safety.* Tying in to workers' compensation and OSHA concerns, the agreement should specify who is responsible for ensuring compliance with applicable safety codes and itemize any requirements that relate to safety at home, including electrical requirements, smoke detectors, fire extinguishers, surge protection, and positioning of equipment.

Ms. Bray also adds this advice: "If you are in an employment-at-will state, and do not have an employment contract with the employee, the telecommuting agreement [policy] should reinforce the 'at will' nature of the relationship. The agreement should contain language indicating it merely sets out rules of conduct or expectations of the telework arrangement, rather than creating or amending any other employment contract."

From the managers interviewed and other expert resources contacted, we compiled this list of the elements your telework agreement should include:

- Names of the parties involved—typically, teleworker and immediate supervisor
- Date signed and effective date for telework
- Telework location
- If agreement is fixed or as-needed
- Statement that teleworker has received, and will abide by, written telework policies
- Statement that telework is voluntary, a privilege—not a right
- Clarification of the employee's job function, title, compensation, and benefits, as well as a statement specifying that these are not altered by the telecommuting arrangement
- Predetermined notification timeline by which either party can terminate the telework arrangement, listing any minimum standards regarding office configuration and safety and security features

- Statement that the teleworker will maintain a safe and healthy home work environment
- Statement that the supervisor or other employer-designated party can periodically inspect work location and the minimum notification to be given to teleworker of said inspection
- Requirement that teleworker abide by work performance standards
- Hours and days of telework
- Times and methods of teleworker/office contact
- Requirements (if any) for teleworker's presence in office
- Statement that data and work-related material are property of employer and must be immediately returned in the event of employment termination
- Costs the employer will and will not reimburse (telephone, Internet, etc.)
- Specific equipment the employee will purchase, provide, and maintain at employee's own expense
- Specific equipment the employer will provide, service, and maintain, including how such equipment should be procured
- Insurance coverage the employer will provide, as well as any coverage the employee is expected to purchase
- Rights and limits of workers' compensation coverage for accidents in the home office, and the reporting procedure
- Availability, means, and responsibility for technical assistance
- Office contact—"buddy," coworker, mentor, assistant, coordinator
- Statement that teleworker will not conduct personal business during times designated for work
- Requirements to secure work-related documents, materials, and equipment by mutually determined methods
- Scope of the work to be accomplished
- Estimated time to complete specific projects, if applicable
- Project start and end dates, if applicable
- Progress report requirements and work evaluation criteria—the employee's specific and measurable accountabilities, including projected review dates
- Work evaluation criteria

7. *A detailed plan and schedule for the start-up of the prototype.* The plan should identify both the necessary activities and the staff responsible for completing them.
8. An *inventory* of "before telecommuting" equipment and telecommunications costs, sick leave use, office space use (sq. ft.), employee effectiveness and morale, for comparison with end-of-pilot results in these same key areas.

9. *A method for monitoring and reporting progress* during the prototype period for the purpose of making corrections and adjustments to the pilot. To whom should participants, including managers, teleworkers, and non-teleworking coworkers report if they see something that is not working or have suggestions for changes? Who would have the authority to implement changes—an individual or the teleworking group as a whole?

10. *Assignment of responsible staff to conduct the pilot program.* While the telework champion would typically keep upper management apprised of the program's progress, you would also need to assign duties such as overseeing of suggestions for change, assessments of requests by individual teleworkers to drop out of the program, scheduling and chairing forums and meetings, and handling publicity. You would want an IT person in charge of technical and security follow-ups—work-at-home maintenance, update of anti-virus software, repairs, and so on.

FYI . . .

Glenn Lovelace noted that initially some TManage teleworkers were phoning the office two or three times a day until they became comfortable with their teleworking situation. He said that as an employer he would prefer someone who e-mailed once a week to a teleworker who phoned several times a day.

Step 6. Equipment and Supplies

At this point, you need to provide equipment and install technology. Prior to purchasing supplies and equipment for your work-at-home employees, you'll want to determine financial responsibility (which expenses are the employer's, which the teleworkers'), and what supplies, equipment and services each teleworker will need.

Determining Financial Responsibility Almost every employer we interviewed said that they purchase the equipment and the connectivity for work-at-home employees. Virtually every consultant recommended this. Not only will the savings outweigh the expense you incur in productivity, retention, and improved employee morale, but you also retain rights and controls you would not when the employee uses her or his equipment.

Issues like monitoring, security and recovery of sensitive company-owned material become that much more cumbersome, if not impossible, when the equipment, supplies, and expenses have been paid for by the employee—especially a terminated one.

In a 2001 techies.com survey of 1,953 members, respondents revealed that of those who telecommute, 75 percent say their employer supplied them with a laptop, more than half were supplied special software installations, 40 percent of the employers covered expenses for office supplies and the same number supplied 800-number access to the main office; 32 percent paid for the home office's ISP, while fewer than 20 percent supplied additional equipment such as printer, scanner, fax, or PC.[15]

FYI ...

An unforeseen challenge that Allina Metro Hospital confronted was the constant upgrading and maintenance of the technical equipment used by telecommuters. They had expected the purchase of PCs, phone lines (later upgraded to ISDN lines), home office furniture and equipment, and voice mail technology, to be a one-time cost. However, they quickly learned that if they did not afford telecommuters enough resources to do their work effectively and efficiently and to solve most of their problems on their own, the telecommuting program would not produce the results to justify its effort and cost. According to Operations Manager Barbara Leitz, "We came out ahead because of productivity [increases]."

Timothy Kane, president of ITAC and founder of Kinetic Workplace, confirms that his firm pays for its employees' hardware:

> We highly encourage our firms to have their employees laptop-enabled as opposed to a PC, so they don't have the issue of personal 'stuff' on the hard drive. If they must have a PC we recommend the employer pay for it. If the employee is terminated the employer then has the right to recoup their business information instead of worrying about the company material remaining on the employee's home equipment.

Art & Logic provides all necessary hardware, software, and support for its teleworking employees. Their reasoning is hard to dispute. According to founder Paul Hershenson, "We would be doing that if they were working in our office, so why would we not just because they are at home?"

Other firms and agencies are pursuing a variety of options. Some of these are described in the following pages.

- KCTS Television offers $2,000 in interest-free loans annually to each employee for the purchase of home computers and equipment. Information systems staff is available by telephone to support employees having difficulty making the computer connection from home.

- For *permanent* home workers at Surrey County Council, all equipment is provided and maintained by SCC. For those who work at home *occasionally*, equipment is not routinely provided, although the number of departments that are providing equipment for even these occasional teleworkers is rising, depending on the situation.

- At InterWorks, the responsibility is the employer's, offering the virtual Telecentro site, with a platform of services and products of InterWorks available 12 hours each day, and the site available 24/7.

- Merrill Lynch provides equipment and connectivity. The teleworkers provide their own ergonomically correct furniture.

- Allina Metro Hospital purchases and takes financial responsibility for all hardware and software for work-at-home medical transcriptionists. They insist, for security reasons, that home workers use only the firm's PC and that no one else be allowed to use the computer.

- Pearson Education pays for its work-at-home employees' software, phone, and fax. Who pays for the hardware varies by business unit.

- Work-at-home i2 employees are reimbursed by the firm for $1,200 in home office furniture. Says Telework Project Manager Yvette Lucio, "If the teleworker chooses a $1,200 chair that is her decision." The teleworker is also reimbursed for a cable or DSL modem, an extra phone line, and $200 in setup fees. If teleworkers do not use their own computer, they take home the one they were using at the office. (i2 is very laptop-oriented.) If an employee does not stay with telework at least one year, however, she must return, on a graduated scheduled, a portion of the reimbursement money.

- At Auto Desk, who pays what is manager-driven. Typically, each manager is given a $1,000 per-teleworker spending limit. The company provides all computers, though, and usually the phone and connectivity.

- At Pasona each teleworker is solely responsible for her own equipment.

- Because Willow CSN's CyberAgents are independent contractors, they purchase their own equipment and furniture, an expense that ranges between $1,200 and $3,700.

- BT takes complete responsibility, rather than relying on their employees.

- At Faulkner Group an extra phone line, a computer with Internet access, office furniture, and a fax and printer are installed for each eWorker. There are no ISDN lines in the office and therefore none are installed at the employees' homes. To date there have been no requests for payments for utilities from the eWorkers.

- For Health Alliance of Cincinnati, the employee purchases a desk, a chair, and the required medical transcription books to work from home. This requires an outlay of approximately $300–$400.
- According to Florida's state telecommuting guide: "to effectively perform their assigned tasks, state employees are allowed to use state equipment at the home office." This use must be approved by the supervisor and must be protected against damage and unauthorized use. State-owned equipment is serviced and maintained by the state. Employees may use their own equipment, but its maintenance would be the responsibility of the employee. The purchase of surge protectors for state equipment is paid for by the state, as are the installation and monthly fees for a second "business phone" in the home office if deemed necessary.

  The state's 1997 telework survey reported that 31 of 119 supervisors purchased additional equipment for the sole use of telecommuters, totaling approximately $45,000, the majority of which was for laptop and personal computers.[16]
- At Nortel Networks, the company pays for all equipment and high-speed data services. When an employee signs up to telecommute, she or he can go online and choose ergonomic furniture that is paid for and delivered by the company. Nortel also provides 24/7 technical support so that the telecommuters receive the same level of computer/telephone service as an employee in the office.
- Clayton University allocates no money for telework equipment and upkeep, though each department can choose to budget for it and many do. Some teleworkers have their own PCs or laptops, and they all have call forwarding. The school has implemented Web-based e-mail so that teleworkers can access their e-mail from any location.
- Sopheon provides mobile workers with docking stations and all other teleworkers with PCs. All teleworkers are equipped with printers, telephone sets, modems, and/or routers. In addition, some teleworkers are provided with headsets and recording devices. The firm pays one-time set-up charges associated with telecommunications services as well as recurring telephone service and business long distance charges. All full-time telecommuters or hotelers (80% telework) are given a furniture allowance of $1,000+ to cover the purchase of an office chair, desk, and document storage container, all of which must meet Sopheon's ergonomic guidelines. Sopheon's policy states that if an employee leaves the company on his/her own accord within one year of signing a

telework agreement, the employee will reimburse Sopheon for 100 percent of one-time setup charges and 50 percent of approved furniture and printer purchases.

The state of Utah's Division of Facilities Construction and Management (DFCM) describes what the state pays for and what is expected of the teleworker in its policies and procedures. They stipulate that an employee who must receive business calls or transmit data regularly as a function of the job will typically be authorized a separate telephone line or lines for business use that will be paid for by DFCM. Teleworkers requiring only occasional communications will be expected to use their own telephone lines, with any additional costs for business use of the personal line to be reimbursed. In regards to those workers whose additional phone lines are paid, installation of these facilities and equipment must be ordered through DFCM and the costs billed to DFCM and regularly reviewed by management.

Utah State employees must obtain supplies for use at the telecommuting work site from the primary office location. Generally, out-of-pocket expenses will not be reimbursed, although exceptions must be approved before any expenditure. Except for unique, one-time situations, copying costs will be borne by the employee, if copying is not done from the state office.

DFCM provides only the PC hardware and software, communication facilities, and other ancillary equipment required to perform job functions successfully in a telework environment. Equipment shall be allocated according to need and availability. While telecommuting equipment may vary among individuals, the equipment must always conform to standards set by DFCM.

DCFM is responsible for upgrades, customization, licensing, and maintenance of hardware and software of all state-owned items. Maintenance on state equipment is provided on a carry-in basis only. Furniture is not supplied by the state, unless proscribed and approved by the immediate supervisor.

If employees make nonstandard or unapproved hardware or software modifications to state-owned equipment or use their own or state-owned hardware or software in unauthorized ways or for unauthorized purposes, any problems or damage resulting from such modification or use shall be the responsibility of the employee. If state resources are required to resolve such a problem, the employee will be expected to reimburse the state's cost for labor, hardware, software, and other expenses. Repairs to employee-owned equipment shall be the employee's responsibility.

The state's ITS Division has outlined a very extensive, very specific reimbursement and responsibility process. These policies and procedures clearly state that the state, as employer, will not be liable for damages to the employee's personal or real property while the employee is working at telecommuting unless damages are as a direct result of malfunctioning state-owned equipment. They also stipulate that the state will not be responsible for any costs associated with using an employee's home as a telecommuting site such as maintenance, insurance, and utilities.

Authored by Gene Puckett, Deputy Director, their policies state that an employee who must receive business calls or transmit data regularly as a function of the job will typically be authorized a separate telephone line or lines for business use, whose installation and purchase will be paid for by the department.

Teleworkers will not be reimbursed for their first commute to their primary work location (state office building) on any given day. Subsequent commutes on the same day will be reimbursed.

While clearly stating that repairs to employee-owned equipment are the employee's responsibility, Puckett spells out the specifics of the employer's responsibility for state-owned hardware, software, and other equipment:

1. ITS shall provide only the PC hardware and software, communication facilities, and other ancillary equipment required to perform job functions successfully in a telework environment. Equipment shall be allocated according to need and availability. Telecommuting equipment may vary among individuals, and will conform to standards set by ITS.

2. Equipment shall be issued for off-site use only with proper, signed documentation in place. Documentation shall identify brand and model name, serial number, and address location. It shall also identify the responsible individual and be signed by the teleworker and the issuing employee.

3. For teleworkers spending at least 40 percent of their work time in a telework environment, ITS will provide: desktop or notebook PC, as determined by employee, management, and LAN Group; ISDN line and Cisco 766 router, if required by job function; ISDN phone set or analog phone, as required by job function; docking station, extra monitor, keyboard, and mouse if required and desired for notebook users.

4. For teleworkers spending less than 40 percent of their work time in a telework environment, ITS will provide: earlier-generation desktop PC with modem, as available; analog (IFR) lines, as required by job function.

5. Notebook PC teleworkers retaining personal workspaces at the State Office Building (SOB) will be allowed only one docking

station, extra monitor, keyboard, and mouse. Notebook PC teleworkers using shared workspaces at the SOB will be allowed one docking station, extra monitor, keyboard, and mouse for use at telework site as well as access to equivalent equipment in their shared workspace. They will also be allowed to place their current technology PC at the telework site and have the use of equivalent equipment in their shared workspace.

6. All off-site equipment allocations and configurations shall be approved by section management in negotiation with LAN Services Group management.

7. ITS shall be responsible for upgrades, customization, licensing, and maintenance of hardware and software. Modifications may not be made without prior approval from the appropriate support group.

8. Only hardware and software purchased, installed, and maintained or otherwise approved by ITS will be supported by ITS support organizations. Maintenance on state equipment will be provided on a carry-in basis only.

9. Furniture, answering machines, fax machines, copiers, and the like will not be supplied by the state.[17]

Determining equipment and supply requirements. While the Work at Home Supplies checklist is a handy tool (see box), what each specific teleworker requires depends on the type of work to be accomplished from home. Issues that must be worked out include the need for intranet and Internet access and what the contact method and speed would be—dial-up, DSL, or broadband—and what software applications would be required. (Computer security issues are addressed in Chapter 4, "Feeling Safe and Secure.")

In *The Techniques of Really Smart Telemanagers*, consultant Michael Dziak points out that the technology tools selected for your remote workers would depend on the tasks typically performed for their position. While a collection agent might only need telephone, files, paper, writing utensils, reference materials and standard office supplies, a sales executive may need to add a second phone line, battery backup, Internet access, fax, speakers and sound card, video/audio mixer and palm device. A graphic artist or corporate executive may additionally need videoconferencing equipment and CAD/CAM graphics hardware.

Dziak states that a rule of thumb for selecting technology is that the remote worker has access for remote work to at least the same technology tools and performance available in the main office for the tasks selected. He points out that computer response time should be as good as or better than that of the office equipment and a modem

---

CHECKLIST FOR WORK-AT-HOME SUPPLIES AND EQUIPMENT
(Teleworker may or may not want or need all of these)

- Desk
- Chair
- PC
- Workstation
- Printer & cartridge
- Fax
- Scanner
- Copier
- Wrist rest, mouse rest
- 2nd phone line
- Headset
- Voice mail or answering machine
- Filing cabinet
- Bookcase
- Lamps
- Surge protector
- Extension cord
- Dry erase, white or cork board

- Pens, red pens, pencils
- Markers
- Copier paper
- Legal or other paper or notebooks
- Rolodex
- Calculator
- Stapler and staple puller
- Staples, paper clips, push pins
- Post-it notes
- In/out baskets
- File folders, hanging file folders
- Envelopes, regular & manila
- Ring binders
- Stereo system
- Easy chair

---

should be chosen that is faster than the teleworker thinks will be needed.[18]

An excellent resource for telework tools is Gil Gordon's Telecommuting, Telework and Alternative Officing, www.gilgordon.com. This superb site, with product details and links, compiles information on the latest telework technology products. While some of these, such as AffinityVideo Net's booking service, would be purchased for use at your firm's office location, many others such as Team Board's electronic whiteboard, Acuity's ichat software and Aegis Virtual Office are designed for use at the teleworker's remote work location or a combination of corporate and telework locations. You will want to view three different sections of the site—Collaboration software/tools, Virtual office support and Real estate/virtual office tools.[19]

By the end of step 6, you should have completed teleworker/supervisor agreements and begun telecommuting. This pilot program should be monitored and periodically evaluated, taking corrective action as necessary.

Step 7. Evaluation of Pilot Program and Recommendations

Once the pilot program is completed, the coordinator and advisory group should analyze the data collected to assess the human, economic, and organizational factors related to telecommuting. The results to be evaluated will include the costs and benefits of the pilot and the progress toward the defined telework goals.

Pilot program results can be assessed by written or online survey, focus groups, and individual interviews. The following general aspects need to be evaluated to determine the overall success of the pilot and the likelihood of your continuation of telework:

- Has recruitment been more successful as a result of offering telework?
- Has retention of valued employees improved?
- Has the need for office space been reduced?
- Has there been a reduction in sick leave and overtime?
- Has there been a change in attitude/morale with teleworkers as well as their peers since the inception of telework?
- Are telecommuters productive and available?
- Are coworkers overburdened by teleworkers' absence from the office?
- Has there been an increase in the ability to respond to ADA and affirmative action guidelines as a result of telework?
- Have you realized any tax credits or other financial rewards as a result of telework?
- Has your firm been able to comply with regulations such as the CAAA concerning congestion and infrastructure problems?
- Have your teleworkers benefited financially?
- Have your teleworkers' work/family problems been alleviated?

Prior to, during, and subsequent to your pilot program you will need to assess the program's success through evaluations by participants—teleworkers, non-teleworking employees, managers, support staff, and possibly even vendors and customers.

The state of Colorado recommends that the teleworking firm hold separate focus groups for teleworkers and telemanagers at three-month and six-month intervals. Of teleworkers, they recommend you inquire:

- How long they have been teleworking
- How frequently
- How teleworking has affected productivity
- How teleworking might have affected performance rating
- What each worker's supervisor's attitude is towards their teleworking and if that has changed since the beginning of the pilot
- How non-telecommuting coworkers have responded
- What they see as some of the benefits and disadvantages
- Suggestions for improvement of the telework program

- How their job duties have changed as a result of telework
- How morale is affected by it
- How technological needs are being met
- How the selection materials might be improved
- How the training materials might be improved
- If they would recommend telework for others at the firm
- How their families have responded
- If telework has impacted on their use of sick or vacation time
- If their work schedule has been affected
- If they are working more or less
- If they are bearing any personal costs as a result of telework, and if that is okay with them
- How many commute hours they save with telework and what they do with that time

Of telemanagers they recommend you inquire:

- How long has your staff been teleworking?
- How frequently do they telework?
- Has teleworking affected productivity?
- Could teleworking affect their performance rating? If so, how?
- What is your attitude towards teleworking, and is this a change?
- What did you think of the selection materials? Any suggested improvements?
- Would you recommend telework to other managers?
- How do your fellow managers not involved in the project respond to teleworking?
- Are you and your staff's technological needs being met?
- How is their morale affected by telework?
- How do their non-telecommuting coworkers respond to telework?
- What are some of the benefits and disadvantages?
- How can the program be improved?
- What did you think of the training? Any suggestions?
- Has telework impacted sick or vacation time?
- Has your staff changed their work schedule as a result of telework?
- Are they working more or fewer hours?
- Have your staff's job duties changed due to telework?
- Are there any costs you are bearing for your staff when they telework?

Let's not forget the input of coworkers, those who worked in-office during your telework pilot. Their feedback is invaluable, not only for the observations and insight on how the process worked, but also as a way to reaffirm to them the value you place on their contribution and their opinion.

Here is what you will want to ask of the non-teleworking coworkers:

- Have you had to schedule, plan or organize your work differently because coworkers telecommute? Was this a problem, or were there advantageous aspects to this change?
- Has communication with teleworkers been difficult? If so, why, and how did you resolve it?
- Have work interruptions and distractions increased, decreased, or remained the same as a result of telework?
- Has your workload increased since telework?
- Have you had to take on any new tasks or learn any new skills as a result? Any positive aspects to this change?
- Has the availability of office resources to you been altered— printer, supplies, fax, etc.?
- How do you feel about the productivity of the teleworkers?
- What about their availability?
- Has telework had a generally positive or negative impact on the department or office as a whole?
- Does management seem supportive of telework?
- Do you believe telework has been good for the organization? Why or why not?
- Do you wish to see telework continue?
- Given the opportunity, would you telecommute?

As with other written materials, sample evaluations are found in Appendix B.

The conclusions and recommendations together with the supporting data should be documented in a report that is presented by the advisory group to the telework coordinator. Once consensus is achieved, the results are presented to senior management.

NOTES

1. State of California Telecommuting Advisory Group, *Telecommuting Work Option,* June 1992. This group was composed of the following organizations and their representatives: Nancy Baldwin, chair, Department of Youth Authority; Nan Powers, CA Energy Commission; Frank Tanka and Frank Marr, Department of Personnel Administration; Sue Teranishi, Franchise Tax board; Judith Toledano, CA Public Utilities Commission; A.J. Watson and Noel Durham, Department of Justice; Del Delgado, State Controller's Office; Everett Haslett, Department of Social Services; Linda Clevenger, CA Unemployment Insurance Appeals Board; Lowell McPherson and Johnnie Zuick, State Teachers Retirement System; and Lauren Sevrin and David Fleming, Department of Social Services.

2. Harvey Levitt, "Creating an Effective Telework Plan: What Works, What Doesn't and Why" [database online 1999], http://www.decisionone.com/

d1m/se/V_ID_text.cfm?s_page=http://www.decisionone.com/d1m/news/ white_papers/white_paper_04.shtml&srch_text=creating%20an%20effective %20telework%20plan.

3. MATAC, "How to Set Up a Telecommuting Program," [database online, August 22, 2000], http://www.matac.org/rocket.htm. The Metro Atlanta Telecommuting Advisory Council (MATAC) is an organization of employers, businesses, and individuals with a common interest in the education, use, and promotion of telecommuting practices, incorporated as a not-for-profit chapter of the International Telework Association and Council.

4. Bob Fortier, "Telework America Online Curriculum" [database online 2000], http://www.telecommute.org.twa2000.

5. Transportation Management Association Group, "TeleManagers Hand-book," September 1997 [database online, June 19, 2001], http://www. tmagroup.org/telmgmt.html. TMA Group describes itself as "partnering with the public and private sectors to implement transportation and mobility options to ensure a better quality of life for Williamson County." Its member firms and organizations are Williamson County Economic Development Council, Williamson Square Development, Crescent Resources, Inc., Williamson County, Nations Bank, First Tennessee Bank, Hampton Inn & Suites, Trace Realty, United Cities Gas Company, RPM and Associates, Brentwood Chamber of Commerce, Bowlby & Associates, City of Franklin, TN, Cool Springs Marriott, CPS Corporation, Hilton Suites, Telco, Calvin Lehew & Company, and Magli Realty Company.

6. Ibid.

7. Oregon Office of Energy, "Sample Teleworker Self-Assessment" [database/pdf online], http://www.energy.state.oregon.us. See Appendix B for complete document to copy.

8. ALLearnatives, "Tips for Telecommuters" [database online, April 14, 2001], http://www.tipsfortelecommuters.com/telecommuting/18.html.

9. AT&T, "Telework Webguide" [database online, August 29, 2000], http://www.att.com/telework/index.html.

10. Colin Tierney, "Factors in Selecting Personnel" [database online, January 2001], http://www.soft.net.uk/tierney/selper.htm.

11. Gil Gordon, "The Manager's Role in Selecting Telecommuters: How to Deliver the News" [database online, April 4, 2001], http://www.gilgordon. com/downloads/managers.txt.

12. Ibid.

13. Michael Dziak, Inteleworks, Inc.,"The Techniques of Really Smart TeleManagers" page 32. Dziak's telework consulting firm, InteleWorks, Inc., offers this booklet as part of their much-lauded RemoteControl System Pro, an 8-week telework implementation packet. Included in the purchase is one hour of Dziak's telework consultation service. For more information visit the In-telework site: http://www.inteleworks.com/Smallbsns.html#Contents.

14. Florida Department of Management Services, "Review of the State Em-ployee Telecommuting Program," December 1997.

15. Techies.com [database online, 2001], http://home.techies.com/Common/ Content/2001/09/04/mc_highspeed.html.

16. Florida Department of Management Services, "Review of the State Em-ployee Telecommuting Program," December 1997.

17. Gene Puckett, State of Utah [database online, January 2000], http://www.its.state.ut.us/contents/resources/policiesprocedures/polprofiles/ pptwo02.prn.pdf.

18. Michael Dziak, "The Techniques of Really Smart Telemanagers," September 2000, pp. 27–28.
19. Gil Gordon Associates [database online, August 21, 2003], http://www.gilgordon.com/resources/products1.htm.

Clearing the Hurdles

No matter how prepared we are for telework—how much planning, time, effort, and expense we put into its preparation—telework will not succeed without the training and support of the most important aspect, the people involved. Creating and maintaining good personal relationships is a key, if not *the* key issue of successful telework implementation. Senior executives who refuse to buy in, managers who refuse to give up control, teleworkers who feel isolated or out of the loop, coworkers who resent the teleworkers' time out of the office—all these can destroy an otherwise successful telework venture.

Making everyone a part of the program, keeping everyone aware of the decisions and the reasons for them, and working at every phase of the program to bring the various parties together is vital to continued goodwill.

Let's take a look at four key issues:

1. The teleworkers' need to stay in touch
2. The non-teleworking coworkers' attitudes towards telework and teleworkers
3. Managerial resistance
4. Change in management style from management by sight to management by performance

TELEWORKERS' NEED TO STAY IN TOUCH

One telecommuter, writing in to the Ask ITAC feature of the International Telecommuting Association site, complains: "we are often referred to by our coworkers as 'you telecommuters.' Since we only have voice mail at work and no physical phone that can be answered at the office, it is guaranteed that you will get our voice mail if you call the office number. This is used as an excuse to avoid talking to us. Please help."

Telework expert June Langhoff offers several suggestions, beginning with a dialogue *arranged by management* to get the issues out in the open. She suggests that teleworkers try to get into the office more often and ask to be included in after-hours events and parties to catch up on office chitchat and reestablish important ties. "If your office doesn't have such events, start something on your own," she adds. Ms. Langhoff also mentions that one company has a monthly potluck dinner that brings teleworkers and in-office folks together; another offers company sports events.

Her final suggestion to teleworkers (one that telemanagers would do well to pass along to their subordinates): "If your coworkers don't call you, take the initiative and call them. They may initially feel uncomfortable calling you or be concerned that they're bothering you at home. Make sure you make it clear to everyone that you're just as available from home as you were when in the office."[1]

(Sign up for ITAC Telework News, a free monthly e-newsletter edited by Ms. Langhoff, at www.telecommute.org/newsletter/newsletter1.1.shtml.)

Smart Valley Inc. recommends a telecommuters' support group within which the teleworkers can share their experience. This would not be managed or participated in by your firms' representatives, but rather a group managed by the workers themselves, meeting perhaps at lunch or after work, informally.

To assist teleworkers in maintaining high visibility, the University of Central Florida's Department of Human Resources suggests the telemanager look for above-average performance when monitoring employee performance, encouraging the teleworker to set higher goals, and assigning more complex projects. They emphasize the telemanager should advise upper management of the teleworking employees' achievements. It is also important, they say, that the teleworkers take advantage of "opportunity assignments" and take part in presentations.

FYI . . .

One consultant suggested including the teleworking employees by teleconference in such office events as singing "Happy Birthday" to a coworker.

COWORKER ATTITUDES

One of the most common reasons for coworker resentment of teleworkers is that the coworker has been turned down for telework.

We cannot overemphasize that telework qualifications and requirements must be clearly defined; those employees not chosen for telework
must be individually and clearly apprised of the specifics of the managerial concerns that caused the rejection.

As discussed in Chapter 8, "The Implementation Process," an employee can be told that if "such and such" be improved so that "such
and such" goal is met she might be considered for telework in the
future.

Telework consultant Michael Dziak emphasizes the importance of
helping non-teleworkers play a role in the telework program. He states
that each teleworker should have an in-office buddy and affirms that
telemanagers must "identify any negativity from non-teleworkers, providing them with needed attention and team-based performance
awards."

In discussing the issue of peer jealousy, Tennessee's TMA Group
affirms that typically the source is misconceptions about who is bene-
fiting from telecommuting and how participants were selected. They
offer these five steps as solutions:

1. *Prevent the perception of work imbalance:* In situations where non-
   telecommuters must pick up the slack when telecommuters are
   out, perhaps a compromise work trade-off can be developed on
   those days when telecommuters are in the office.
2. *Integrate telecommuting into current procedures:* The new rules and
   their benefits must be perfectly clear to all those affected.
3. *Neutralize opposition:* Identify a non-believer who is highly visible
   and respected in the work group and attempt to neutralize her
   negativity, turning it into positive support.
4. *Form alliances with your peers:* Other telecommuting managers can
   become a powerful resource.
5. *Implement effective feedback systems:* At certain points in a
   telecommuting program, it is critical that you make an assessment
   of progress and attitudes toward telecommuting. A properly designed instrument can quantify overall program performance in
   meeting its objectives and provide a red flag for areas that need
   attention.[2] (See Chapter 8 evaluation instructions and find sample
   evaluations in Appendix B.)

The state of Florida, in its telecommuting guide, stresses that non-
telecommuters should not be expected to do extra work in the office
while the telecommuters are working from their homes.[3]

The processes you have already established, as part of your pilot
program, should have included contact guidance—how to contact the
teleworkers, and when.

Florida's guide reiterates those ideas and adds others:

- Provide guidelines for contacting the telecommuter when an issue arises in the office that requires immediate action. Don't expect the non-telecommuters to work on their own assignments and also handle problems for the telecommuters who are working at home.
- Establish guidelines for answering the telecommuters' phones while they are teleworking. Include staff such as the administrative assistants, secretaries, and receptionists in the process of deciding what they will say in answering the phone. ("Mary is unavailable," rather than "Mary is working at home today," for instance.)
- Establish guidelines for telecommuters to call the office at regular intervals. Determine whether it will be the telecommuter's responsibility to call for messages, or if it will be the responsibility of someone in the office, such as an administrative assistant, to call the telecommuter. Provide support staff with the home phone numbers of telecommuters. Forwarding the telecommuters' lines to voice mail is one method of handling calls, insuring calls are answered without creating extra work for the support staff. Calls might also be forwarded to the home office phone (if this is a second line, or the message is professional and does not convey a residential atmosphere).
- Consider keeping a log of the incoming calls answered by the support staff for the telecommuter. This will assist in determining how much extra work has been generated as a result of the telecommuting program. The log will also provide documentation showing when the call came into the office and when it was given to the telecommuter.

MANAGERIAL RESISTANCE

Most consultants, educators, and executives with whom we spoke indicated that managerial resistance is a strong and commonplace impediment to telework.

Peter Thomson, director of Henley Management College's Future Work Forum says that managing telework is critical to its success but is also "the biggest barrier to success." "Managers have to learn to trust people and allow them the freedom to manage themselves," he insists. "This is something that good managers are able to do but poor or inexperienced managers find a challenge."

Shenandoah University's Dr. Miles Davis believes that managers tend to manage the way they are raised. His definition of management is "getting work done through others." Of the four management facets of planning, organizing, leading, and controlling, he explains that controlling is the one that changes through telecommuting.

He says that because managers are evaluated by what their subordinates do, a manager may think: "I want to have my hands around that." He said telework-resistant managers have the assumption that a teleworking person is doing something different "than when I am there." He believes management books need to be updated to cover teleworker management.

Russell Miller and Keith Segerson of the George Mason University Mason Enterprise Center and Fairfax Telework Center talked with us about management resistance. While their experience has been with federal employees, their views are pertinent to private sector managers also. They conjectured that while real estate savings may seem a benefit of worthy note, some managers might fear being perceived by others as losing power—that their workers' absence would suggest a reduction in the number of workers over whom they "reign." They also wondered if some managers might not fear giving up workspace that could be usurped by other agencies or departments and not returned when expansion required.

How Do You Counter Resistance?

The beauty of the pilot program, as we indicated in Chapter 7, is that you are choosing a telework champion, along with managers already sold on telework and the most self-directed employees. The effect of these choices is not only that you have the group most likely to succeed, but also that the participating managers will inevitably communicate to their peers (some of whom may be adamant opponents of telework) their enthusiasm for the telework program and the positive effects of the pilot.

That's why communication is so crucial every step of the way. Once the pilot program has succeeded and managers have seen for themselves that telework does work—that employees actually can be counted on to be productive and trustworthy while out of the office environment—most will "come around" to support telework.

John Vivadelli, founder of hoteling reservation software firm Agilquest and board member of ITAC, talks to managers before they have made the decision to implement telework. How does he counter their resistance?

He says: "I ask the managers to take a walk down the hallway, around the workplace and see how many employees are at their workstation or in their offices. I assure them they will find no more than 50%." This activity, he clarifies, points out vividly that employees are already being managed remotely—that managers are not really "managing by seeing."

Helen Solomons emphasizes that, in her talks with managers about telework, she doesn't approach them with the benefit telework offers for society or the ecology. "I just show them the bottom line, the hard facts and figures." She adds that when she brings together a managerial focus group to discuss the implementation "shall we or shan't we" issue, she makes sure to include at least one manager who is adamantly opposed. "Because, " she says, "they will tell you everything. You will have every objection right up front."

Consultant and telework author Michael Dziak concurs. "What I love to do, " he says, "is my firing line effect." I have all the executives and managerial decision makers sit all in a row. I sit in a chair in front of them and have them fire questions at me."

Miles Davis is able to respond with firsthand telemanagement experience. Prior to joining Shenandoah University, Davis served in a management capacity at EDS (Electronic Data Systems Inc.), supervising consultants in 40 countries, some of whom he never met.

At EDS he discovered: "The more remote the employees were, the more I had to schedule the relationship." He conducted weekly individual e-mail meetings, and approximately once a month held group conference meetings so that they could hear each other's voices and interact with each other—what he called his "Charlie's Angels Thing." He found that, contrary to his having management problems, this became a self-policing community, that as the team members interacted with each other and developed relationships it became clear to each of them who did not complete work on time and well, and he would hear about it from the others.

MANAGING TELEWORKERS

In researching the opportunities for formal telemanagement training, we found little available in the traditional college and university setting. Numerous schools responded with "we have no course on that but do discuss it somewhat in our ... [business management or human resources management] class."

One example is Temple University's Fox School of Business and Management. Their graduate program includes course HRA 556, "Electronic Relationships and Virtual Organization." Describing how electronic technologies are changing the nature of organizations, some of the coursework emphasizes telework, virtual teams and the virtual organization.[4]

We found that in academic, as opposed to research institutions, telecommuting and telemanagement are starting to be recognized by instructors as something that should be addressed, and students are very interested. However, the prospect of actually putting course work together to actively assist in managing teleworkers is several years down the road. In the immediate future, executives and their subordinate telemanagers are going to need to rely on their own human resource department, telework consultants and/or publications such as this one, to set up their own formalized training for telework.

We spoke with Dr. Miles Davis, assistant professor of Management at Shenandoah University in Winchester VA, who teaches telemanagement, and whose background includes managing teleworkers. "The students are very interested in telemanagement," he says. " I believe in being hands-on with my teaching. I ask them what if this happened, what would you do?"

Davis says that the reason the academic community has not embraced the teaching of telework yet is the predominance of a faculty age group not familiar with the concept. He points out, however, that the tenured instructors are starting to retire and that will change the focus. He also explains that the academic institutions, rather than the research institutions, are leading the way because they tend to hire more from the business community than from the traditional academic background.

Dr. Bradley Alge, assistant professor at the Krannert School of Management at Purdue University, tells us about their telemanagement instruction:

I teach a course titled, "E-people: Human-technology interaction in a digital world," which is offered in our MBA program as part of our E-Commerce concentration. The course covers a variety of managerial challenges related to technologically mediated work: e.g., virtual teams, telecommuting, privacy, knowledge management/information sharing.

So, yes, I would say that the Krannert Graduate School of Management at Purdue University is recognizing the need to train students in how to deal with the many issues raised with respect to E-Business in general, and remote/telework specifically.

Professor Marilyn M. Helms, Sesquicentennial Endowed Chair and professor of management at Dalton State College in Dalton, Georgia, recommends that their school's MIS courses teach telemanagement. She says that there is a keen interest there in telework since the 2001 World Trade Center disaster.

We visited Hartwick College in Oneonta, New York, which offers an innovative program that not only teaches telework implementation and management but also offers sophomore students an opportunity to learn remotely and online through a simulation-based program called "Management and Organization." Each student and team are responsible for the management and growth of their bike shop business, must do Excel spreadsheets and Power Point presentations, seek technical or business assistance online, and either grow, sell, or merge their business. Hartwick's senior class, "Management for Human Resources," teaches management of remote sites and workers, videoconferencing, and telework implementation.

Dr. Helen Solomons, human resource and telework implementation consultant with Harrison Associates, is also adjunct professor at Villanova University in Philadelphia, where she teaches a graduate-level telemanagement course. Most participants are human resource managers, champions of telework who do not how to present it to their senior managers.

Henley Management College of Oxfordshire England offers the MBA online or by distance learning and partners with numerous UK firms to offer customized management training programs. Their Future Work Forum was established in 1992 as a focal point for people interested in changing working patterns and the implications that this has for managers in organizations. The forum, through seminars, workshops, research, and networking strives to help firms and individuals to understand the way that working patterns are being influenced by technology and how managers need to adapt to this new world.

Peter Thomson, director of the Future Work Forum, emphasizes that membership or participation at individual seminars is open to all and not just those studying at Henley for their MBA. He tells us how the forum started.

> I set up the Future Work Forum ten years ago when I left Digital, where I had been personnel director for the UK and Northern Europe. I approached Henley, one of the leading UK business schools, and suggested they might like to host meetings of people who have an interest in the way the work is changing and how this affects management. We decided to call it a forum and to sign up members from major employers who were interested in the future of work and its impact on their business.

Thomson explained further that they run a series of seminars that are not designed to provide any formal qualifications but are aimed at businesspeople who are facing practical problems in implementing telework or other new work practices.

"The fact that it happens at a business school," he emphasizes, "is because I felt it was an appropriate place to set up a center of expertise in this subject, not because there was a demand for courses from the normal customers of the college, who are typically gaining their MBA."

Thompson enthused about the Forum's success: "[The managers] love meeting other people [online or face-to-face] in other firms going through the whole thing." The meetings always have discussion groups, too. There are various levels of participation and membership available. While associate members do not come to physical events,

FWF does offer at least two virtual conferences each year. One recent event, hosted by Jack Nilles, focused on telework in response to the events of September 11, 2001. (For more information, see http://www.henleymc.ac.uk/henleymc01.nsf/pages/futureworkforum?opendocument.)

While telework may be changing the way managers measure performance from management by sight to management by results, all experts emphasized that this is a positive, though sometimes unsettling, step. Most also admit that this process is not really new, but rather the way it should have been accomplished all along.

As mentioned before, Michael Dziak affirms that one of the benefits of teleworking is its potential to amplify pre-existing management deficiencies in your organization. In his "Managing in a Telework Environment," part of his firm's Remote Control System Pro package, Dziak explains that the answer to the question, "How will I know if they're working at home?" should be answered with another question: "How do you know they're really working when in the office?" He goes on to inquire: "How are you measuring your current employee's performance today? Do you know specifically what each individual accomplishes in a given hour, day, week or month?" When considering telework, he emphasizes, the answers to these questions shouldn't be any different.

The state of California's Telecommuting Advisory Group concurs, advising,

> The most successful philosophy for managing telecommuters is that of management by end result. The elements that should be built into this style of management are project schedules and key milestones, regular status reporting, peer and/or project team quality reviews, team participation in decision making, trust, and telecommuter agreements. Part of the training for prospective managers of telecommuters should include a section on the practical implementation of these ideas.[5]

Michael Dziak says that successfully measuring performance of any worker boils down to a simple communications-based process:

- The manager and the worker agree on work output.
- The worker performs the work.
- The manager determines if the work performance meets expectations.

He offers four measurement techniques:

- Piecework
- Electronic measurement
- Agreed-upon deliverables
- General trust and regular remote tasks

Miles Davis agrees with Dziak's simplification. "To manage teleworkers," he explains, "You and your subordinates need to know whom you are each responsible for and what you are each responsible for."

FYI . . .

Bruce Holmes, telework project manager and director of public safety at Clayton University, suggests that project-based telework may be more beneficial than assigned telework days. He discovered that it is harder to manage a teleworker who is assigned a telework day rather than a telework task. Clayton, he said, found that workers did not always accurately gauge the volume of work that could be accomplished in a work-at-home day.

Holmes tells a humorous but clarifying story about their pilot program. "When the program started," he said, "the teleworkers were told they could not return to campus at all on their telework days, but they proved to be so productive at home that they ran out of work. They started sneaking on campus at lunchtime, having coworkers leave the office and meet them somewhere else on campus to give them more work materials. I ran into one teleworker one day, on campus in sweats. 'You weren't supposed to see me,' she responded, clearly agitated about having been found out."

Once a telework agreement is signed, you and your teleworker will know when and from where the employee will be teleworking and what tasks are to be accomplished. All that is left to do is to determine contact means and schedules and the means of delivering the goods. Teleworkers will need the name, e-mail address, phone numbers, and schedule of their supervisor, IT support contact, and designated office contact (their "buddy"). They'll need to determine their home office equipment and supply needs and provide you with a list of what they need the firm to provide, as much as you are allowing them a voice in the choices.

The self-assessment and your assessment will have determined any potential weaknesses in the teleworkers' "ideal telework candidate" profile. You may want to direct them to publications and sites of specific interest to teleworkers.6 Sites such as www.osha.org will provide teleworkers with the specifics of setting up an ergonomically sound work area.

You will definitely want to assign the teleworkers a designated IT department member who can answer any technical support or troubleshooting questions up front and schedule a time for a home visit for equipment installation.

FYI . . .

Willow CSN CEO Asim Saber says that his firm puts their Cyber Agent telework candidates through a rigorous PC skills test. Each candidate answers 50 questions that test motor skills, mouse skills, Windows skills, and general troubleshooting capabilities. The candidate is online- and keyboard-monitored to determine the number of mouse clicks or keystrokes, for instance, it takes for the candidate to perform a requested function. The test also looks at how quickly each candidate can move from one Windows screen to another. "The test is tough," says Asim. "But it has to be. In a telework environment you can't just nudge your buddy."

You'll need to determine a procedural schedule. In other words, will you talk by phone or e-mail every day or just twice a week? Will the teleworkers send you daily e-mailed progress reports, fax over the finished product, or what? If the employee teleworks part time, will review of the completed project be left for a face-to-face meeting on a day when she is scheduled to be in the office?

The state of Arizona suggests that prior to training the telemanager and teleworker need to determine what percentage of the employee's job is devoted to face-to-face contact with other employees or the public. They emphasize the need to know if the contacts can be readjusted for telephone communication or if these tasks need to be performed when the employee is in the conventional office. Other questions include: What percentage of the job requires resources located in the main office? Can those resources be easily removed and taken home for a day? In regard to fieldwork, can trips begin at the home office rather than the main office?[7]

With a mutually agreed-upon list of finite tasks, you will be able to assess very quickly if the employee is having trouble accomplishing assigned work in a telework environment. If your firm's telework policy states that a telework situation may be terminated by either party with due notice (usually 30 days), as it should, your maximum risk will be one month of sub-par accomplishments.

(If you wish some formal assistance with your activities management, software packages are available that allow you and teleworkers to input, view, and keep up to date on their work progress. In the software portion of this chapter, look at three task-management vendors. As with other products mentioned throughout the book, we mention these not to recommend products but to advise you of what is available and encourage you to see them for yourself.)

For a general telemanagement how-to starting point, we turn to AT&T, which in December of 2000 received Keep America Beautiful, Inc.'s Distinguished Service Citation National Award for its employee telework program. This award recognized the telecommunications pioneer for its efforts to minimize wasted emissions, gasoline, and time through its reduction of vehicle miles traveled.

AT&T's telework program has grown from its 1992 inception to a year 2000-high avoidance of 110 million commute miles, savings of 50,000 tons of carbon dioxide, 5.1 million gallons of gasoline, 220,000 tons of hydrocarbons, 1.7 million tons of carbon dioxide, and 110,000 tons of nitrous oxide.

Recent innovations include an intranet telework portal giving readiness assessments and links to AT&T resources; statistical telephone surveys regarding participation, benefits, and environmental impacts; a widely publicized "Earth Day is E-Day" event; and one of the best online resources for the implementation of a telework pilot program. From this lauded telework-expert firm's *Telework Webguide* we garnered the "Telemanager Do's and Don'ts" (see box).

UK Online's *Working Anywhere*[8] and the state of Florida's online *Guide for Managers and Employees Considering Telecommuting*[9] emphasize that managers should:

- Set agreed and achievable targets for staff. Prepare an itemized list (weekly, monthly or even quarterly) of what is expected from the teleworking employee. Establish objectives in a format that is easy to administer, including the teleworkers in this process. Create a document to support your agreement, signed by both supervisor and employee.
- Develop a greater degree of trust, empowering your staff and allowing them to be confident that, if they make mistakes, they will not be penalized.
- Give your remote staff feedback for performance. Establish a matrix or graph and clearly define what the telecommuter needs to accomplish for satisfactory and excellent performance evaluations. Be very explicit about what is expected. Then, track the results. In measuring the performance of the telecommuter, consider the quality of work in reaching organizational goals rather than just counting beans. If you set up weekly goals, schedule weekly meetings. Use this as a dynamic document, capable of changing when necessary. Employees feel they have more control over their destiny when they can track their success.
- Provide telecommuters the same information and news about the company as their office-based colleagues.

TELEMANAGER DOs AND DON'Ts

- *Do* trust your teleworkers.
- *Do* require teleworkers to participate in surveys and evaluations—and participate yourself.
- *Do* use a telework arrangement as an opportunity to strengthen your own management skills.
- *Do* manage by measuring results.
- *Do* telework yourself when you have the opportunity. It will help increase your personal effectiveness and improve your understanding of the ups and downs of teleworking.
- *Do* look at things from your teleworker's point of view. Understand the timeframes involved in completing tasks and the resources required to complete them.
- *Do* include your teleworker in goal setting.
- *Do* delegate assignments fairly among teleworkers and non-teleworkers.
- *Do* include the teleworkers in day-to-day activities; keep on the lookout for clues that a teleworker is feeling isolated, left out or has "cabin fever."
- *Do* encourage informal communication within your team to keep teleworkers and coworkers in touch and up-to-date. Consider establishing a "virtual water cooler" via a shared e-mail folder or organizational intranet.
- *Do* expect that things will not go smoothly all the time.
- *Do* communicate on a regular basis. Let the teleworkers know you're there for them.
- *Do* be willing to increase the frequency of teleworking if it is working well for the employee.
- *Do* be prepared to let the employee terminate the program—or terminate it yourself—if it is clearly not working out.
- *Do* keep an open mind about teleworking. If one arrangement doesn't work, it doesn't mean the next one won't.
- *Do* **communicate**!
- *Don't* conduct curfew checks.
- *Don't* call your teleworker every hour to check on progress.
- *Don't* ignore your teleworker.
- *Don't* ask for constant status reports.
- *Don't* expect unrealistic deadlines for projects.
- *Don't* neglect problems.
- *Don't* set unattainable goals.
- *Don't* manage by close supervision.
- *Don't* expect perfection—there will be adjustments.
- *Don't* allow one unsuccessful attempt to give telework a bad name.
- *Don't* expect everyone to be a successful teleworker.

- Arrange for day-to-day contact, fixing regular time for phone, fax, or e-mail contact, or explore videoconferencing.
- For those teleworking full time, arrange for regular weekly or monthly office visits where possible.
- Agree on the times when teleworkers can or cannot be contacted at home.
- Arrange home visits at times acceptable with the home worker.
- Arrange regular team meetings and facilitate communication among teleworking staff.

The University of Central Florida's Human Resource Department emphasizes the need to coach and develop telecommuting employees' capabilities by always reinforcing positive behavior and by bringing unsatisfactory performance to the employee's attention immediately.

The university also recommends the following:

- Make contingency plans. Set up a "Murphy's Law" strategy (i.e., anything that can go wrong will go wrong) to guide the work group through events that may affect the group as a result of telecommuting. Encourage the telecommuters and non-telecommuters to participate in this process.
- What happens if it's NOT working? Not everyone who tries telecommuting is successful. While the screening survey process tries to qualify successful telecommuters, it's not a guarantee that all selected telecommuters will be happy or successful. Each supervisor should remain aware that there are many good reasons that employees have to end their participation in telework. Help employees understand their value to the organization. Bring the employee back into the office as quickly as possible. Use this as a developmental opportunity to coach the employee in an area of weakness and create an area of strength from that weakness.

UK change-management consultant Colin Tierney emphasizes the innovative aspect of teleworking, pointing out that the teleworker will solve problems, push new boundaries, and make discoveries. For these reasons, Tierney says, the supervisor should schedule regular debriefing sessions during which they can analyze developmental experiences and learning points.

The Telecommuting Advisory Group for California's state employees emphasizes that each agreement should be discussed and renewed annually, whenever there is a major job change such as a promotion or whenever the supervisor or teleworkers change positions. They point out that because telecommuting was selected as a feasible work option based on the combination of job characteristics, employee characteristics, and supervisor characteristics, a change in any one of these requires a review of the telecommuting agreement. They also stress that because this is a management work option, there should be no automatic right of the telecommuter to continue to telework in the event of a change of supervisor.[10]

It should be noted, however, that Dr. Helen Solomons expresses concern with some employers' practice of terminating an employee's telework because that employee has changed supervisors. "Companies are flirting with a legal problem," she believes, "when they have a situation where the employee has been teleworking for two or three years and, because they now have a new boss, cannot work from home any longer. If this worker is a minority, for instance, discrimination accusations could result." She stressed that this type of option can leave the firm wide open to litigation.

It would seem, then, that with a management change resulting in a request to discontinue a subordinate's telework, it might be advisable to seek the advice of your firm's legal staff.

Looking over Their Shoulders

Information about managing teleworkers, or any workers for that matter, would not be complete without at least a mention of monitoring. A more invasive variety of task-management software, monitoring software allows managers of employees, remote or in house, to view in real time what their employees are doing—what Web sites they visit, what keystrokes they make, whom they e-mail, and from whom they receive e-mails and the contents of their phone calls. Much controversy rages around this issue, and while it certainly serves its purposes for security reasons, it is our opinion and the opinion of virtually every telework consultant with whom we conferred that monitoring is not necessary, productive, or welcome *as a response to the introduction of telework.*

As mentioned before, you will primarily be offering telework to those employees who have proven themselves highly self motivated and knowledgeable in the office, monitored or not. Monitoring, except minimally (content filters, for example) and for security reasons, can be demotivating and negatively affect a teleworker's productivity.

Consultant Colin Tierney talks about this. His response to the question "How do you manage a teleworker?" is "How do you manage a manager?" He sees the two situations as analogous, in that both have responsibility to deliver results given a designated resource and are both assumed to be properly resourced, trained, and supported to achieve that result. He reiterates his belief that telework can only work in a spirit of empowerment. He vehemently discourages the Big Brother aspects of the monitoring process.

Tierney emphasizes that while everything the teleworker does can be monitored, recorded, and measured, you need to remember that under-pinning the move to telework is a philosophy of empowerment, of delegating responsibility. He cautions that monitoring should capture essential data without overloading the system and the manager and should be geared more toward output than input. What if the data shows, for instance, that individual workers are operating in less than optimum ways, such as starting late, then rushing to finish? "So what?" responds Tierney. "That is their choice. Take that option away from them and they will soon think that they might as well go back to the old way."[11]

FYI . . .

Of the 40 million online workers in the United States, 19 percent, or nearly 8 million, are monitored when they are on the Internet, and 15 percent have their e-mail monitored by their employer. Of the world's 100 million online workers, 15 percent are Internet-moni-tored, and 12 percent e-mail monitored.

To be sure, those of you whose teleworkers are using telecommuni-cations at home—intranet or Internet, phone or e-mail—in the course of their work for you (which will be most teleworkers), there is abun-dant opportunity to watch every Web site, every keystroke, read each e-mail, and observe each phone call. Right now businesses are generally allowed to listen in on their employee's phone calls and rifle through their e-mail without the employee's knowledge, according to Gregory T. Nojeim, an ACLU legislative counsel.[12]

There are strong concerns, though, and pending U.S. legislation that would drastically curb this practice. Organizations and unions such as the ACLU, AFL-CIO, Communication Workers of America (CWA), American Federation of Government Employees, American Federation of State, County and Municipal Employees, 9–5, National Association of Working Women, Service Employees International Union, National Consumers League, Coalition on New Office Technology and the United Auto Workers, have all come out as strong supporters of pend-ing legislation, the Notice of Electronic Monitoring Act, which would impose financial penalties on employers who monitor employees with-out prior "specified" notification. (For further information on the leg-islated side of this issue see Chapter 3, "Keeping It on the Up and Up.")

Michael Dziak mentioned a very simple monitoring tool, and one that is free—instant messaging. He advised that it could be an excellent tool because a manager can see which teleworkers are online and how quickly they respond when instant messaged. Free instant messaging can be found at Yahoo.com or MSN.com.

Software for Activities Management and Monitoring

The Canadian activities-management product freetaskmanager.com allows you to create tasks for your remote workers, assign them, define status and priorities, view number of hours to completion and percentage of project completed at any point in time, and notify employees by e-mail of assigned tasks. You retain administrator rights and then assign access rights to your remote users as you see fit. If you wish to try the product, the company offers a free package of two projects, five users, and 50 tasks.

Yellowzone Inc.'s YZ Project Manager allows remote users, managers, and executives to access and share critical data on a real-time basis. The software provides online workflow capabilities for managing projects. It also monitors project completion time and time to market. Users will have access to all the critical project information via secured login and password. Managers will be able to monitor productivity for users, groups, and departments. They could also measure real-time individual and team performance. The tool allows constant monitoring of project cost.

The online messaging system will allow users to easily and frequently communicate among each other and monitor user communication. Detailed reporting provides managers with full statistics on project status, cost, and performance. For an online demonstration and presentation, see www.yzmanager.com.

PC2000, a product of David Driskill Associates, is a state-of-the-art management tool for setting employee expectations, performance planning, and performance management. The program, built with the guidance of both managers and subordinates, allows input of both manager and employee and can be viewed online.

The software includes a predetermined bank of general and job-specific standards, scales the weight of each standard, and provides a format for documentation of individual accomplishments and a structured opportunity for self-examination and rating.

Such a combination of task management and performance review features can assist with mutual understanding of expectations and priorities, allow the employee an active voice in the process, and support and quantify forward planning for the next review period.

Spy Software Solutions (www.spy-software-solutions.com) offers monitoring software—VCR-like screenshot recorder, instant message/chat logging, e-mail monitoring, and keystroke recording. I-Spy Now allows the telemanager to remotely monitor computers without having to physically access or install software. iSpyNOW offers the ability to remotely install the spy software from any location and via the logs from anywhere in the world! Simply send iSpyNOW spy software via e-mail and it will install instantly. Then you can remotely view applications and terminate with a single click, reboot, shutdown and logoff remotely, and so on. You can purchase and download directly from their site.

Clear Swift Corporation's MIME Sweeper products includes e-mail and Internet monitoring, both inbound and outbound, and Web page blocking and preview. These, unlike the iSpy type of products, are designed much more for security against hackers, viruses, and the like. (Security is discussed in depth in Chapter 4, "Feeling Safe and Secure.")

THE VOICES OF EXPERIENCE

During our talks with managers and executives who offer telework we asked each the question, What Tips Can You Offer Managers in Their Quest to Successfully Supervise Teleworkers?" Their answers follow.

Sherry Doggett of Health Alliance of Cincinnati affirms, "You have to be very flexible. We all have very different lifestyles. In-house or not, there are certain employees to whom you just give the tools and step away." She always stresses the importance of being consistent "so there are no issues in perception of fairness." She shares that what has worked for them is a buddy mentoring program that puts experienced teleworkers in touch with the new "tele's." She emphasizes that this is most important for second- and third-shift workers.

The state of California's Telecommuting Advisory Group suggests that you implement periodic telework forums, bringing teleworkers together as a group, perhaps with supervisors in attendance, to look at the issues affecting their success and do some brainstorming about problems and their resolution.

Yvette Lucio of i2 stresses that the support of executive management "right from the start" is crucial to telework success.

Caroline Cheales of Surrey County Council advises:

> Teams need regular structured communication and to still identify them-
> selves as a team, not a collection of individuals working alone. The social
> aspects of work are too important to be ignored. Team briefings need to
> have significant social elements and those who are left behind in the office
> need to understand the needs of those they are supporting—that fine
> weather does not mean not working! This is a team issue—not just a 1:1
> issue between worker and manager. If home workers are too remote will
> they feel part of an organization at all? In our experience the work is never
> done.

Our approach to Flexible Working (of which home working is just one option) has also to be flexible. The technology changes, expectations of existing staff and potential recruits are changing as the way we deliver services to our customers changes. Teleworking is just one way to manage these challenges—just one option in a menu of ways of working.

Glenn Lovelace at TManage emphasizes that when it comes to telework his is "not a company but a cause." Stressing that forcing someone to become a teleworker just doesn't work, he offers statistics from a Gardner Group research study that determined that 40 percent of telecommuter programs fail. The primary reasons were the complexity of the programs, lack of technical support, choosing the wrong people, security problems, and lack of financial and management support.

Glenn Fernihough of Faulkner Group lists his tips:

1. Establish a clear policy and rules on who owns the hardware/software and what happens in the event of employment termination.
2. Establish standards of performance that can be measured and then create a regular appraisal against those standards. While this represents good practice anyway regardless of location, the fact is that when people are meeting in the office on an ongoing basis there can be too much informality and familiarity—while eWorking forces management to be more structured and objective in this respect.
3. Make sure that all equipment and software are compatible.
4. Look very carefully at security issues if access to confidential information is involved, like customer lists and buying patterns, costs and revenue statements.
5. Provide regular meetings to avoid people becoming disjointed from the overall team effort that is needed in most successful businesses.
6. Carefully select personnel to ensure that they are the right types for eWorking.

From Bruce Holmes at Clayton University come several tips. He explains that they have had to combat resentment by non-teleworking employees. One in-house worker, for instance, made the comment to a teleworker, "You are on paid vacation." They have successful allayed these attitudes by presenting information programs: "This is what we are doing; this is how we are doing it."

Holmes emphasizes: "Training is critical. You need to clear the air." The University is working toward implementing four-hour teleworking and telemanaging courses, taught by Michael Dziak of InteleWorks.

Holmes tells of an incident where one woman, new to teleworking, bought $300 worth of supplies for her home office and then brought in the receipt and expected the department to reimburse her. This taught them the value of written clarification early on. He adds that consistency is important and managers are the key. He affirms that they did not let a lack of technology slow down their telework. "On the list of 10 most important items for telework, equipment is about number nine," he says.

Art & Logic's founder Paul Hershenson gives this advice:

1. Trust is of number one importance. It is the highest form of motivation, and will be repaid by loyalty.
2. Accountability—It is obvious when somebody is not getting the work done. If the job does not have results that can be measured, the job is not a good candidate for teleworking.
3. A sense of community is vital, as opposed to one-on-one manager and subordinate. Virtual office needs community—email and telephone are not enough because they are just between two people.
4. Pay for the home equipment. If you go to work for IBM in their office they put a computer on your desk. So, if you go to work for us, we put a computer on your home desk.

Several practices that worked for Sopheon Resource Network were monthly teleconferences to alleviate telework isolation issues, IS training for teleworkers prior to their starting telework, a telecommuting task force that makes the decision to allow the employee to telework, an in-house counterpart for each teleworker who can keep her or him in the loop while out of the office, a home site evaluation, and an emergency office evacuation procedure. Sopheon has also made a commitment to bring teleworkers into the corporate office once or twice a year—paid for by the firm—for team meetings and training.

Gene Puckett, Deputy Director for the state of Utah's ITS Division offers the chronological specifics of their telework implementation procedure, including the staff or department responsible for each aspect:

1. The employee and manager first read and understand the Department's Telecommuting Work Option Policy, telecommuting waiver and release form [see Appendix B], and appropriate guidelines and policies, such as the Governor's Telecommuting Directive, State of Utah's Official Telecommuting Policy, and the Telecommuting Guidebook FAQ, etc.
2. The employee and manager meet to discuss the feasibility of telecommuting.

3. The employee and manager negotiate necessary changes, if any, to performance plan, performance measurement methods, etc.
4. The employee and manager discuss what level of telecommuting will be feasible and appropriate.
5. The employee and manager decide what equipment, facilities, etc. the employee will need to effectively work outside the office.
6. The employee and manager then fill out the Telecommuting Waiver and Release form, the each separately complete their own Telecommuting Feasibility Assessment [see Appendix B].
7. The manager then routes the entire document package through the Section Manager to the Director or Assistant Director for review and approval.
8. Once reviewed and approved the Director or Assistant Director forwards copies of appropriate forms to LAN Group for processing, to the Telephone Orders Group for order entry and coordination with the WAN Group, and gives the original to Telecommuting Waiver and Release form to designated Human Resource personnel.
9. The LAN Group then meets with the employee to make specific arrangements for ordering and customizing hardware and software.
10. The Telephone Order Group verifies requirements and orders and arranges for installation of ISDN line, analog line and other equipment as appropriate.
11. The WAN Group now verifies requirements and makes specific arrangements for router and switch configuration, if appropriate.
12. Once the equipment and lines are prepared, the employee attends a LAN Group–sponsored training session. Once trained and comfortable with installation and operation of all hardware and software the employee can begin telecommuting.

Barbara Lietz, operations manager for Allina Metro Hospital's medical transcription services, offers three important pieces of advice:

1. *Documentation:* Begin your telecommuting pilot with a comprehensive policy agreement that outlines specific selection criteria, safety measures, work schedule, confidentiality and *employer* productivity.
2. *Communication:* Agree upon and maintain a communication plan. Choose specific times to talk on the phone, e-mail and visit the office and adhere to that plan. An effective communication plan can make telework less stressful and more beneficial to the employer and the employee than working in the office.

3. *Continuation:* Continued technology improvements, review of telecommuting standards, procedures and responsibilities, and improved resources allow telecommuters to be as well equipped and self-sufficient as employees who work in the office.

The key to Nortel Network's telework success, according to Wendy Herman, is "high quality equipment and connections. Working at home is not a technological frustration for our employees."

Janice Miholics, vice president of Global Work/Life Strategies for Merrill Lynch, offers several tips. The two issues she stressed as important were *treatment* and *communication.* She emphasized that teleworkers should not be treated any differently because they telework, including compensation. She also advised that communication is crucial—even to family and neighbors, who need to be aware that just because you are home does not mean you are available.

As speaker at the ITAC/Placeware Telework Web conference on "HR and Legal Issues in Telework Implementation,"[13] Lynch pointed out her HR *musts* for telework success:

• First, you must understand why telework is being considered.

Then, Human Resources must take the lead in:

• Program objectives
• Selection criteria
• Performance management
• Compensation
• Due diligence

She advised the use of resources such as organizational development specialists, who can manage surveys; compensation analysts; real estate, insurance and risk, legal and health and safety experts; a technology team; and specialists in the area of benchmarking and research.

Lynch believes success is determined by the firm's values and culture, its management commitment and ideas, patience, collaboration, flexibility, and a continuous feedback loop such as a Web site.

Sherry Cronin of Prudential emphasizes the need for technical support and ergonomics. She is emphatic also that teleworking cannot be a substitute for child care.

Teleworkers need to "take breaks, but not visiting the refrigerator every time," she adds. Her view is that "to be really successful you have to realize it's different things for different people. Just ask people what they want."

Teresa Antunes of InterWorks, Portugal, as both a consultant herself and an employer of teleworkers, offers these thoughts:

I have the strongest belief that the telework in Portugal and in Europe is in full expansion. However, there is a certain fear from the managers in implementing projects of telework in their companies and, as a consequence, in employing collaborators that may render their services in the companies in a telework regime—as a part time or a full time job, according to each case.

The companies have to change their strategy in the management of human resources, adjusting the new technology, so that they can become more competitive and keep up with the evolution. It is vital to develop new ways of working and new concepts of working, thus anticipating the future and foreseeing the total mobility of the people. The new working relations and organization, the relationship and the interaction between the people, the citizens, the collaborators and future workers of the companies and enterprises, the use of the work outside the traditional relations, that so far have been implemented and marked their relevance in the enterprises and organizations is coming to an end. Thus, the institutions and the enterprises have to dimension and at the same time to institutionalize permanent incentives and training plans of different types to achieve a qualified body of human resources. To bet heavily on training? Yes! On-line training! Yes.

Through one of our clients we have had the opportunity of initiating in Portugal, about a year ago, innovative courses. We have chosen a line of training that meets people's lack of time, a training directed exclusively to the enterprises, with restricted access. Through a confidential password that was given to each of the trainees the training can take place at any time, in any place. It consists of on-line training sent to all the trainees during the week. Questions can be asked or sent, as well as answers concerning the exercises at any time, at any place!

Willow CSN's Asim Saber believes in interaction and communication to keep teleworkers connected. That is why he has structured Willow's CyberAgent CSR training in-person. The initial orientation is at their Fort Lauderdale Florida Office. "Look at the person to the left and right of you," he states. "They may be your new cyber buddies. "

He continually encourages this interaction, not only with e-mail but also with Christmas parties, focus groups, and other activities. He has formed the Willow National CyberUnion Association, a national non-profit group, to keep everyone in touch. He proudly mentions that two CyberAgents recently married and that there are numerous husband/wife and mother/daughter teams working for Willow. Saber stresses that the key to teleworker motivation is that the worker have "skin in the game (i.e., something of her or his own invested in the work venture—money, home office furnishings, preparation time, or the like)."

Washington Mutual has a very structured, highly successful, telework preparation to share. Prior to moving work to an employee's home, appraisers prepare a business and communication plan, which also details the benefits of the arrangement, both to the bank and to the employee. Management currently addresses any issues related to telework within individual teleworkers' agreements and when assessing performance. Managers track turnaround times, production levels, timeliness, and the quality of work for teleworkers the same way as for in-office staff. If problems emerge, appraisers may be asked to work from the office for a time under closer supervision.[14]

Timothy Kane emphasizes that real estate savings, a strong benefit of telework, will not be realized unless the work-at-home offer is accompanied by hoteling. He believes hoteling can work for any size firm. His company, Kinetic Workplace, with only 15 employees, realized a 50 percent reduction in leasing costs due to the ability to share desk space. He also emphasizes that scheduling is the key to large-scale hoteling. While this small firm needs no concierge or scheduler—"Everyone just comes in and finds a vacant seat"—he affirms that some companies and some employees need an arrangement whereby the employees contact a Web site or a person to schedule the needed space.

T. J. Johnson, technical assistance team leader for the Washington State Department of Transportation, speaks not only as a supervisor of telecommuters but as one of the managers in charge of the state's program to encourage statewide telework. In discussing the state's program to get people off the highways, or at least out of their SOVs (single-occupant vehicles), he told us that employers ask for assistance in the form of public education. He said, "Do it for your planet" didn't work. What did work was an emphasis on relief of stress. They designed a relaxation theme, with a motto of "there's more than one way to get there." After six months, public awareness of the issue and the campaign had increased by 75 percent. Washington has now realized a 400 percent increase in the telework, with a threefold increase in the number of work sites involved.

The U.S. Office of Personnel Management offers three keys to success:

1. *Managers with a willingness to experiment.* Most of the managers interviewed for their May 2001 telework report mentioned that they had approached the experience with reservation. Their concerns focused on the employees' availability for face-to-face interaction, potential resentment by the rest of the staff, and anticipated communication problems. They had been willing to take a chance to see whether their reservations would materialize; to a person, they reported that their concerns were shown to be unfounded.
2. *Motivated, self-starting employees.* Virtually all of the employees reported that they had initiated the first discussion with their supervisor about the possibility of teleworking. They had thought

about it, worked out the details of their specific situations, and then approached their supervisor with a specific proposal.

3. *Clearly defined expectations at the outset.* All parties agreed on reporting requirements, expected outcomes, and frequency and nature of communication. Having expectations in place and understood from the beginning was critical to the success of the telework experience.[15]

Florida's Department of Management Services emphasizes that the time a manager spends communicating with the telecommuters will dictate the caliber of work produced. Their recommendation has three parts:

1. *Timetables:* Work with employees to develop attainable and time goals, listing tasks for completion and deadlines.
2. *Review Work Status:* Set up intermediate periods to determine the progress of the teleworkers' tasks. This assessment may be at designated points during the program, upon completion of certain tasks, or on recurring timetables such as every Monday.
3. *Coach and Develop Teleworkers' Capabilities:* Always reinforce positive behavior, but bring unsatisfactory performance to the employee's attention immediately. Use all available communication—voice mail, e-mail, phone, or face-to-face.[16]

Washington State Department of Transportation's Rail and Public Transportation Division allows staff to document schedule variations with e-mail notices to a general folder. Each employee also writes a brief weekly report that lists items accomplished the previous week and planned for the next week. The reports are e-mailed to each member of the group to enhance spontaneous communications that might otherwise be lost, as some teams are fully staffed in the office less than two days per week.[17]

Neil McClocklin of BT states his advice simply: "Invest in the support, and the education and training."

ONE FINAL THOUGHT

In closing, we ask you to ponder the InteleWorks, Inc., definition of telework. Succinct and original, it incorporates the values they and numerous other managers, executives, and consultants define as crucial to telemanagement success: "Telework is *entrusting employees* to carry out the organizational mission with the proper tools in the location most conducive to higher productivity." *Telework–it's all about trust.*

NOTES

1. June Langhoff, as contributor to Ask ITAC [database online, 1998], http://www.telecommute.org/interactive/. Ms. Langhoff, author of *The Telecommuter's Advisor: Real World Solutions for Remote Workers* (Aegis Books, 1999), describes her Telecommuting Resource Center, www.langhoff.com, as "a guide for telecommuters, telecommuter wannabees, managers of remote workers, and all sorts of people who work at a distance."

2. Transportation Management Association Group, "Telemanagers Handbook" [database online, September 1997], http://www.tmagroup.org/TelMGMNT.html.

3. Florida Department of Management Services, "A Guide for Managers and Employees Considering Telecommuting" [database online], http://fcn.state.fl.us/dms/hrm/telecom/telegde.html.

4. Fox School of Busienss and Management, Temple University [database online], http://www.sbm.temple.edu/courses/g-hra.html.

5. State of California Telecommuting Advisory Group.

6. Books such as Michael Dziak's *Telecommuting Success* (Jist Works, 2002), Debra Dinnocenzo's *101 Tips for Teleworkers* (Bernett-Kolhler Publishers, 1999), and Jeff Zbar's *Safe at Home* (copyright 1998-2002 Jeffrey D. Zbar, Inc.) all offer insight into some of the problems inherent in working from home—isolation, distraction, safety, and so on.

7. State of Arizona Telecommuting Zone [database online, June 8, 2001], http://www.teleworkarizona.com/telework_files/selectin.htm.

8. UK Online's "Working Anywhere: Exploring Telework for Individuals and Organizations" is a 1998 collaboration of their Department for Education and Employment (DFEE), Department of Trade and Industry (DTI), and Department of Environment Transport Regions (DETR). This booklet offers statistics, expertise, and case studies on telework, at http://www.ukonlineforbusiness.gov.uk/Advice/publications/teleworking/home.html.

9. Florida Department of Management Services, "Telecommuting: A Guide for Managers and Employees Considering Telecommuting," http://fcn.state.fl.us/dms/hrm/telecom/telegde.html.

10. State of California Telecommuting Advisory Group, *Telecommuting Work Option*, June 1992.

11. Colin Tierney, "Factors in Monitoring and Evaluation" [database online], http://www.soft.net.uk/tierney/moneva.htm.

12. "ACLU Applauds Bipartisan Legislation to Protect Employees' Privacy," July 20, 2000, http://www.aclu.org/workplacerights/workplacerights.cfm?ID=804&C=179.

13. http://www.placeware.com. See their seminars and live events archives for the two ITAC Web conferences on telework implementation.

14. Washington State University Cooperative Extension, and Commuter Challenge, *Telework Resource Kit*.

15. Ibid.

16. Florida Department of Management Services, "Telecommuting: A Guide for Managers and Employees Considering Telecommuting," http://fcn.state.fl.us/dms/hrm/telecom/telegde.html.

17. WSU Cooperative Extension, and Commuter Challenge, *Telework Resource Kit*.

Appendix A
Labor Union Opinions and Sample Agreements

(All CWA-related labor union contract materials in this appendix have been graciously provided by Debbie Goldman of Communications Workers of America.)

CWA TELECOMMUNICATIONS CONFERENCE ON COLLECTIVE BARGAINING, DECEMBER 8–9, 1994

Author/editors - CWA Research Department

Telecommuting continues to be a much discussed but little practiced phenomenon among unionized workers in the telephone industry. Currently, the companies mention telecommuting most frequently in connection with their responsibilities under the Clean Air Act amendments of 1990. This paper will review our basic concerns, discuss the impact on call-out language currently in the contracts, and review the Clean Air Act with regard to telecommuting.

Telecommuting

Telecommuting means working from a location remote from your traditional reporting location. Most typically, this means working from your home or from a satellite office. The continuing advances in technology and the ability of the phone system to transmit data means that large portions of computer based jobs can be performed away from the traditional job site. A telephone, a fax, and a computer with a modem give many workers access to all the same data and information that they would be working with in a traditional office.

Currently, portable computers allow technicians or their supervisors to "shoot troubles" and make repairs from remote locations. Telecommuting could be used as a replacement for call-outs, or the entire job could be performed from home or from a non-traditional work location. In any case, we must be careful to secure proper protection for the members as we address telecommuting.

Clean Air Act

The Clean Air Act (CAA) amendments of 1990 are designed to improve air quality when regions have reached a "severe" or "extreme" designation by the Environmental Protection Agency (EPA). A region can be a city or a multi-city area. When the severe or extreme designation is reached, the Act directs employers with 100 or more workers to reduce their "average passenger occupancy" by 25 percent. This can be achieved by car pooling, workers using mass transit, bicycling, walking, compressed work weeks, flex-time, a return to neighborhood offices, or telecommuting.

The regions that currently are designated as severe or extreme are Baltimore, Chicago, Houston, the Los Angeles Basin, Milwaukee, the New York/New Jersey/Connecticut region, the Philadelphia/Wilmington region, and San Diego. The federal rules are implemented at the state level, and failure to comply could result in loss of federal highway funds to the state and fines to the employers if they don't make "good faith" efforts to comply.

While the companies have appropriate concerns about compliance with the Clean Air Act, it is important to note that telecommuting is not mandated by the Act or the states charged with enforcing it. Car-pooling, mass transit, compressed work schedules or flextime all offer a more traditional way to address the air quality issue. *Telecommuting should be evaluated as to the benefits it provides to the members, not as a tool for compliance with the Clean Air Act.*

Possible Benefits

If the job is structured properly, telecommuting could help workers who wish to have greater autonomy, work time flexibility and independence. Telecommuting would also be of great benefits to those who are homebound because of various disabilities. However, the vast majority of non-management workers should not expect to achieve the autonomy and independence in telecommuting that have been denied them in the traditional office.

Other benefits that could accrue to workers are the elimination of commuting time and the attendant costs, a reduction of expenses associated with clothing and the costs of meals outside of the home.

Potential Problems

One of the largest problems for workers who telecommute from home is the problem of isolation and how it affects the worker and the work product. Structure and direction provided in a traditional work setting will be absent for those who telecommute. "Buddy training" or group discussions on new processes or work applications will be unavailable to isolated workers. Contacts with fellow workers, which often help to make sense of the individual's job with regard to the larger task being performed, will be missing.

Other problems associated with home-based telecommuting are the type of equipment to be placed in the home, who would pay for the equipment, and the costs associated with operating that equipment. Would the individual be assured of receiving safe and ergonomically sound equipment and furniture?

Would the employee be forced to pay for a portion of for all of the equipment and furniture? Would the employee be compensated for the costs of utilities to run the equipment and to light, heat, and cool the house? Would the company provide a separate telephone hookup and equipment or would the employee's personal equipment be used? Would the employer pay rent for that portion of the house or apartment that is being used to provide a worksite for the company? Who is responsible in case of theft or damage to the equipment? Who pays for the increased cost of insurance?

Problems with regard to personal privacy are also raised for the worker who telecommutes from home. Many employers assert the right to search lockers, test body fluids, and interrogate their employees. What would this mean to the worker who telecommutes? Will the employer have the right to search the telecommuter's home if they suspect theft or drug use? Will prohibitions against alcohol at the work site mean no beer in the icebox? Will the employer have the right to visit the worksite whenever they wish?

Issues with regards to electronic monitoring could also be a problem for the telecommuter. New standards of productivity could work directly against the autonomy that home-based work might otherwise provide. Corporate assumptions about improved productivity being a byproduct of telecommuting could place a heavy burden on the workers.

The conflict between family demands and workplace demands is also a potential problem for telecommuters. Telecommuting is not a solution to childcare problems. Taking care of young children is a task that requires one's full attention. Working a job also requires one's full attention. If telecommuters think that the two can be combined, experts suggest that they will soon be disappointed. In fact, some employers require the child to be placed in a childcare facility before the employee can work from home.

Callout Pay

Another issue of concern is payment for traditional call-outs. If the worker has the ability to resolve the problem in 15 minutes from a laptop, what is the incentive for the company to pay the traditional four hours call-out pay? There are rumors throughout the phone system that some technicians and even some supervisors are currently doing this work from home during non-work hours. This issue has not traditionally been part of the telecommuting discussion, but it is important that it be addressed by the contract.

Telecommuting in (Telephone Exchange Carrier Firm Named Here)

Since early 1993, a small group of Credit Reps and Service Reps at (*this carrier firm*) have engaged in a telecommuting experiment. In (*city named here*),

CWA engaged in a telecommuting trial that had five Credit Reps working four days a week from their home. The experiment lasted for over a year and the workers were generally pleased with the experiment. The company agreed to assume liability for the equipment and any accidents that the employee suffered. Injuries to other members of the household were to be covered by homeowners insurance. CWA had access to the members participating and kept in close contact with them. The experiment has been discontinued because the company has introduced new hardware and software to process the credit data and was unwilling to place the new systems in the employees' homes.

CWA participated in a similar experiment for 15 Service Reps in (*another city named here*). The employees involved seemed quite satisfied with the work arrangement. The most frequently mentioned advantage was the lack of travel, and the most constantly heard complaint was losing touch with the day-to-day operation of the office. This experiment has been discontinued by (*the employer firm*) because they are consolidating the Service Rep function and eliminating about 16 centers.

From this limited experience, we can see that (*the above-named firm*) places several factors above telecommuting as a corporate goal. Consolidation and an unwillingness to pay the expense of the new equipment for the telecommuter clearly rank high and may signal that telecommuting is not a serious concern for the company.

Guidelines for Telecommuting Experiments

Any agreements with regard to telecommuting should be treated as "pilot projects" with special provisions to monitor their applications in our industry. Any continuation of a project shall require the union's consent. The following guidelines should be a part of any pilot project:

- The union must be an equal partner in all aspects of the trial including design, implementation, and evaluation. The union may terminate any and all projects, subject to reasonable notification.
- All telecommuters will spend at least three days a week in the office.
- The company agrees to abolish subcontracting in the area of work where the telecommuting is involved.
- Time will be made available so that all telecommuters will meet regularly with their union steward.
- A message from the union will appear when the telecommuter brings up the computer screen.
- Remote monitoring will not be excessive and notice of the monitoring will be provided to the employee.
- Non-quantitative work performance measurements will be sought.
- Telecommuters will be provided training to keep them current with all emerging technologies in their field.
- A proper childcare program will be available to the employees.
- Home visits by managers will be restricted to no more than two a month and will only occur if 24 hours notice has been provided.
- The employer will indemnify the employee against any and all claims made with regard to the work performed at home or the equipment used to perform it.
- The employer will pay a telecommuting differential to cover the additional costs of any insurance increase, electricity, or heating and cooling costs.

Because of our limited experience, we should continue to approach telecommuting cautiously and limit our experiments to no more than one per state. We should also propose that the company pay for a union-selected human resources consultant to evaluate each trial project.

OLYMPIC GAMES TELECOMMUTING TRIAL

(Source: Debbie Goldman, Communication Workers of America)

(Telephone exchange carrier employer firm named here) and CWA agree to the following trial program for telecommuting during the period of the

Olympic and Para-Olympic Games to be held in Atlanta, Georgia, in 1996. This trial will cover participating employees covered under the (*employer firm*)/CWA Bargaining Agreement dated May 31, 1995. The length of the trial will be two months, July and August 1996. The trial is intended to benefit the Employees, Company and Community.

Hours of Work

- Employees standard work schedule is unaffected by telecommuting. The daily schedule will be established by management, as specified in the Bargaining Agreement.
- Employees will be compensated for the approved overtime as defined by the (*employer firm*)/CWA May 1995 Agreement.
- Employees required to deviate from their normal schedule will immediately notify their supervisor, providing the reason and probable duration of their deviation from their normal schedule.
- Names and hours worked of all employees who telecommute or perform work from their homes during regular or overtime hours will be provided to the Union local every payroll period.

Travel Time/Expenses

- A telecommuting employee required to travel during their normal work hours will have expenses reimbursed for personal vehicle mileage or the preferred mode of transportation as defined by the Company.
- Should an employee be required to report to their regular reporting location, and not their telecommuting location, for a full tour to perform their normal daily work assignment they will not be entitled to pay for the time of the commute or expenses.

Compensation and Benefits

Compensation and benefits are not affected by this telecommuting trial. Employees will be paid according to the wage zone at their (*employer firm*) work location, even though their home or telecommuting location may be in a different wage zone.

Communication to Employees by Union

Telecommuting employees shall be granted paid time during each scheduled tour to call the Union's daily pre-recorded message.

Proprietary Information

(*Employer firm*)'s policy on proprietary information, as outlined in CSI 3.01, Guidelines and Procedures for Safeguarding Proprietary Information, must be followed. Supervisors are responsible for reviewing CSI's for computer security and safeguarding proprietary information with each employee participating in this trial.

Company-Provided Equipment

If the company provides equipment for this trial the following procedures will apply:

- Company will repair or replace damaged, lost or stolen equipment.
- Employees may not use company-provided equipment for personal use or allow non-(*employer firm*) employees to use it.
- Employees must return equipment to (*employer firm*) when requested by their supervisor or at the end of the telecommuting assignment. The employee can elect to bring in the equipment or have it picked up by the company.
- Employees will be responsible for providing access for repair of company-provided equipment as required.

Employee-Provided Equipment (at the Election of the Employee)

- Expenses (e.g., maintenance repair, insurance) are employee's responsibilities.
- Company and personal files must be kept on separate and removable computing media, clearly marked as company or personal.
- All company information and company network connections must be secured.
- Employees are responsible for the protection of proprietary information.

Work Environment

- Time required to establish the necessary environment for telecommuting at the employee's home will be compensated as work time.
- The Company will arrange for the delivery of documents from/to the home and office.
- Participants must provide a supportive and ergonomically correct office environment including but not limited to adequate workspace, security and sound control, adequate telephone and electrical outlets, and separation from on-going domestic activities. Costs of providing any additional telephone lines will be paid by the Company.

- Management will provide a minimum of 24 hours advance notice prior to a visit to the employee's home. Employees will be provided with the telephone number of the local union and advised they can notify the Union of the planned visit if they desire and the employee may invite the Union representative to also attend during the visit if they desire.

Monitoring

Monitoring will be performed as deemed necessary by management based on the guidelines set forth in the Bargaining Agreement, i.e., during employee's regularly scheduled tour with prior notification to the employee.

Employee Selection Criteria

Participants in the trial will be determined based upon the selection criteria agreed to between the local management team and the appropriate CWA representatives.

Performance Evaluation Criteria

Productivity will be tracked on a daily basis. Performance standards and procedures in place at the employee's normal work location will be the same with the work at home trial.

Employee Expenses

Reimbursable expenses include:
- Business telephone calls
- Basic office supplies, such as paper, pens, and fax and computer paper
- Any other business expenses that may arise, employees must obtain supervisory approval before incurring them in order to be reimbursed.

Safety and Accidents

- Workers' Compensation liability for job-related injuries and illnesses and eligibility for Accident Disability Benefits continue during the employee's approved work schedule/assignment throughout the duration of the trial.
- (*Employer firm*) is not liable for any injuries to family members, visitors, and others in the employee's home or telecommuting

location. Telecommuting employees should seek advice from their personal insurance carrier to consider coverage for third party injuries arising out of or relating to the use of the home under (*employer firm*)'s telecommuting policy.

Termination of the Telecommuting Assignment/Trial

- A steering committee will be established for each Business Unit participating in the trial. The participants will be: Labor Relations, a Business Unit Manager, Union local President, and Union job steward for the job involved.
- This committee must agree on all startup and administrative issues not provided for in this stipulation and shall develop procedures for handling and resolving disputes not covered by the collective bargaining agreement such as unforeseen costs due to telecommuting including claims resulting in personal equipment damage if caused by company-provided equipment.

Violations by Employee

Violations by an employee of the specific procedures outlined above shall only entitle the Company to remove the employee from the telecommuting trial.

CONFIRMATION LETTER FROM EMPLOYER FIRM TO CWA, RE: WORK-AT-HOME TRIAL, SEPTEMBER 17, 1992

(Source: Debbie Goldman, Communication Workers of America)

This will confirm our prior understanding in which it was agreed, with respect to the Residence Collection Centers employees in the bargaining unit covered by Appendix C, recognized as being represented by your Union, that the Company and the Union would establish a work-from-home trial in accordance with the provisions set forth below:

1. The work-from-home trial will commence during 1993 and run for a twelve-month period, but may be extended as mutually agreed by the Company and the Union. Four Credit representatives will participate.
2. A work-from-home participant is defined as a person routinely performing his/her job functions in the individual's home. For

(employer firm named here) work-from-home applications, this includes performing all applicable job functions during a scheduled tour.

3. The trial is entered into in recognition of the fact that the work-at-home customer is the fastest growing segment of the residence telecommunications market. The purpose of the trial is to aid the Company and the Union in gaining the knowledge needed to learn how to best serve the work-at-home customer and to enhance our credibility in advising work-at-home customers on applicable telecommunications technology. Work-from-home trial participants will assist the parties in examining and evaluating several work-from-home issues, including, but not listed to: customer satisfaction; employee satisfaction; productivity; environmental factors; and, technology requirements.

4. In order to qualify as a work-from-home trial participant, employees must meet the following criteria:
   a) Employee must be a Credit Representative who volunteers to work from home.
   b) Employee must have a satisfactory or better work and attendance record.
   c) Employee must be able to do satisfactory work with minimal supervision.
   d) Employee must commit to a six-month time frame, but may volunteer to extend participation for duration of the trial.
   e) Employee must be willing and able to dedicate a certain amount of home space, approximately 6' x 4' for the work area and equipment.
   f) When ability and other qualifications as determined by the Company are equal, seniority will prevail in the selection of the work-from-home participants for the trial.

5. The Company will provide all furnishings required to set up the work area and equipment (e.g., table, desk, chair)
   a) Management approval of location is required, including lighting, electrical outlets, etc.
   b) Employee must obtain agreement to install, and the Company must have the availability of, facilities for up to three additional lines (e.g., landlord refused additional work or city ordinance prohibits the employee from working at home).
   c) Employee will not be reimbursed for electricity used.

6. Occasionally, an employee will receive scheduled visits, with a full day's notice, from a supervisor and, unless the employee objects, a Union steward. Such home visits normally will not exceed one or two times a month. The Union steward's visits will be on Company time and mileage reimbursement will be pro-

vided to the steward because information gathered will be added to the trial evaluation data.

7. Today Credit Representatives and their managers have electronic mail available. Electronic mail (E-mail) will continue to be available for communication with the work-from-home employee during the trial. The Union steward may utilize E-mail as is appropriate to communicate with the work-from-home Credit Representative.

8. The Company will, at all times, retain ownership of all supplies and equipment furnished by the Company. If the employee is released by the Company from the program for any reason whatsoever, is not capable of participating, or the trial is terminated, the equipment will be returned to the Company.

9. The employee will be reviewed on the Code of Business Conduct, Safeguarding Proprietary Records and Computer Inquiry IV, by management. Employees are not allowed to use Company equipment or facilities for personal use without authorization from the Company.

10. The employee must be flexible in workdays/hours needed. Employees will continue to be required to select from the headquarters tour availability schedule on a seniority basis. Employees will be scheduled to work from home three or four days a week. Their hours will coincide with their headquarters location hours. In other words, if the employee's headquarters location handles calls between 7:00am and 7:00pm, the employee is expected to work their eight-hour tour in that timeframe. However, should the needs of the business or individual system problems arise, the employee may be expected to report to his/her headquarters location within a reasonable period of time. In the event of a system failure and the employee is unable to report to his/her headquarters location, said employee will be paid and not charged with an absence and/or vacation day.

   For the purposes of this trial, it is expected that care of child(ren) requirements will not interfere with work performance. The Company may make overtime available to the employee in accordance with the Company's then-existing policy or practice on overtime for the work group.

11. The employee must be willing to participate in interviews and focus group review sessions prior to and as the trial progresses.

12. The employee may be removed from the program if not performing satisfactory work from home or not otherwise meeting or complying with other Company standards, policies, practices or procedures. The Union will be notified when an individual's performance or attendance places them in jeopardy of being

removed from the Work-From-Home agreement so the parties can work together on preventing cancellations. Any disciplinary discussions will include Union representation in accordance with Paragraph 3.09 of the Collective Bargaining Agreement.

13. It is understood that all training, updates and revisions will be covered and reviewed during in-office days.

14. Individuals who work at home will be treated as employees of the Company, not independent contractors.

15. The Union and the Company will mutually evaluate results throughout the trail to determine if the program will continue.

TELECOMMUTING TRIAL PROGRAM STATEMENT
(agreement between CWA and telephone exchange
carrier employer)

(Source: Debbie Goldman, Communication Workers of America)

The telecommuting trials jointly agreed to by *(employer firm)* and the CWA in 1992 Bargaining are an employer and CWA effort to test and evaluate the concept of telecommuting in an operations environment. The Company and the Union recognize the challenge that each employee faces as workplace demands, career objectives, family needs and personal goals compete for time and attention. Telecommuting is a possible resource to help meet those challenges and environmental concerns, as well as providing potential cost savings. Accordingly, the Company and the Union have agreed to trial telecommuting during the life of the Working Agreement. All trials must be approved by the Local President and Operations Manager and concurred in by the State CWA Representative. Should a situation develop that cannot be resolved, the Company and Union will have the right to terminate the trial with 30 days notice.

Communications with Employees

Appropriate and adequate communication is crucial to a successful telecommuting program. This must include accessibility and connectivity. Telecommuters must be accessible to customers, management and suppliers as if they were in the office; likewise, customers, management and suppliers must remain accessible to the telecommuter. At the same time the telecommuters must be able to connect to information sources and databases as if they were in the office if they are to perform the same functions.

- **Meetings**—Plan for meetings when telecommuter is working in the office, or discuss an alternative date with employee. For on-the-spot meetings, consider linking the telecommuter by conference call.

- **General Information**—Share through normal channels with telecommuters while they are in the office.
- **Special Announcements/Information**—Contact by telephone should be primary. E-mail and voice mail do not take the place of personal contact.
- **Individual Meetings**—In addition to group meetings, it is very necessary for the telecommuter to have one-on-one meetings with his/her manager both for developmental purposes and sharing information. These meetings should be scheduled when the telecommuter is in the office.

Pay Issues

Employees who telecommute shall be paid according to the Working Agreement. When working from the telecommuting location (e.g., home), that location will be considered the place of reporting. Pay will still be based on the office location and no payment for change in place of reporting will apply. Telecommuter will not receive a special commuting allowance when working at the telecommuting location. If the Company directs the telecommuter to report to another location after his/her telecommuting tour has begun, a commuting allowance will be due. All overtime pay policies will stay the same. When the telecommuter's schedule includes flexible scheduling concepts, contract language will be followed. (*see Scheduled Hours.*)

Performance Standards

Performance standards and measurements for telecommuters will be the same as those of employees working in the office doing the same job.

Scheduled Hours/Vacations

Employees who work at home will have scheduled hours and vacation consistent with their work unit/group and the provisions of the Working Agreement. During this trial, the employee would telecommute for no more than 3 days per week; exceptions would be considered on a case-by-case basis between the local management and the local union representative.

Selection Process

Telecommuting opportunities will be offered by seniority to the senior qualified employees. The number of employees offered telecommuting will be decided on the basis of cost and provisioning capabilities. Telecommuting trials will continue from 6 months to a year.

Telecommuting is a voluntary program and may be terminated by the Company or employee upon reasonable notice in writing.

Proprietary Information

Employees who work at a telecommuting location will take all precautions necessary to secure proprietary information and to prevent unauthorized access to any Company system from the telecommuting location. Telecommuting employees have the same responsibility for security of data and information at the telecommuting location as they have at their regular office location.

Safety

(*Employer firm*) employees who work at home will have a designated work space maintained by the employee and subject to joint inspections with reasonable notice, by a company representative and the local union representative, to insure safe working conditions and compliance with safety guidelines and ergonomic guidelines. Accident reporting also must be in compliance with the Company Safety Results Plan and Benefit Plan.

Facilities/Furniture/Supplies

Costs for room rearrangement, home modifications and furniture other than that provided by the company will be the responsibility of the telecommuter and must meet local building codes. Additional or modified wiring with grounding may be necessary. Lighting must be adequate and windows should not cause glare on a display screen. Extension cords should not be used where they may cause trip hazards.

Adequate space, which is not a part of the main traffic flow during working hours, must be available for a workspace. When the work surface is supplied by the telecommuter, it must be large enough to provide space for needed work items (e.g., keyboard, display screen and accessories, etc.) Work surfaces provided by the employee must be no lower than 27" and no higher than 30" in height. Five point chairs will be provided by the company, if necessary. When it is necessary for the Company to provide a work surface, the working space size must be 5'x 5' to accommodate a desk and chair.

The Company will provide office supplies and equipment as required to perform daily job functions. Furniture, equipment and supplies provided by the Company in connection with telecommuting arrangements will remain the property of the Company. Company employees who work at a telecommuting location will take all precautions necessary to insure that company-provided items are secured and protected from damage.

Training

Training will be provided for Company telecommuters, their managers and their peers prior to beginning the telecommuting process. Telecommuters, their managers, peers and union representation should also regularly schedule meetings to discuss the progress and challenges faced with telecommuting. (*see Individual Meetings Under Communications.*)

Working Conditions

Telecommuting is not the answer to childcare or dependent care. Provisions for those responsibilities must be made prior to beginning telecommuting.

Other potential distractions to the telecommuter should be considered and conflicting demands resolved in advance of participation in the trial.

Research

Telecommuters must agree to assist in research necessary to evaluate the telecommuting program.

Quarterly reports on the status of each trial will be provided to the Administrative Assistant to the Vice President of CWA-District 3 and Vice President-Labor Relations, (*employer firm*).

MASTER CONTRACT FOR BARGAINING UNITS 1, 3, 4 and 11
(agreement between the State of California and the California State Employees Association [CSEA])

[Reprint permission graciously given by Anne Reise, legal representative for CSEA local 1000. This contract, effective January 31, 2002 to July 2, 2003 is currently being renegotiated.]

Article 21 – MISCELLANEOUS

21.1. Telecommute/Telework Program
A. Telework is defined as performing work one (1) or more days per pay period away from the work site to which the employee

is normally assigned. Such locations must be within a pre-approved workspace and during pre-approved work hours inside the teleworker's residence, telework centers, or other offices of the State, as approved pursuant to the department's telework policy and guidelines.

B. Where operational considerations permit, a department may establish a telework program. If the telework arrangement conforms to telework criteria established in the department's telework policy and guidelines, no employee's request for telework shall be unreasonably denied. Upon request by the employee, the denial and the reason for denial shall be in writing. Such programs shall operate within the policies, procedures, and guidelines established by the Telework Advisory Group, as described in the Telecommuting Work Option. Information Guidelines and Model Policy, June 1992. [To peruse this state telework material online, go to http://www.dpa.ca.gov/telework/guidelines/tele2002.shtm]

C. Formal written telework or telecommuting policies and programs already adopted by departments before the date of this contract will remain in effect during the term of this Contract. Upon the request of the Union, the departments will provide a copy of their formal written telework policy.

FRAMEWORK AGREEMENT ON TELEWORK

[For this reprint we thank Wim Bergans, Press Officer and Emanuela Bonacina, Assistant Press Officer for European Trade Union Confederation. This agreement, signed in Brussels Belgium July 18th, 2002, is the brainchild of representatives from the European Trade Union Confederation (ETUC).[1] The Union of Industrial and Employers' Confederations of Europe (UNICE),[2] the European Association of Craft, Small and Medium-Sized Enterprises (UEAPME),[3] and Central Europe Experts Pool (CEEP).[4]]

1. General Considerations

In the context of the European employment strategy, the European Council invited the social partners to negotiate agreements modernizing the organizations of work, including flexible working arrangements, with the aim of making undertakings productive and competitive and achieving the necessary balance between flexibility and security.

The European Commission, in its second stage consultation of social partners on modernizing and improving employment relations, invited the social partners to start negotiations on telework. On 20 September 2001, ETUC (and the liaison committee EUROCADRES/CEC [Council of European Managerial and Professional Staff, and the European Managers Confederation])[5], UNICE/UEAPME, and CEEP announced their intention to start negotiations aimed at an agreement to be implemented by the members of the signatory parties in the member States and in the countries of the European Economic Area. Through them, they wished to contribute to preparing the transition to a knowledge-based economy and society as agreed by the European Council in Lisbon.

Telework covers a wide and fast evolving spectrum of circumstances and practices. For that reason, social partners have chosen a definition of telework that permits to cover various forms of regular telework.

The social partners see telework both as a way for companies and public service organizations to modernize work organization, and as a way for workers to reconcile work and social life and giving them greater autonomy in the accomplishment of their tasks. If Europe wants to make the most out of the information society, it must encourage this new form of work organization in such a way, that flexibility and security go together and the quality of jobs is enhanced, and that the chances of disabled people on the labor market are increased.

This voluntary agreement aims at establishing a general framework at the European level to be implemented by the members of the signatory parties in accordance with the national procedures and practices specific to management and labor. The signatory parties also invite their member organizations to candidate countries to implement this agreement.

Implementation of this agreement does not constitute valid grounds to reduce the general level of protection afforded to workers in the field of this agreement. When implementing this agreement, the members of the signatory parties avoid unnecessary burdens on SMEs [Small and Medium Sized Enterprises].

This agreement does not prejudice the right of social partners to conclude, at the appropriate level, including European level, agreements adapting and/or complementing this agreement in a manner that will take note of the specific needs of the social partners concerned.

Member organizations will report on the implementation of this agreement to an ad hoc group set by the signatory parties, under the responsibility of the social dialogue committee. This ad hoc group will prepare a joint report on the actions of implementation taken. This report will be prepared within four years after the date of signature of this agreement.

In case of questions on the content of this agreement, member organizations involved can separately or jointly refer to the signatory parties.

Brussels, 16 July 2002

2. Definition and Scope

Telework is a form of organizing and/or performing work, using information technology, in the context of an employment contract/relationship, where work, which could also be performed at the employer's premises, is carried out away from those premises on a regular basis.

This agreement covers teleworkers. A teleworker is any person carrying out telework as defined above.

3. Voluntary Character

Telework is voluntary for the worker and the employer concerned. Teleworking may be required as part of a worker's initial job description or it may be engaged in as a voluntary arrangement subsequently.

In both cases, the employer provides the teleworker with relevant written information in accordance with directive 91/533/EEC [this October 1991 European Council legislation dictates an employer's obligation to inform employees of the conditions applicable to the contract or employment relationship.] The specificities of telework normally require additional written information on matters such as the department of the undertaking to which the teleworker is attached, his/her immediate superior or other persons to whom she or he can address questions of professional or personal nature, reporting arrangements, etc.

If telework is not part of the initial job description, and the employer makes an offer of telework, the worker may accept or refuse this offer. If a worker expresses the wish to opt for telework, the employer may accept or refuse this request.

The passage to telework as such, because it only modifies the way in which work is performed, does not affect the teleworker's employment status. A worker refusal to opt for telework is not, as such, a reason for terminating the employment relationship or changing the terms and conditions of employment of that worker.

If telework is not part of the initial job description, the decision to pass to telework is reversible by individual and/or collective agreement. The reversibility could imply returning to work at the employer's premises at the worker's or at the employer's request. The modalities of this reversibility are established by individual and/or collective agreement.

4. Employment Conditions

Regarding employment conditions, teleworkers benefit from the same rights, guaranteed by applicable legislation and collective agreements, as to comparable workers at the employer's premises. However, in order to take into account the particularities of telework, specific complementary collective and/or individual agreements may be necessary.

5. Data Protection

The employer is responsible for taking the appropriate measures, notably with regard to software, to ensure the protection of data used and processed by the teleworker for professional purposes.

The employer informs the teleworker of all relevant legislations and company rules concerning data protection.

It is the teleworkers' responsibility to comply with these rules.

The employer informs the teleworker in particular of any restrictions on the use of IT equipment or tools such as the Internet and sanctions in the case of non-compliance.

6. Privacy

The employer respects the privacy of the teleworker.

If any kind of monitoring system is put in place, it needs to be proportionate to the objective and introduced in accordance with Directive 90/270 on video display units. [European May 1990 directive covering the prevention and identification of risks for work with display screen equipment, including minimum requirements for equipment, work environment and computer interface.]

7. Equipment

All questions concerning work equipment, liability and costs are clearly defined before starting telework.

As a general rule, the employer is responsible for providing, installing and maintaining the equipment necessary for regular telework unless the teleworker uses his/her own equipment.

If telework is performed on a regular basis, the employer compensates or covers the costs directly caused by the work, in particular those relating to communication.

The employer provides the teleworker with an appropriate technical support facility.

The employer has the liability, in accordance with national legislation and collective agreements, regarding costs for loss and damage to the equipment and data used by the teleworker.

The teleworker takes good care of the equipment provided to him/her and does not collect or distribute illegal material via the Internet.

8. Health and Safety

The employer is responsible for the protection of the occupational health and safety of the teleworker in accordance with Directive 89/391 [European Council legislation, June 1989, introducing measures to encourage improvements in the safety and health of workers while in the process of performing their job tasks] and relevant daughter directives, national legislation and collective agreements.

The employer informs the teleworker of the company's policy on occupational health and safety, in particular requirements on video display units. The teleworker applies these safety policies correctly.

In order to verify that the applicable health and safety provisions are correctly applied, the employer, workers' representatives and/or relevant authorities have access to the telework place, within the limits of national legislation and collective agreements. If the teleworker is working at home, such access is subject to prior notification and his/her agreement. The teleworker is entitled to request inspection visits.

9. Organization of Work

Within the framework of applicable legislation, collective agreements and company rules, the teleworker manages the organization of his/her working time.

The workload and performance standards of the teleworker are equivalent to those of comparable workers at the employer's premises.

The employer ensures that measures are taken preventing the teleworker from being isolated from the rest of the working community in the company, such as giving him/her the opportunity to meet with colleagues on a regular basis and access to company information.

10. Training

Teleworkers have the same access to training and career development opportunities as comparable workers at the employer's premises and are subject to the same appraisal policies as these other workers.

Teleworkers receive appropriate training targeted at the technical equipment at their disposal and at the characteristics of this form or work organization. The teleworker's supervisor and his/her direct colleagues may also need training for this form of work and its management.

11. Collective Rights Issues

Teleworkers have the same collective rights as workers at the employer's premises. No obstacles are put to communicating with worker's representatives.

The same conditions for participating in and standing for elections to bodies representing workers or providing worker representation apply to them.

Teleworkers are included in calculations for determining thresholds for bodies with worker representation in accordance with European and national law, collective agreements or practices. The establishment to which the teleworker will be attached for the purpose of exercising his/her collective rights is specified from the outset.

Worker representatives are informed and consulted on the introduction of telework in accordance with European and national legislations, collective agreements and practices.

12. Implementation and Follow-up

In the context of article 139 of the Treaty [refers to European Council's 1999 Framework Agreement on the Rights of Workers on Fixed-Work Contracts], this European framework agreement shall be implemented by the members of UNICE/UEAPME, CEEP AND ETUC (and the liaison committee EUROCADRES/CEC) in accordance with the procedures and practices specific to management and labor in the Member States.

UNITED STATES PATENT AND TRADEMARK OFFICE (USPTO) PATENTS TELEWORK PROGRAM

[This January 29, 2003 agreement between USPTO and the labor union Patent Office Professional Association (POPA) was supplied by Brigid Quinn, Deputy Director Office of Public Affairs, U.S. Patent and Trademark Office]

The Patents Telework Program (PTP) is an ongoing work arrangement that allows eligible employees under the Commissioner for Patents in the POPA bargaining unit to work at an alternate work site during paid work hours to conduct their officially assigned duties without diminished employee performance. As used herein, "alternate work site" is defined as a location in the employee's home designated by the employee as the location they will use to perform their official USPTO duties, or another location approved by the Agency. The PTP will be evaluated on an ongoing basis.

The goal of the PTP is to establish a program under which eligible employees of the POPA bargaining unit may participate in telework to the maximum extent possible without diminished employee performance as set forth in Section 359 of Public Law 106-346, October 23, 2000.

A. Implementation Procedures

A1. Employee Participation

1. The pool of participating employees will be comprised of sixty (60) percent of primary examiners and equivalent employees (GS-14 and above) working under the Commissioner for Patents. This pool is based on the number of employees the Agency can allow to be away form the worksite during normal business hours and still maintain sufficient resources on site to train junior examiners, provide internal and external customers service and maintain the normal functions and performance of the agency. One hundred percent of this pool of employees will be allowed to participate so long as they meet the requirements of this agreement. The PTP allows participants to work from the alternate worksite one day per week.

2. The USPTO has many other flexible programs in place such as compressed work schedules, increased flex-time program (IFP), and compensatory time programs which allow work outside of normal business hours and work on weekends in lieu of Monday to Friday. The PTO must maintain sufficient experienced staff levels during normal business hours to train junior staff and provide internal customer service. In order to participate in the PTOP, and to ensure that the PTO can meet its needs, PTP participants must work at the PTO site for a minimum of 3 days per week of at least 6 hours per day, between 6:30am and 6:00pm. The three days must be worked Monday through Friday. Approved leave, including religious compensatory time and compensatory time earned for the purpose of maternity/paternity, may be used to meet the minimum required hours. Other forms of compensatory time may not be used, except in the case of absences of 1 week or longer.

3. Participants may not work at the alternate work site and at the USPTO on the same day unless directed to do so by the SPE.

4. On days employees telework, they will complete 6 hours of their workday between 6:30am and 7:00pm, Monday-Friday. A maximum of 10 hours may be worked on a telework day. If the employee works less than 6 hours, all hours worked must be completed during this band. Any other hours worked on this day must be completed during the hours appropriate to the work schedule for the employee. All forms of approved leave, including compensatory time, may be used to meet the required hours on telework days.

5. All examiners are expected to provide customer service to both internal and external customers by being accessible and available

during working hours. Participants who use their own telephones will forward their work phone calls to their home phone on telework days or will give their home phone number to their supervisor and art unit or equivalent. Participants working at the alternate work site must check voicemail near the beginning and midpoint of their telework day.

6. Participation in the PTP is voluntary.
7. To withdraw from the Program, including for the purpose of promotion or retirement, employees will e-mail their supervisor and the program coordinator. Management will notify POPA of new vacancies within 1 biweek.
8. Participants cannot work paid overtime or compensatory time on the day they work at the alternate work site during the program.

A2. Selection Criteria

Within each Technology Center or other business unit within Patents, priority of selection shall be given first to participants in the former Work at Home Pilot Program under the Millennium Agreement [see next document in this appendix](for the first application period only); then according to the grade of the employee, and next, according to the amount of time served in the employee's current and previous higher grades (as in the case of downgraded employees) while an employee of the USPTO. Employees must meet eligibility requirements set forth herein.

There will be eight separate selection pools under the Commissioner for Parents. Each of Technology Centers 1600, 1700, 2600, 2800, 3600, and 3700/2900 will be one of seven separate selection pools and the eighth pool will consist of the combined organizations under the Deputy Commissioner for Patent Examination Policy and the Deputy Commissioner for Patent Resources and Planning. The slots will be apportioned between the 8 pools based on the ratio of the number of those eligible employees in each pool divided by the total number of those eligible employees under the Commissioner for Patents. Slots that are not filled in any of the 8 pools will be redistributed throughout the remaining pools in a manner that redistribution does not impede the Agency's ability to accomplish its mission.

A3. Application Process

1. There will be an application period prior to the commencement of the PTP program. Thereafter, any eligible employee may apply. USPTO will place an announcement of the application period on the bulletin board email or through the chain of command and intranet page with the appropriate links to a copy of this agree-

ment and any other program guidelines developed, and an application including instructions on how to apply for the program.

2. For the first application period, individual notification will be given to the prior participants in the former Patents Work at Home Pilot Program under the Millennium Agreement.

3. USPTO will provide written notification (e.g. via e-mail) to all employees who file an application for the program of their acceptance or non-acceptance at least 2 weeks prior to the commencement of the program. Written notification of non-acceptance will include the reason for non-acceptance, when the reason for non-acceptance is a reason other than seniority.

4. USPTO will provide POPA with the names of all employees participating in the PTP.

5. Vacancies will be filled at the end of the first, second, and third quarters of the fiscal year. Newly selected employees will be trained prior to participating.

A4. Requirements for Participating in the program

Participants are required to comply with the following:

1. Be a GS-14 or higher and if an examiner, have Full Signatory Authority.

2. Have and maintain at least a Fully Successful rating of record.

3. Are not currently under an oral and written warning improvement period in any critical element of the Performance Appraisal Plan. If an employee's performance diminishes and the employee is placed on an oral or written warning improvement period, he or she will be removed from the telework program. Employees will be reinstated in the program not later than 4 weeks following successful completion of the performance improvement period for matters of workflow and production. For other matters, employees will be reinstated not later than 3 months following successful completion of the improvement period. Employees will be reinstated even if the number of participants temporarily exceeds the number defined in A1.1 above.

4. Sign the Patents Telework Program Work Agreement (See Attachment I.)

5. The USPTO will give employees being removed from the program two weeks advance notice, unless exigent circumstances exist.

A5. Medical Exception

USPTO will consider requests from employees to work at home based on short-term medical needs within a reasonable time period, generally

15 days. These employees must meet all eligibility requirements, except for seniority. Applicants must submit documentation from a licensed physician or equivalent medical professional describing the medical condition and how the ability to telework one day per week will alleviate the condition.

Approval will be for the duration of the medical need, up to 4 months. Training and needs of the Agency will be considered in making a determination on the application. Approval of these requests will not be considered as evidence of the Agency treating an employee as handicapped. Exceptions granted under this provision will not be counted in the participation level set forth in A1.1.

B. Files and Documents

B1. Participants will be able to work on patent applications and documents at the employee's designated alternate worksite without any hardware or software support. Only for the purposes of this program, participants will be permitted to remove USPTO patent applications and documents from the USPTO in order to perform their officially assigned duties at the alternate work site. The participant is responsible for the transportation of the patent applications and documents to and from the alternate work site. Participants are also responsible for taking sufficient work for the time worked at the alternate work site.

B2. At its discretion, the agency may provide equipment, software, and other materials to participants for use at the alternate worksite. Employee use of these items will be voluntary. The USPTO may require return or exchange of this equipment. Catastrophic time may be granted for loss of work due to failure of USPTO-provided equipment. The USPTO is not responsible for non-USPTO-provided equipment and non-examining time will not be granted for installation of software or if problems occur. If the participant has installed USPTO-provided e-mail capability, the participant must access e-mail periodically throughout the workday during USPTO business hours when working at the alternate work site.

B3. The USPTO maintains ownership and control of any and all equipment, software, other materials, and data provided to the participant.

B4. USPTO will provide telephone calling cards to cover the cost of long distance business-related phone calls for participants if necessary to perform assigned duties. Participants will maintain a log of calls made at the alternate site using the telephone credit card by date, telephone number, and category and will turn the phone logs in to their supervisor on a monthly basis. Participants will not be reimbursed for use of their own phone. If no phone calls are made using the agency's credit card, then no log needs to be turned in.

B5. Any USPTO-owned equipment, including the telephone calling card, is for official use. Use of the equipment for private purposes is prohibited except as permitted by USPTO.

B6. The participants will use PALM ExPo [computer application that tracks and provides the status of paper patent application files] to charge cases out to the alternate work site location as specified in Attachment 2. In the event that PALM ExPo is not working, the participants will notify their supervisor by appropriate means of the applications they are removing to the alternate work site and when they are returned. No patent application or document shall remain at the alternate work site longer than ten (10) business days, unless prior supervisory approval is granted. Participants on scheduled leave longer than three workdays should return all patent applications and documents to the USPTO.

C. Rights and Responsibilities

C1. Participation in the PTP will not change the conditions of employment established by past practices, law, rule, regulation or any previous agreements except as specified in these guidelines.

C2. Employees participating in the PTP will have their performance evaluated under the criteria set out in the Performance Appraisal Plan.

C3. All USPTO-owner materials associated with this program must be returned to the USPTO or arrangements for their return must be scheduled with the designated agency official within 5 business days from the end of an individual's participation.

C4. Participants that are renters are responsible for ensuring that their lease allows the installation of all the necessary equipment and lines for the program.

C5. The participant is responsible for ensuring compliance with all local laws or rules governing an office in their home.

C6. Participants may work any full time schedule approved by the USPTO, subject to the requirements of this agreement.

C7. When working at the alternate work site, the examiner must perform patent-examining functions and related activities, as defined in the Gainsharing agreement [1986 USPTO/POPA collective bargaining agreement, can be viewed at http://www.popa.org/pdf/cba.pdf]. Non-examiners must work on tasks directly related to their job functions as defined in their performance appraisal plan when working at the alternate work site.

D. Evaluation

D1. Prior to renegotiation of the agreement, the program will be evaluated to determine the continuing feasibility of the Telework program arrangement to ensure that the duties officially assigned are performed without diminished employee performance as required by Public Law and the Agency's ability to serve the public is not adversely affected.

D2. During the evaluation period, the program will be evaluated on criteria including but not limited to:

- Cost effectiveness/organizational costs
- Employee satisfaction
- Customer service
- Performance (individual and organizational)

D3. Participants will participate in surveys and focus sessions. Participants will adjust their work schedule as necessary to participate in the PTP evaluation. Co-workers and supervisors may also be surveyed. If conducted, the USPTO and POPA agree to provide each other with studies, evaluations, agreements, surveys, questionnaires, etc. that they develop related to evaluation of the PTP reasonably in advance of the next semi-annual meeting or renegotiation of this agreement.

D4. The parties agree to meet at least once each six months to discuss issues related to the program. In addition, either party may reopen this agreement every 2 years so long as notice is provided to the other party at least 30 days prior to the 2-year anniversary of the effective date of this agreement.

E. Additional Guidelines

E1. In order to continue in the program, participants must follow the USPTO standards governing ethical behavior, conduct, and confidentiality regardless of where the official duties are performed. An employee may be removed from the program for up to 12 months if the employee has received a disciplinary or adverse action. If management believes the employee should be precluded from participating in the program for longer than this period, the agency will include this decision in the disciplinary/adverse action. On a case-by-case basis, the Agency may temporarily remove an employee being investigated for serious violations of the above standards, including proposed actions. Temporary removal will last no longer than 100 days from the date of removal, unless the issue is referred to the Inspector General or the Department of Justice.

E2. Abuse of the program guidelines may result in removal from the program.

E3. Participants will apply approved safeguards to protect all USPTO records and data from unauthorized disclosure, access, damage, or destruction and will comply with the Privacy Act requirements.

E4. If the alternative worksite is the participant's home, the participant must designate a room or location in their home for placement and use of the material for the PTP.

E5. Participants will complete a self-certification of the safety of their alternate work site. See **Attachment 3.** [*authors' note: attachment not included in this book.*]

E6. Primary examiners participating in the PTP will notify the junior examiners who they train of their schedule or will schedule appointments with junior examiners who they train.

E7. Generally, employees in the PTP will be given advance notice of at least two USPTO business days for all meetings, legal lectures, training, or other events that require their attendance at the USPTO.

E8. When the USPTO has an unusual need for a patent application or other document that is located at the alternate worksite, the employee with whom the patent application or other document is located may be directed to provide the patent application or other document or other requested information to the Office within one USPTO business day. An unusual need is one that does not occur on a regular basis and cannot wait for the employee's scheduled return to the USPTO or be resolved through other means. If the day the application needs to be retuned is a day the participant is scheduled to be away from the Office, transportation time to and from the official duty station will be treated as duty time. When there is a normal need for an application or document, the participant will bring the application or document into the Office on his or her next workday at the USPTO.

E9. The USPTO will provide participants in the PTO standard office supplies for use at the alternate worksite.

E10. Participants are responsible for any utility cost, heating, and lighting at the participant's home. Participants are responsible for any re-wiring, updating, and improvements necessary to bring the electrical connections in a participant's home up to the required standards.

E11. Participants will maintain reasonable care of all USPT-owned material. The USPTO acts as the insurer for damage, theft or other loss (e.g. fire, flood, etc.) of the USPTO material.

E12. Participants are covered under the Federal Employee's Compensation Act if injured in the course of performing official duties at the alternate work site. If so injured, the participant will notify their supervisor or another designated USPTO official as soon as possible (in accordance with FECA).

E13. Upon notification, the USPTO may investigate all accident and injury reports that occur at the alternate work sites.

E14. The USPTO will not be liable for damages to an employee's personal or real property during the course of performance of official duties or while using USPTO material in the employee's residence or elsewhere, except to the extent the USPTO is held liable by the Federal Tort Claims Act claims or claims arising under the Military Personnel and Civilian Employees Claims Act.

E15. All participants in the PTP program will indicate on their timesheet (690-E) which days were worked at the alternate worksite.

E16. Participants may take approved leave and use approved compensatory time on a telework day.

E17. Participants working at the alternate work site will be granted the same holidays as employees at the USPTO. Early or partial dismissals or delayed arrivals due to road conditions or conditions that affect part or all of the USPTO worksite normally do not affect the status of the employees working at an alternate work site. The employee will continue to work during these closures and will not normally be granted administrative leave. If these conditions limit the employee's ability to perform their duties, supervisors will consider requests for administrative leave.

E18. Participants must identify their telework day in advance and obtain prior Supervisory approval of that day. Approval will be granted based on Office needs for coverage of work and needed employee interactions and training. If the participant teleworks on the same schedule each week, a single notification of that schedule to the supervisor is adequate. In order that participants not be disturbed during non-duty hours when at the alternate worksite, participants will notify their supervisor when their work-day commences, or prior thereto, of the hours to be worked.

E19. Except for a participant's chain of command and those administering this program, the USPTO will ensure that a participant's address is not divulged to other USPTO personnel or member of the public without the participant's consent.

F. Miscellaneous

F1. This agreement does not affect the dispute between the parties over the termination of the work at home pilot under the Millennium Agreement.

F2. This program shall commence no later than 2 months of the effective date from this agreement. The effective date is the date of Agency Head approval or 31 days after signing of this agreement, which occurs first.

Attachment 2
ALTERNATE WORKSITE SAFETY GUIDANCE

This list constitutes general safety guidance to be maintained at the alternate worksite.

Workplace Environment

1. Temperature, noise, ventilation, and lighting are maintained at levels that enable you to perform your normal duties.
2. Stairs with four or more steps are equipped with handrails.
3. Electrical systems at the alternate worksite are in good working order.
4. Chairs are sturdy and safe to sit on.

5. Phone lines, electrical cords, and extension wires are not in pathways and walkways.
6. Air vents on computers and other electrical equipment are not obstructed.
7. Lighting is adequate for reading.
8. If the alternative workplace is at an employee's home, it must be equipped with smoke/fire detectors that are in proper working order.

PATENT TELEWORK PROGRAM
WORK AGREEMENT

The following constitutes an agreement between the U.S. Patent & Trademark Office and (print name) _____, an employee participating in the Patents Telework Program.

The employee's official duty station is U.S. Patent & Trademark Office Technology Center/Organization _____ Arlington, Virginia. The alternate work site address is:

_____
_____

The phone number at the alternate work site is _____

The alternate work site is described as follows: (designate room or area of room to be used for Patents Telework Program)

_____
_____
_____

In General

1. The employee has read and agrees to adhere to Patents Telework Program Guidelines (attached hereto.)
2. All pay, leave and travel entitlements will be based on the employee's official duty station.
3. The employee must follow established USPTO procedures when requesting and taking leave, compensatory time or credit hours.
4. The employee agrees to complete surveys and attend focus group meetings and interviews to help evaluate the Patents Telework Program.
5. The employee will permit other USPTO employees and contractors to access the alternate worksite during the hours from 9:00am to 5:00pm Monday-Friday (excluding holidays) upon two

business days notice to the employee for the purpose of installing, repairing, maintaining, or removing work equipment, software, or other USPTO property or to investigate an accident or a
Workers' Compensation claim or to investigate other work-related or safety problems arising from the administration of the
Patents Telework Program. The parties may mutually agree to a
time outside of these hours.

6. Participants agree to comply with USPTO instructions regarding
   the return or removal of program materials. Other than for patent
   applications or other documents needed by the USPTO on the
   next business day, participants will have at least 3 business days
   to comply with those instructions.

7. The employee has read the Alternate Worksite Safety Guidance.
   To the best of the employee's knowledge, the alternate worksite
   is safe and will be maintained as such.

8. If a telephone line is installed at government expense at the
   alternate worksite, the employee agrees to maintain telephone
   service for their private use.

Safeguarding Patent Files and Information

9. Patent applications are covered under a privacy agreement with
   legal penalties. Patent applications and certain sensitive documents including budget and procurement documents can only
   be worked on at the employee's home. Documents under secrecy
   orders or containing national security markings cannot be removed from the USPTO.

10. The employee will keep in confidence patent applications and
    information therein in accordance with 35 U.S.C. 122.

11. The employee will safeguard patent files during transit and at
    alternate work site.

12. The employee will comply with the procedure for checking in
    and checking out patent applications.

13. The employee will ensure that only authorized personnel access
    the patent files taken from the USPTO.

14. The employer must return all patent files, work product, drafts
    and notes to the USPTO within two business days of the em-
    ployee ending participation in the program, regardless of
    whether participation ends voluntarily.

Telephone Credit Card Usage

15. The employee will use the office-issued telephone credit card for
    official purposes only.

16. The employee understands that misuse of the telephone credit card may subject the employee to disciplinary action.
17. The employee agrees to maintain a log of calls made at the alternate work site using the telephone credit card by date, telephone number and category and to turn the phone logs in to their supervisor on a monthly basis.
18. In case of theft or loss of the telephone credit card, the employee agrees to immediately notify USPTO, Office of Administrative Services, Telecommunications Branch, 703-305-8331.

I certify that I have read and will comply with the aforementioned provisions:

_____

Print name

_____

Employee's Signature   Date

_____

Patents Telework Program Administrator   Date

Agreement on Initiatives for a New Millennium Between the United States Patent and Trademark Office and the Patent Office Professional Association

[Signed in July 2001, and generally referred to as the "Millennium Agreement," this document provides that, contingent upon approval of a 10 percent special pay request for patent examiner and related-positions, POPA agrees to the phased removal of paper-search files, a work-at-home pilot project, and a customer service element in employees performance plan. For purposes of clarification of the above telework agreement we have reproduced only those portions of the Millennium agreement directly referring to work at home. Should you wish to view the complete agreement it is available online at http://www.popa.org/pdf/pay-final.pdf]

H. Work at Home

Patents Work at Home (PWH) is a six-month pilot work arrangement that allows examiners to work at home during paid work hours to conduct their officially assigned duties. As used herein, "alternative work site" is defined as the location in an employee's home designated by the employee as the location they will use to perform their official USPTO duties.

The Patents Work at Home pilot program has two components – one in which the participant is provided with a fully supported workstation, another in which the participant does not have a fully supported workstation. At least three participants per technology center will have a fully supported workstation. The USPTO will work in partnership with POPA to provide hardware and/or software so that other participants in the pilot will have access to Actionwriter or OACS (whichever is used by the employee at the Office, while working at home). Selection of the hardware and/or software to provide access to Actionwriter or OACS to other participants working at home will be developed within one month of the effective date of the special pay rate.

a. **Implementation Procedures**
   1. Examiners will be allowed to work from home one day per week (up to 12 hours). At least one of the workdays at home per pay period must be a Monday-Friday. No overtime, comp time, or credit hours may be worked at home during the pilot.
   2. Employee participation is voluntary.
   3. The pilot will begin within one month of the effective date of the special pay schedule.
   4. The first phase of the program will be for 6 months. The number of participants to begin the program will be 10% of the Primary Examiners and GS-14 Classifiers per Technology Center, unless there are not enough volunteers, and 10% of GS-14 and above employees in other units within Patents (e.g., PCT, Special Program Law Office), unless there are not enough volunteers. Unless significant problems have been identified, after six months, the number of participants on the program will increase to 15% of the Primary Examiners and GS-14 Classifiers per Technology Center, unless there are not enough volunteers, and 15% of GS-14 and above employees in other units within Patents, unless there are not enough volunteers. A pilot program for non-patents POPA bargaining unit employees will be developed to commence six months after the commencement of the pilot in Patents. Within each Technology Center or other unit within Patents, priority of selection to be a participant shall be determined first by the grade of the employee, and finally by the amount of time served in the employee's current and previous higher grades (as in the case of downgraded employees) while an employee of the USPTO.
   5. Prior to commencement of the pilot program, management will provide POPA with the names of all employees participating in the program. Management will promptly notify POPA of any vacancies.
   6. Participants in the PWH program are required to:

- Have Full Signatory Authority (or be a GS-14 classifier)
- Work a full time work schedule during the pilot
- Be performing at least at Fully Successful in the current rating of record and for an employee's cumulative most recent four full quarters of work.

7. Participants in the fully supported workstation portion of the PWH program must have DSL service available to their home.

b. Equipment and Files

1. Participants will work from USPTO applications. For the purposes of this program, employees will be permitted to remove USPTO applications from the office in order to perform their officially assigned duties at home. The participant is responsible for the transportation of the application to and from home.
2. USPTO will provide the fully supported workstation equipment used in the fully supported workstation component of the pilot program.
3. The USPTO maintains ownership and control of any and all hardware, software, telecommunication equipment and data used in the fully supported workstation component of the program. Repair and maintenance of all government-owned equipment in a participant's home is the responsibility of the USPTO.
4. USPTO will provide telephone calling cards to cover the cost of long distance business related phone calls.
5. For full or partial equipment failure, lost work (catastrophic time), computer shutdown when using high speed access, training, and installation, participants will be treated the same as employees working on-site at the USPTO; however, it is recognized that the participants may be more limited in the ability to perform alternative work during those interruptions.
6. All USPTO owned equipment is for official use. Use of the equipment for private purposes is prohibited except as permitted by USPTO.

c. Rights and Responsibilities

1. Participation in the six-month pilot of PWH will not change the conditions of employment established by past practices, law, rule, regulation and any previous agreements except as specified in the agreement and the guidelines.
2. Employees participating in the PWH pilot programs will have their performance evaluated under the criteria set out in the PAP.
3. Participants must commit to the program for a period of at least 6 months. Participation in the program may be terminated after the 6 months or under exigent circumstances.

4. For the six-month pilot period, when working at home, the examiner must perform patent examining functions and related activities, as per the Gainsharing agreement.
5. Participants that are renters are responsible for ensuring that their lease allows the installation of all the necessary equipment and lines for the pilot.
6. The participant is responsible to ensure that they comply with all local laws or rules governing an office in their home.

d. Pilot Program Evaluation

The USPTO and POPA agree to meet on a periodic basis at least every six months to assess the progress of the program, address any questions and/or concerns that arise from the implementation of PWH and discuss needed changes.

After the first phase of the program is completed (6 months), there will be a 30-day evaluation period conducted by the USPTO and POPA in partnership to assess the progress made to date.

During this period, the program will be evaluated on, but not limited to:

• Cost effectiveness/organizational costs
• Employee satisfaction
• Customer service
• Performance (organizational and individual)

USPTO and POPA agree to provide each other with all studies, evaluations, agreements, surveys, questionnaires, etc. that they develop related to PWH, contemporaneously with the insurance of such materials.

e. Distribution of PWH Agreement

1. Prior to the commencement of the pilot, an announcement will be placed on the "What's New" e-mail and intranet page with appropriate links to a copy of this agreement and any other program guidelines developed, and an application including a complete set of instructions of how to apply for the pilot program. This information will also be disseminated through the chain of command. Enrollment in the program will be ongoing as long as openings are available.
2. USPTO will provide written notification to all employees that file an application for the program of their acceptance or non-acceptance.

f. Guidelines for PWH

1. In general
   a. Participants are reminded that all standards governing ethical behavior and confidentiality remain in effect regardless of where or when the official duties of the USPTO are performed.

b. Participants will apply approved safeguards to protect all USPTO records and data from unauthorized disclosure, access, damage, or destruction and will comply with the Privacy Act requirements.

c. Employees must designate a room or location in their home which will be their alternative work site for placement and use of the equipment for the PWH program.

d. Employees will be required to complete a self-certification of the safety of their alternative work site within their home.

e. Employees will be the property custodians for all USPTO-owned equipment placed in their home.

2. Participants must notify their supervisors by appropriate means prior to beginning a workday at home.

3. Where a participant finds it necessary to report to the official duty station on a day in which the participant normally works at home, the participant may adjust the work schedule to choose another day on which to work at home. Changes to the schedule should be communicated to management in a reasonable manner, which may include voice messaging and e-mail among others.

4. Employees will be given advance notice of two USPTO business days for all meetings, legal lectures, training, or other events that require their attendance at the USPTO.

5. Where the USPTO has an unusual need for an application that is located at an employee's home, the employee with whom the application is located may be required to provide the application or other requested information to the Office within one USPTO business day. An unusual need for an application is one that does not occur on a regular basis and cannot wait for the employee's scheduled return to the USPTO or be resolved through other means.

6. If a participant is working at home on any day from Monday to Friday, the participant should access voice mail at least once a day during USPTO business hours. If the participant is equipped with a fully supported workstation, the participant will access both voice mail and e-mail at least once a day during USPTO business hours when working at home.

7. Participants will notify their supervisor by appropriate means of the applications they are taking home. When the files are returned, the participant will inform the supervisor by appropriate means.

8. If the program is expanded to permit participants to work additional time at home, participants may be required to share an office so long as participants are only required to come into the workplace two days a week. The USPTO may require those two days to occur Monday through Friday.

9. If the employee is unable to work at home because of equipment failure which the employee discovers during the first two hours of any day's tour of duty, the employee will notify a designated USPTO official as soon as the employee is able to do so. The USPTO may require the employee to report to the official duty station. Transportation time to the official duty station in these circumstances will be treated as time during which an employee cannot access their computer and cannot reasonably perform another task. Alternatively, the employee may request annual leave or may request use of accrued compensatory time rather than report to the official duty station. If the employee chooses to report to the official duty station for reasons other than emergency equipment failure discovered that day, transportation time is the responsibility of the employee and will not be treated as duty time.

10. If an equipment failure or condition resulting in non-access to necessary equipment occurs after the first two hours of any day's tour of duty at home and renders an employee unable to work for the remainder of that day, management may excuse the remaining portion of the day by granting administrative leave or approving non-production time. Depending on the circumstances, the employee may choose to report to the official duty station for the remainder of the day. Transportation time to the official duty station in there circumstances will be treated as time during which an employee cannot access their computer and cannot reasonably perform another task. If the employee has other work that may be performed without the use of the downed automated systems, the employee is expected to do that work before any non-production time is granted.

11. Repair and maintenance of all government-owned equipment placed in a participant's home are the responsibility of the USPTO.

12. The USPTO will designate an official(s) for the employee to contact to report equipment failures or problems during all work hours (5:30am-10:00pm). The employee will report such failures or problems as soon as they are discovered.

13. The USPTO will provide the necessary equipment to accomplish the duties of the position prior to the employee beginning participation in the PWH with supplies equivalent to that provided to non-participating bargaining unit professionals.

14. The Office will provide the necessary equipment to accomplish the duties of the position prior to the employee beginning participation in the PWH. The USPTO is not responsible for any utility cost, heating, or lighting at the alternative work site in the employee's home. The USPTO will not be responsible for any re-wiring, updating, or improvements necessary to bring the

electrical connections in an employee's home up to the required standards for PWH.

15. Except for an employee's chain of command and those who require the information for installation and repair of USPTO-owned equipment located in the employee's home, the USPTO will ensure that an employee's address and telephone number is not divulged to other USPTO personnel or members of the public without the employee's prior consent.

16. The participant agrees to maintain reasonable care of all USPTO-owned equipment. The Office acts as the insurer for damage, theft or other loss (e.g. fire, flood) of the Office's equipment.

17. The employee is covered under the Federal Employee's Compensation Act if injured in the course of actually performing official duties at home. If so injured, the employee will notify the supervisor or another designated USPTO official as soon as possible (in accordance with FECA.)

18. For the six-month pilot, the USPTO will investigate all accident and injury reports, following notification, that occur at the alternative work sites within employees' homes.

19. The government will not be liable for damages to an employee's personal or real property during the course of performance of official duties or while using Government equipment in the employee's residence, except to the extent the Government is held liable by the Federal Tort Claims acts claims or claims arising under the Military Personnel and Civilian Employees Claims Act.

20. An official electronic USPTO 690E (or equivalent timesheet) will be provided to participants who are provided with a fully supported workstation having capability to communicate electronically with the USPTO. At the end of each biweek, the participant agrees to e-mail the timesheet form to the participant's supervisor. The supervisor will notify the participant via e-mail of any changes made to the electronic timesheet form.

21. Participants provided with a USPTO-owned computer at home agree to use the current Examiner's Electronic Toolkit, as appropriate.

22. The USPTO and POPA agree to continue to work in partnership to develop further guidelines for this program.

Work and Family Provisions in Canadian Collective Agreements

Human Resources Development Canada, Government of Canada.

[For this reprint we thank Gay Stinson, Director of Policy Development, Human Resource Development Canada (HRDC) Labour Program. The study

is made up of five chapters, discussing organization of working time, mater-
nity, paternity and adoption provisions, leave and vacations, childcare and
employee benefits. We have reproduced only the Methodology, Objectives of
the Study, and the Telework portion of Chapter One, Organization of Working
Time. The complete study can be viewed online at http://labour-travail.hrdc-drhc.
gc.ca/doc/wlb-ctp/CP_Rochon/acknowled_en.html]

The opinions expressed in this study do not necessarily reflect the
views and policies of Human Resources Development Canada or the
Federal Government.

Methodology

This study is based on contract clauses found in *major Canadian*
collective agreements, defined as collective agreements covering more
than 200 employees in sectors under federal jurisdiction or more than
500 employees in sectors under provincial jurisdiction. Relevant provisions were identified and statistics compiled by means of the Workplace
Information Directorate's (WID) Collective Agreement Information Retrieval System (CAIRS) database as well as the *Negotech*, an electronic
document dissemination system which includes contract summaries as
well as full-text collective agreements. A large sample of the roughly
1100 major agreements available at the WID library was also analyzed.
In all, over four hundred major collective agreements were identified
and studied, many of which are quoted in the following chapters and
appear in the list of agreement references at the end of this study. Each
agreement quoted is identified by a number between parentheses,
which refers to its classification code in the Labour Program's Collective Agreements library.

Objectives of the Study

This study has been undertaken in the context of the federal
government's commitment to "make workplace policies . . . of federally
regulated employers more family friendly."[1] Its main purpose is to
examine to what degree provisions related to the balancing of work and
family responsibilities have been considered in the context of collective
bargaining. It identifies and analyzes family-friendly provisions contained in major Canadian collective agreements. This involves a critical
evaluation of the wording, the scope and the practical application of
various clauses.

This information is meant to help employers, unions, labour practitioners and researchers gain a better understanding of policies and
practices conducive to the balancing of work and family responsibilities; identify some of the more innovative practices; assess the feasibil-

ity of implementing such arrangements in a variety of contexts; and discern some of the emerging bargaining priorities regarding this issue. This document should also inform a wider audience of the current issues and implications surrounding family-friendly policies and practices in Canada.

Chapter 1: Organization of Working Time

E. Telework (Home-Based Work)

Telework, also referred to as telecommuting, is an arrangement whereby an employee, at least on a periodic basis, fulfills his or her regularly scheduled job responsibilities at a remote location which is not operated by the employer (a teleworkplace)—usually an employee's own residence.

Working from home is not a new phenomenon, since it has been practiced for decades in certain sectors, such as the garment industry. However, the rapid development of computer and information technologies in recent years has made teleworking feasible in an increasing number of job categories.

Telework can be advantageous for employees by allowing them: to organize their work day around their personal and family needs; to decrease work-related expenses; to reduce commuting time; and to work in a less stressful and disruptive environment; it may also help to accommodate employees who, because of particular disabilities, are unable to leave home. Although telework cannot normally be combined with child or eldercare-related tasks, it may nevertheless let employees work in closer proximity to their children and relatives, offering some peace of mind and giving the family a chance to spend more time together at lunch time as well as before and after school.

Apart from improved productivity, efficiency and employee morale, employers can also benefit from lower overhead costs and from reduced disruption in case of bad weather and other emergencies. The fact that employees who telework can use this added flexibility to capitalize on their personal peak productivity periods can also favorably influence a company's bottom line.

Despite these benefits and the attention that telecommuting has attracted in the media, very few collective agreements contain telework provisions. Those that exist are mostly concentrated in the public sector and in various Crown corporations, particularly in British Columbia.

The paucity of telework clauses is partly due to the fact that not all occupations are amenable to such an arrangement. Moreover, employers may be concerned by the initial implementation costs, potential legal liabilities, and difficulties in supervising and appraising the performance of teleworkers. Unions may disapprove of work-at-home clauses if they perceive them as leading to greater isolation of employees, reduced job security and promotion opportunities, and diminished health and safety protection.

Joint Union-Management Committees on Telework

In some cases, union and employers have agreed to establish committees to study issues related to telework and to propose appropriate regulations and policies. This is usually a first step, which may lead to the implementation of a future telework arrangement.

(01474)   The Company and the Guild agree to strike a committee of two representatives from each party to examine telecommuting issues and recommend changes to the collective bargaining agreement, where required.

(07313)   The Employer and the Union agree to establish a Joint Committee to discuss the matter of implementing telecommuting on a trial basis. The Joint Committee shall consist of not more than three (3) representatives of the Employer and three (3) representatives of the Union. The Committee shall report its finding and any recommendations to the respective bargaining committees for the renewal of the next Collective Agreement. Where a recommendation is approved by the principals of both parties it may be implemented prior to the next round of collective bargaining.

The parties may also agree on a set of criteria and conditions to guide future union-management discussions regarding particular telework arrangements.

(02130)   It is agreed that if potential Telecommuting opportunities arise during the life of the Collective Labour Agreement, the following items, as a minimum, shall be discussed with the goal to achieve mutual agreement.

1. The provisions of the Collective Labour Agreement remain in effect for the employee.
2. Telecommuting will commence and continue based on mutual consent of the company and the employee.
3. The employee retains some form of workspace at the main Company location and electronic access to co-workers and Union officials.
4. Equipment necessary to perform the duties of the job shall be provided and installed at Company cost as determined by the Company.

The parties agree that this letter is not authorization to begin offering Telecommuting work to C.A.W. members at Northern Telecom. It provides a basis for discussion of critical areas that would require agreement after fully considering the needs of the employee, the Company and the Union.

DETAILED TELEWORK CLAUSES

Some agreements contain more detailed telework clauses. These usually specify eligibility and selection criteria and work schedules, together with the terms, conditions and duration of the arrangement. The parties can also negotiate specific safeguards for employees, to ensure there are no deleterious effects on their workload, employment status, and job security.

Eligibility and Selection Criteria

In general, a number of criteria are set to determine which employees will be eligible to telework and how candidates are to be selected.

(07262) Each teleworking proposal will be considered on an individual basis after taking into account the nature of work, and the needs of the employee, supervisor and the City. Only employees with proven satisfactory performance in the position may be considered for teleworking opportunities. Any proposal for teleworking that is not approved may be subject to review and the reasons for denial will be provided upon request by the employee. A statement, outlining the teleworking arrangements and clear performance expectations will be discussed with and signed by the employee and supervisor. A copy of the agreement will be forwarded to the Union. All teleworkers will receive training and counseling on how to telework effectively.

(04026) The participation in this alternative work arrangement shall be limited to functions that, according to the Company, can be carried out from home. Participation shall be limited to regular employees and require the mutual consent of the volunteers and their managers.

SELECTION CRITERIA

The Company shall select participants on the basis of their seniority from qualified volunteers who meet the following selection criteria:

- Participants shall have a safe, closed room in their principal residence for their work, which meets the standards established by the Company for Teleworking.
- In order to limit operating costs, participants must have their principal residence in the same headquarters, in an adjacent headquarter or within 72 air mile km of their formal reporting center. Certain specific situations may be reviewed by the Associate Director, Industrial Relations and the National Representative of CEP.

- Participants shall have the required experience to work totally independently from their residence.

Equipment and Other Costs

The cost of supplies and equipment required by teleworking employees is usually borne by the employer. However, as illustrated in the first example below, the employee may also be responsible to provide at least some of the necessary equipment.

(04115) In each telecommuting arrangement, the supervisor and employee determine the need for telecommuting equipment. The employee normally provides all telecommuting equipment.

EXCEPTION: The Corporation will provide telecommuting equipment if justified based on the needs of the Corporation and the nature of the work assignment.

If the supervisor determines that the employee should have Corporate-owned equipment in his/her off-site location, the equipment may be provided with the Department Manager's approval. If approved, the installation, repair and maintenance of telecommuting equipment becomes the Corporation's responsibility. The supervisor tracks the equipment's use in meeting the department's specific goals.

(06755) The Corporation will provide the equipment necessary to perform the tasks identified for telecommuting. Liability for cost, maintenance or replacement of the equipment will be the Corporation's. The employee will be expected to properly handle and house the equipment. Such equipment and supplies shall remain the property of the Corporation and must be returned if the employee's employment is terminated or if the telecommuting arrangement is terminated.

The employee who works from home is responsible for providing dedicated office space with adequate office furniture for use during telecommuting days.

(04026) The Company agrees to assume all costs which it has approved and which are directly related to the equipment, terminals, furniture, and required telephone links, as well as to the installing and moving of the equipment, terminals, and furniture from or to Company premises.

The Company agrees to continue reimbursing employees for all work-related expenses, in accordance with its practices and the Collective Agreement, except expenses incurred by employees in traveling to and from their reporting center during the Teleworking period.

All teleworking participants shall inform their personal insurer that they have Company equipment and other property at their home.

Schedules

Telework clauses sometimes indicate how the hours of work will be set, and how many days per week are to be spent by the employee at the teleworkplace and at the regular office respectively. Contract language tends to leave substantial flexibility in scheduling.

(06755) Employees shall telecommute no more than three (3) days a week without mutual consent of the employee and the excluded manager. The Corporation and the employee will mutually set the hours of work.

(04026) Work hours shall be established in accordance with the Collective Agreement. To meet service requirements, split shift schedules could be established and offered to Teleworkers who volunteer. Split shift tour will be of two equal half tours during the period from 0600 to 2100 with an interval between tours not to exceed 5 hours.

During the teleworking period, employees shall work at their usual work center one day every two weeks or according to a different frequency when specific needs so warrant. If employees must return to their work center during their tour of duty for reasons beyond their control (e.g. equipment failure), the Company shall pay for their return trip by public transportation or the equivalent.

Safeguards for Teleworking Employees

Unions often insist on including a number of safeguards for participating employees when negotiating telework agreements. The most basic requirements are that teleworking must be both voluntary and cancelable. Additional measures regarding the employment status, work responsibilities and job security of telecommuting employees are also important issues normally discussed by the parties.

(06755) Telecommuting is voluntary and may be terminated with two (2) weeks' notice by either the employee who is telecommuting or the excluded manager. The parties agree that no employee shall be required to telecommute.

While involved in telecommuting, individuals continue to be employees of the Corporation and retain all rights and benefits of the Collective Agreement. Employee status, salary, benefits and job responsibilities will not change due to participation in telecommuting.

(06746) Telework shall not affect the terms and conditions of employment of any employee and the provisions of all collective agreements and relevant legislation continue to apply to an employee who teleworks.

Telework shall not affect the employment status of any employee. In other words, telework in or of itself will not prevent a person from remaining or becoming an employee.

(04026) Employee shall participate for a minimum period of six months, unless there are exceptional circumstances. In such circumstances, and after discussions between the Company and the Union, either party may end the participation of an employee by providing the other party with 14 days' notice. When an employee's participation in telework ends, the employee shall return to his regular job at his usual reporting center or, if his usual reporting center no longer exists, to the work center where his group has been relocated.

(07262) Teleworking is voluntary on the part of the employee, and is subject to mutual agreement between the employee teleworking and the City. Teleworking arrangements are subject to cancellation by the employee of the City, upon the provision of thirty (30) calendar days' written notice, or as otherwise mutually agreed upon.

Teleworking will not erode full-time positions into part-time positions, nor shall any permanent employees be laid off as the result of teleworking.

The collective agreement provisions apply to teleworkers subject to this Letter of Understanding. Hours of work for teleworkers shall be in accordance with the collective agreement.

Workload and productivity levels for teleworkers will be reasonable and comparable to office workers.

Teleworkers are entitled to access City office space, internal correspondence, job postings, and other information available to their office counterparts.

Teleworkers maintain the same employment/promotional opportunities as their office counterparts.

Management Contacting/Visiting Employee

To ensure managers and supervisors have access to telecommuting employees, employers can bargain contract language allowing for telephone contact, in-person visits and on-site inspections. In the latter case, inspections may be deemed important to make sure that equipment is functioning properly and that all safety precautions are being taken in the teleworkplace.

(07262)   During mutually agreed upon core hours, the City may access the teleworker in person, or by telephone. The City will provide the teleworker with twenty-four (24) hours' notice of a site inspection.

(04026)   Employees shall allow the support manager and project coordinator to visit their place of work so they can analyze the technical performance of systems and take any necessary corrective measures. Such visits shall be planned with employees.

The manager responsible may meet employees at their home anytime during their tour of duty. Employees shall be given reasonable prior notice (15 minutes.)

Conditions and Employee Responsibilities

Considering that employers have very limited control on the teleworkplace and that telecommuters have a great deal of autonomy from their supervisors, special conditions and requirements regarding employee responsibilities are sometimes negotiated. These conditions are normally meant to ensure employees will be able to perform adequately, while limiting employer liability in terms of occupational health and safety and other legal responsibilities.

(06746)   The employee is responsible to:

1. Ensure that the telework arrangement is consistent with all municipal or regional district bylaws and regulations;
2. In consultation with the Local Occupational Health and Safety Committee or Union and Employer designated safety representatives, ensure that the telworkplace is adequately equipped and maintained from a health and safety point of view;
3. Ensure that the equipment and supplies provided by the Employer are used only for the purpose of carrying out the Employer's work;
4. Ensure that the environment of the teleworkplace is such that the employee is able to respect the terms and conditions of employment, as well as relevant collective agreements, legislation, regulations and policies;
5. Ensure that dependent care arrangements are in place and that personal responsibilities are managed in a way that allows them to successfully meet their job responsibilities. Telework is not a substitute for dependent care.

(04026) Participant employees involved in Teleworking shall meet the performance criteria and quality standards established by the Company. These criteria and standards shall be at least those they were achieving before participating in Teleworking.

The Company's confidential documents and exclusive information shall be kept under lock and key outside work hours.

The Company's confidential documents and exclusive information that become outdated shall be returned to Bell and destroyed on Bell premises.

The telephone and computer systems may be used only by Teleworkers and strictly for their work for the Company.

Long distance calls should be kept to a strict minimum and may be made only for Company purposes.

If major problems arise which prevent Teleworkers from operating normally (network access is impossible, communication system deficient, etc.), the Company reserves the right to interrupt the employees' participation in Teleworking temporarily and to call them back to their usual place of work until everything is completely restored.

Should a failure occur at a participant's home, the participant shall be responsible for contacting his manager as quickly as possible. The participant shall not incur loss of wages due to circumstances beyond his control.

Participants shall attend meetings, training sessions and other scheduled activities. They shall be advised insofar as possible at least two days in advance. If applicable, the premium pay for change in tour of duty shall apply.

Participants shall be considered to be at work in the same way as if they were at their normal place of work. They shall therefore take all reasonable measures to ensure their safety, in accordance with Company practices.

Collective Agreement References
[In order of appearance in above material]

(01474) Pacific Press (Division of Southam Inc.) and the Communications, Energy and Paperworks Union of Canada, local 115-M (Vancouver Newspaper Guild, 1993-1998)

(07313) City of Burnaby and Burnaby Civic Employees Union (CUPE,) local 23 (1997-1999)

(04115) Manitoba Hydro-Electric Board and International Brotherhood of Electrical Workers, Local 2034 (1997-2000)

(06755) British Columbia Buildings Corporation and British Columbia Government and Service Employees' Union (1997-1999)

(04026) Bell Canada and Communications, Energy and Paperworkers Union of Canada (1998-2003)

(06746) Government of British Columbia and British Columbia Government and Service Employees' Union (1997-1999)

(07262) City of Edmonton and Civic Service Union 52 (1998-1999)

(02130) Northern Telecom Canada Ltd. And National Automobile, aerospace, Transportation and General Workers Union of Canada (CAW,) locals 1839 and 1915 (1997-2000)

NOTES

1. Established in 1983, ETUC is recognized by the European Union as the only representative cross-sector trade union organization at European level. Its 60 million members represent 78 national trade union confederations from 34 European countries, as well as 11 European industry federations.

2. Created in 1958 to promote the common professional interests of its member firms, the Union of Industrial and Employer's Confederation is comprised of 40 business federations from 27 European countries covering the continent from Ireland in the West to Turkey in the East, Iceland in the North and Malta in the South.

3. Europe's SME (small and medium-sized enterprise) employer association represents the interests of craft, trade and SME organizations in Europe. Of the 19 million enterprises in the European Union UEAPME represents more than 7 million. Across all of Europe (to include those just applying for EU membership) this non-profit organization represents 10 million SMEs with nearly 50 million employees.

4. Also referred to as Central Europe Experts Pool, CEEP dates back to 1961. Headquartered in Brussels, the association is made up of public-interest organizations, whether at the local, regional, national or European level.

5. Managerial and professional staff make up approximately 15-20% of the workforce in the various EU member states. There are 2 principal organizations that represent their interests at European level: EUROCADRES represents all those managerial and professional staff within ETUC-affiliated unions. It claims to represent 5 million professional and managerial staff in all branches of industry, public and private services and administrative departments; CEC brings together separate national bodies representing managerial and professional staff from 11 European countries.

Appendix B

Sample Telework Documents

Applications, Assessments, Guidelines, Policies, Surveys, Home Office Evaluations

FLORIDA STATE EMPLOYEE TELECOMMUTING PROGRAM TELECOMMUTING APPLICATION

Employee Name_____ Class Title:_____

Office Location_____ Home Location_____

Office Phone_____ Home Phone_____

Supervisor_____ Miles from office to home_____

1. Briefly describe your current job duties (*use additional sheets if necessary*)

2. Rate each of the following job characteristics according to your current job requirements. If there is a high requirement for this aspect of your job, then mark an **X** in **HIGH** column. If it has little importance, mark an **X** in the **LOW** column.

JOB REQUIREMENTS	HIGH	LOW
Ability to control and schedule work		
Clear and understandable work assignment objectives		
Work autonomy		
Concentration required		
PC or computer terminal work		
Amount of face-to-face contact required		
Amount of telephone communication required		
Amount of in-office reference material required		
Amount of data security required		

Note: high rating for items 1-5 and low ratings for items 6-9 indicate likelihood that the job is compatible with a telecommuting arrangement.

3. Describe how your current job duties will be adapted to telecommuting.

4. Describe how telecommuting will assist you in meeting the goals and needs of your work unit and the department and benefit the State.

5. How often would you want to telecommute? (*Please check*)

❏ About once every two weeks	❏ Three or four days a week
❏ About once every week	❏ Five days a week
❏ Two days a week	❏ Occasionally for special projects

6. What kinds of work would you expect to do while telecommuting? *(Check as many as apply and provide an approximate percent of time for each)*

check	**KIND OF WORK**	*Percent of Time*
	Writing	
	Word processing	
	Data management and computer programming	
	Reading	
	Talking on the phone	
	Sending and receiving electronic mail	
	Field visits and meetings	
	Planning and organizing	
	Administrative support work	
	Batch work	
	Evaluation, research and analysis	
	Other – *please specify*	

7. If applicable, describe the workspace in your home that you intend to dedicate to performing your work.

8. What equipment would you need to enable you to telecommute? *(Check all that apply.)*

Check	**EQUIPMENT**	Need	Currently Have
	Personal computer or laptop		
	Printer		
	Software		
	Modem		
	Additional phone line		
	Office furniture		
	Fax machine		
	Copy machine		
	SunCom phone line		
	Other – *please specify*		

9. What distractions or obligations might make it difficult to work at home? How are you planning to resolve these obstacles?

Employee's Signature_____ Date_____

Supervisor's Comments:

	Yes	No
Are the job duties to be performed conducive for telecommuting?		
Is the employee's job performance conducive for telecommuting? (*Consider the employee's work habits and past job performance*)		
Can arrangements for the equipment be made without presenting a financial hardship on the agency?		
Is the employee's home office space appropriate for performing work?		
Can a cost savings be realized from this telecommuting arrangement? (e.g. office space reduced). *Please specify.*		

❑ Approved   ❑ Denied

Approval is based on the following conditions: (cost, equipment, core hours, schedule, etc.)

_____   _____
   Supervisor's Signature   Date

Notice: a telecommuting agreement must be signed and processed before the telecommuting arrangement becomes official. The signed Agreement should be filed in the employee's personnel file.

STATE OF UTAH
DEPARTMENT OF ADMINISTRATIVE SERVICES
INFORMATION TECHNOLOGY SERVICES DIVISION
TELECOMMUTING FEASIBILITY ASSESSMENT

Employee name:

1. Why do you want to telecommute?

2. Describe briefly how you intend to accomplish the major functions of your job in a telework environment. What obstacles do you anticipate? How do you plan to overcome them?

3. What hardware platform do you anticipate using at your telework site? Current PC? Newer desktop? Notebook? Older desktop? What additional hardware?

4. What software, if any, beyond that included in the LAN group's standard platform, will you need? For what purpose?

5. What type telephone line will you need? Multiple POTS lines? ISDN line? Do you need an ISDN phone set? Why or why not?

6. What personal equipment, if any, do you plan to use? For what purpose?

7. What other facilities or accommodations will be required to facilitate your telework? What do you estimate the one-time and recurring costs will be?

8. Initially, what days and hours do you intend to work at your telework site? At your normal office location? How do you and your manager intend to negotiate changes to your schedule?

	Location	Hours
Saturday		
Sunday		
Monday		
Tuesday		
Wednesday		
Thursday		
Friday		

9. What backup and coverage issues exist? How do you propose to address them?

10. How do you intend to facilitate communication with your manager while you telecommute?

11. Where is your telework site? What is the address?

12. Describe your telework site with special attention to safety and ergonomic factors.

13. What other factors or information should be considered?

To Be Completed By Manager

Employee name:

1. What functions of this employee's job cannot be done in a telework situation? How do you plan for your group to accomplish those functions?

2. Why do you want, or not want, this employee to telecommute?

3. Are this employee's documented work habits and/or performance conducive to telework? What concerns do you have?

4. What adjustments have been made to this employee's performance plan to facilitate measurement of performance in a telework situation? What other adjustments are needed? What have you done to insure that the employee understands how performance and work product will be measured?

5. What other factors or information should be considered?

OREGON OFFICE OF ENERGY
SAMPLE TELEWORK APPLICATION

Instructions: Employee completes application and gives to supervisor. Supervisor conducts preliminary review and gives to Information Services. Information Services reviews and returns to supervisor. Supervisor meets with employee to discuss approval or denial

Employee Information:

Name _____Central office phone _____

Division _____Supervisor _____Phone _____

Proposed telework location: ❏ Home ❏ Satellite Office ❏ Telework Center

or Other (*please specify*) _____

Telework Address _____ City _____

Telework Phone _____ Fax _____ Pager_____
Telework office e-mail (*if different from central office*)_____

In addition to your supervisor and other management personnel, the following personnel would be authorized to have your telework phone number:

_____

Telework Statistics:

Proposed start date: _____Hrs. travel saved per week _____

_____×_____×_____=_____
# of round trips   miles per   miles per   gallons saved/week
/week   round trip   gallon

Telework Schedule:

Which days do you propose to telework? ❏ Mon ❏ Tues. ❏ Wed.
❏ Thurs. ❏ Fri.

Or variable/seasonal (*specify*) _____

Alternate days: ❏ Mon. ❏ Tues. ❏ Wed. ❏ Thurs. ❏ Fri.

Daily Schedule: Total hours per day_____
                       Start: _____AM/PM Finish _____AM/PM
                       Lunch_____AM/PM to _____AM/PM
Core hours you can be reached_____AM/PM to_____AM/PM

Tasks or assignments to be completed on telework days (*i.e., planning, reading, budgeting, data entry, word processing, contacting customers, analysis, preparing contracts, etc*)

Dependent Care:

Do you have dependents requiring care during telework hours? ❏ Yes ❏ No

If yes, would you have dependent care to relieve you from primary-care responsibilities during telework hours? ❏ Yes ❏ No

Accessibility Information:

How can you be contacted when you telework? ❏ Phone ❏ Voice Mail

❏ E-mail ❏ Other _____

Equipment/Services To Be Used at the Worksite:

What equipment and software do you propose to provide? (*check all that apply.*)

❏ Phone ❏ Voice mail ❏ Second phone line ❏ Office furniture

❏ Fax ❏ ISP ❏ Pager ❏ Computer type & model _____

❏ Printer type & model _____❏ Modem type & model _____

❏ Operating System _____❏ Software _____

❏ Surge protection type _____ ❏ Other _____

Remote access requested? ❏ Yes ❏ No

Applicant Acceptance of Telework Policy:

I have read the telework policy and understand the requirements and obligations I am expected to accept and meet as a teleworker:

_____   _____
                applicant's signature   date

Information Services Review:

System resources (e.g. computer equipment, software) are consistent with organization's standards: ❏ Yes ❏ No

System meets requirements for remote access: ❏ Yes ❏ No

Comments:

_____   _____
              signature   date

Supervisor Review:

Application accepted _____ Date _____

Application denied _____ Date _____
Reason for denial :

SOUTH CAROLINA STATE EMPLOYEE TELECOMMUTING GUIDELINES

Telecommuting is a work arrangement where selected state employees are allowed to perform the normal duties and responsibilities of their positions, through the use of computers or other telecommunications equipment, at home or at an alternate work location apart from the employee's usual location of work. Telecommuting may be a part time or full time arrangement; however, the employee may be expected to report to the official work location on a scheduled or an as-needed basis.

General Statements:

1. Telecommuting is a management option and not a universal employee benefit. It is the Agency's option to allow an employee to telecommute through the Agency's telecommuting policy.

2. An employee's participation in the Agency's telecommuting program is voluntary.
3. The agency head should identify a member of her staff to be the Telecommuting Coordinator.

Eligibility Requirements for Telecommuting:

1. The Agency should identify the job classes or positions with duties or portions of duties considered appropriate for telecommuting.
2. To be eligible to apply for telecommuting an employee should have completed six months of satisfactory employment with the Agency. This six-month requirement may be waived at the discretion of the Agency Head or his designee. The Agency may identify a list of skills and characteristics deemed necessary for the employee to be a successful telecommuter. Employees in a warning period of substandard performance are not eligible for telecommuting.

Application for Telecommuting:

1. An eligible employee shall complete an Application for Telecommuting and submit the request to his supervisor for review and final approval by the agency head or his designee. The Application for Telecommuting shall include the minimum requirements in the State Employee Telecommuting Guidelines.
2. Requests for telecommuting will be considered on an individual basis to determine if the employee has the necessary skills and abilities to be a telecommuter and if the duties, or a portion of the duties, of the employee's position, can be adequately performed by telecommuting. Telecommuting is not considered a substitute for child or elder care.
3. The Agency must approve the request prior to the employee beginning to telecommute. Upon approval, the employee agrees to follow all requirements of the Agency's Telecommuting Policy and any additional requirements agreed upon by the Agency and employee.

Conditions of Employment:

1. The employee's duties, responsibilities, and conditions of employment remain the same as if the employee were working at the Agency's official work location. The employee will continue to comply with Federal, State and Agency laws, policies, and regulations while working at the remote location.

2. Telecommuting will not adversely affect an employee's eligibility for advancement or any other employee right or benefit. The employee will be compensated for all pay, leave, overtime, and travel entitlement as if all duties were being performed at the employee's usual work location.

3. Work hours, overtime compensation (for non-exempt employees), compensatory time, and leave benefits will not change as a result of telecommuting. Requests to work overtime or use sick, annual or other leave must be approved by the Agency in the same manner as when the employee was working at the employee's usual work location. An employee shall not work overtime unless authorized in advance by the Agency or as otherwise authorized by the Agency's overtime policy.

4. The employee agrees to designate a separate work space in the remote site for the purposes of telecommuting and will maintain this area in a safe condition, free from hazards and other dangers to the employee and the Agency's equipment. To ensure the safety of the workspace, the employee agrees to complete and return to the Agency a Telecommuting Work Space Checklist, which will certify the employee's alternate workspace complies with health and safety requirements. The employee must submit this checklist to the Agency before she may begin to telecommute. The employee agrees that the Agency shall have reasonable access to the workspace for the purposes of inspection of the site and retrieval of Agency-owned property.

5. The alternate work location is considered an extension of the employee's usual work location; therefore, workers' compensation will continue to exist for the employee when performing official work duties in the defined workspace during approved telecommuting hours. Any work-related injuries must be reported to the employee's supervisor immediately.

6. The Agency may provide all or part of the equipment necessary for accomplishing work assignments.

7. The Agency will cover the cost of installation, repair, or maintenance of State-owned equipment at the alternate work location; however, the Agency typically should not cover the cost of repair or maintenance of the employee's personal equipment.

8. The Agency's security controls and conditions for use of the State-owned equipment for the official work location will also apply to alternate work locations. All official Agency records, files and documents must be protected from unauthorized disclosure or damage and returned safely to the official work location. The employee will return all Agency equipment, files, and documents to the Agency immediately upon termination of telecommuting or of the employee's employment.

9. No employee engaged in telecommuting will be allowed to conduct face-to-face, agency-related business at his home office. An employee understands that she will be liable for injuries or damages to the person or property of third parties or any members of the employee's family in the alternate work location.

Termination of Employment:

The agency may terminate the telecommuting arrangement at any time with or without cause, and this determination is final in terms of administrative review.

Reporting Requirements:

The Agency will provide an annual report to the Office of Human Resources on the Agency's utilization of telecommuting

HR.COM
TELECOMMUTING POLICY (TEMPLATE)

Policy:	Telecommuting
Policy number:	(*insert number*)
Effective date:	(*insert date*)
Pertains to:	all regular full time employees

This company is committed to being flexible to the personal circumstances and preferences of their employees.

Telecommuting schedules must be arranged with the employee's immediate supervisor. Approval for these schedules is at the discretion of the supervisor as it is not possible for all positions to be removed from the regular working environment. Any employee working from home is asked to schedule their day according to regular working hours in order to be accessible to fellow workers and company clients. This includes checking in with the office regularly and keeping your supervisor informed of your working hours and location as well as your status on assignments and projects.

Employees are required to be present for all departmental meetings and to be in the office a minimum of (*insert number of days*) per (*week or month*). Being present in the regular work environment creates consistency and communication among the team.

Any employee found to be abusing the telecommuting privilege will be disciplined up to and including dismissal.

SOUTH CAROLINA STATE EMPLOYEE TELECOMMUTING SAMPLE POLICY

The purpose of this sample policy is to provide a general framework for telecommuting in State agencies. It does not attempt to address the special conditions and needs of all individual agencies. When developing a telecommuting policy, an agency should consult with its legal counsel to determine if the language meets the agency's specific needs.

The language used in this policy does not create an employment contract between the employee and the agency. The agency reserves the right to revise the contents of this policy, in whole or in part.

Section A: General

South Carolina State Government supports State agencies that use alternative work arrangements, including telecommuting, that result in greater efficiency and cost savings to the State. Telecommuting is a workplace option that allows work to be done at an alternative workspace. As defined by this policy, there are varying levels of telecommuting, including employees:

- Working from an alternate work space (e.g., regional service center, district office, employee's home) for one to four days a week
- Extending the workday through remote access from the alternate workspace or on the road
- Using remote access occasionally during the workday when out of the office or traveling
- Working in the field with no daily office work
- Working from an alternate work space, for a few hours a month, a few hours a day, or more often
- Providing remote technical support services during a weekend to fix the network versus having to drive in from home (e.g., information technology staff) and
- Working from home when an employee is temporarily or permanently homebound (e.g., an employee recovering from illness or surgery or for a reasonable accommodation for an employee with a disability)

Telecommuting provides employees the opportunity to increase productivity, especially for those employees whose jobs include frequent travel or jobs which have defined tasks with clearly measurable results. Telecommuting is not considered a substitute for child or elder care. It is the policy of South Carolina State Government to encourage and promote the use of telecommuting work options. This policy recognizes the societal, management, and personal benefits available through a carefully planned and managed telecommuting program.

Section B: Authority

The agency director has the authority to establish a telecommuting program within the agency based on Proviso 72/73 of the 2000-2001 Appropriation Act and the South Carolina State Employee Telecommuting Guidelines established by the South Carolina Budget and Control Board. Each agency director or her designee has the ability to set the work schedule and work location for agency employees. Each telecommuting program should be implemented following the South Carolina State Employee Telecommuting Guidelines and all other appropriate Federal, State, and agency laws, regulations, and policies.

Telecommuting is a management option and not a universal employee benefit. It is the agency's option to allow an employee to telecommute.

Section C: Telecommuting Coordinator

The agency director or his designee shall identify an employee to be responsible for the day-to-day coordination and management of the agency's telecommuting program. The Telecommuting Coordinator will oversee the telecommuting program. This program will include training for employees and supervisors and will ensure compliance with laws, policies, procedures, and guidelines.

Section D: Training

All prospective telecommuters and supervisors should be educated on remote electronic access techniques, South Carolina State Employee Telecommuting Guidelines, and the agency's Telecommuting Policy before they become involved in telecommuting.

Section E: Selection of Job Classes and Positions

The agency shall identify and maintain a current list of the job classifications and positions that the agency considers appropriate for telecommuting. These job classifications and positions should include tasks that are amenable in whole or in part to being performed away from the official work location.

Section F: Employee Eligibility

To be eligible to apply for telecommuting, an employee must have completed six months of satisfactory employment with the agency. This six-month requirement may be waived at the discretion of the agency head or his designee. The agency may identify a list of skills and characteristics deemed necessary for the employee to be a successful telecommuter and may require the employee to meet these standards. An employee in a warning period of substandard performance is not eligible to telecommute.

Section G: Application and Employee Selection

Participation in telecommuting should be based on the ability of the employee to perform tasks that can be completed from an alternate workspace, such as a home office, and management's assessment of the employee's ability to complete these tasks satisfactorily. An employee shall complete an Application for Telecommuting and submit the request to his supervisor for review with final approval given by the agency director or his designee. The Application for Telecommuting will be consistent with all South Carolina State Employee Telecommuting Guidelines and agency requirements for telecommuting.

The agency director or his designee will establish employee selection criteria and select employees. Selection of employees shall not be arbitrary or based on seniority, but shall be based on specific, work related criteria established by management. Potential telecommuters must be screened carefully and shown to have the characteristics necessary to be a successful telecommuter. These characteristics include, but are not limited to, high motivation, self-discipline, and excellent communication skills. The agency should avoid considering for a telecommuting program an employee with chronic attendance or tardiness problems, the inability to stay organized or focused, poor performance, or the failure to keep others informed of her whereabouts. The agency director or his designee must approve the request prior to the employee beginning to telecommute.

Section H: Telecommuting Employee's Conditions of Employment

The employee's duties, responsibilities, and conditions of employment remain the same as if the employee were working at the employee's official work location. The employee will continue to comply with all Federal, State, and agency laws, policies, and regulations while working at the alternate workspace. Telecommuting will not adversely affect an employee's eligibility for advancement or any other employee right or benefit. An employee will be compensated for all pay, leave, overtime and travel entitlement as if all duties were being performed at the employee's usual work location.

Section I: Hours of Work, Overtime Hours and Time Reporting

Work hours, overtime compensation (for non-exempt employees), or compensatory time, and leave benefits will not change as a result of telecommuting. Requests to work overtime or use sick, annual or other leave must be approved by the agency in the same manner as when the employee works at the employee's usual work location. An employee shall not work overtime unless authorized in advance by the agency or as otherwise authorized by the agency's overtime policy.

Telecommuters need regular contact with supervisors and co-workers and access to specialized files or equipment. In addition, the supervisor must take action to prevent the telecommuter from becoming isolated from office staff. Therefore, management should ensure regular communication through weekly or monthly meetings, teleconferencing, or in-office days. Office needs will take precedence over telecommute days. An employee must forgo telecommuting if needed in the official work location on a regularly scheduled telecommuting day. The agency may require that the employee attend certain called meetings throughout the workweek. The manager or supervisor should provide reasonable notice whenever necessary. However, the employee may be required to report to the official work location without advance notice, as needed.

Section J: Designating the Alternate Work Space

The employee agrees to designate a separate workspace in the remote site for the purposes of telecommuting and will maintain this area in a safe condition, free from hazards and other dangers to the employee and the agency's equipment. To ensure the safety of the alternate workspace, the employee agrees to complete and return to the agency a Telecommuting Work Space Checklist, which will certify the employee's designated alternate workspace complies with health and safety requirements. The employee must submit this checklist to the agency before he may begin to telecommute. The employee agrees that the agency shall have reasonable access to the designated alternate workspace for the purposes of inspection of the space and retrieval of agency-owner property.

Section K: Workers' Compensation

The approved alternate workspace is considered an extension of the employee's official work location; therefore, workers' compensation will continue to exist for the employee when performing official work duties in the defined alternate workspace during approved telecommuting hours. Any work-related injuries must be reported to the employee's supervisor immediately, and the employee must complete all necessary or management-requested documents regarding the injury.

Section L: Security of State-Owned Equipment and Documents

The agency must establish security controls and conditions for use of the agency equipment. All official agency records, files and documents must be protected from unauthorized disclosure or damage and returned safely to the official work location. The employee will return all agency equipment, files and documents to the agency within a designated timeframe upon termination of telecommuting or of the employee's employment.

Section M: State-Owned Equipment

Support, maintenance, repair and replacement of State-owned equipment issued to telecommuters are the responsibility of the agency. In the event of equipment malfunction, the telecommuter must notify his supervisor immediately. If repairs will take some time, the telecommuter may be asked to report to the official work location until the equipment is usable.

Section N: Employee-Owned Equipment

Use of an employee-owned computer is the decision of the telecommuter with the understanding that on-site or telephonic support will be provided from any agency resource. Additionally, the purchase of appropriate software and installation and configuration are the responsibility of the telecommuter. All support will be the responsibility of the telecommuter. Configuration, maintenance and repairs to personally owned equipment would be the responsibility of the employee.

Section O: Termination of Participation

An employee's participation in the agency's telecommuting program is voluntary. The agency or employee may terminate the telecommuting arrangement at any time with or without cause, and termination is final in terms of administrative review. If the employee unreasonably terminates the telecommuting agreement, the agency may require her to reimburse any expenses that the agency has contributed to establish the alternate workspace.

Section P: Assessment and Evaluation

The agency will provide an annual report to the Budget and Control Board's Office of Human Resources. A telecommuting employee and his supervisor will be required to provide information to assess and evaluate the success of the telecommuting arrangement.

TOOL BOX OPTIONS

Test Period

At the end of this time, the employee and supervisor will evaluate the success of the telecommuting arrangement. The supervisor will make a recommendation to the agency head or her designee to continue, modify or terminate the telecommuting arrangement.

Scheduling

When applicable, the agency must approve an established schedule for an employee's work hours. Any deviation from this approved schedule must be approved in advance. The agency must be able to contact the employee at all times during scheduled work hours.

Office Inspections

The agency reserves the right to inspect the designated alternate workspace to insure that all safety requirements are met.

Business Telephone Access

If appropriate and necessary for the employee's job duties, the agency will arrange for the installation of a business telephone line or a dedicated data circuit at the alternate workspace. These lines are to be used solely for conducting agency business.

The employee understands that the agency will not reimburse the cost of home-related expenses, including but not limited to heat, water, electricity and insurance.

Computer Responsibilities

The employee agrees to abide by any rules promulgated by the agency concerning the use of computer equipment (including protecting the employee's home personal computer against computer viruses) and understands that these rules may be changed at any time. The employee agrees to follow the agency's procedures for network access and to take all necessary steps to protect the integrity of systems including but not limited to:

1. Not making passwords available to anyone else, not allowing others to see passwords when the employee is working, and not posting passwords where others can see them; and
2. Software used at the remote work site must be approved by the manager before installation. The agency owned software may not be duplicated.

By order of the Secretary of the Air Force   Air Force Instruction 36-8002
                                                                        1 July 1998
                                                                        Personnel

TELECOMMUTING GUIDELINES FOR AIR FORCE RESERVISTS AND THEIR SUPERVISORS

Compliance with this publication is mandatory

Notice: this publication is available digitally on the SAF/AAD www site at http://afpubs/hq.af.mil (*authors' note: some portions of this document, such as military addresses, jargon and other materials not deemed of assistance to our book's readers have been omitted.*)

OPR: HQ ARPC/XP   Certified by: HQ USAF/RE
Supersedes AF1 36-8002, 1 June 1998

This publication establishes the recommended guidelines that implement telecommuting for Reservists. Air Force Policy Directive, *Reserve Training and Education* and Air Force manual, *Reserve Personnel Participation and Training Procedures*, are the official publications for managing the Reserve participation program. Telecommuting is authorized as a method of participation by AFMAN 36-8001. This publication applies to the members of the Air Force Reserve, to include the Individual Mobilization Augmentees (IMAs), unit reservists and participating individual Ready Reserve (IRR) personnel. This publication does not apply to the Air National Guard (ANG).

In the event of conflict with Air Force or major command regulations, the applicable regulation will take precedence over this instruction.

SECTION A—GENERAL INFORMATION

- **Background**
  1. Telecommuting is a management tool that allows the United States Air Force to authorize Reservists to work away from their official duty location. Telecommuting is a complementary way of doing business, which moves work to the people instead of moving the people to the work. In general, it means working from an alternate work location away from the official duty location. The most common technologies used for telecommuting are the telephone, facsimile, computer and modem.
  2. The approval authority should grant telecommuting only when it is in the best interest of the Air Force. Telecommuting is a privilege and not a right for the Reservist. Do not authorize travel in connection with this type of duty.
  3. This instruction recommends that participants use a pre-authorized work agreement for accountability.

- **Definition**

  Telecommuting is a management tool. It allows written pre-authorization by Reserve unit commanders or IMA program managers (or their written designees) to allow Reservists to work in an official capacity for pay and/or points away from the official duty location in either active duty (AD) or inactive duty (IDT) status. The alternate work locations must have the necessary tools and environment to enable Reservists to accomplish assigned duties. All data, documents, or products developed are the sole property of the US Government and will be prepared for filing in accordance with command guidance if it is to be a permanent record.

- **Percentage of Training Use**

  The approval authority and the supervisor determine the percentage of telecommuting work for an individual Reservist. Under no circumstances should a Reservist perform all their duty by telecommuting. It is the intent that every Reservist participates in a military environment by performing duty in uniform at their official duty location.

- **Rules and Responsibilities**
  1. The IMA program manager or the NAF/wing/group commander (or their designees) are approval authorities for telecommuting and work agreements.

2. The immediate active duty or Reserve supervisor is responsible for:
   i. Recommending the telecommuting project to the approval authority
   ii. Preparing required documentation and obtaining any necessary signatures from the telecommuter
   iii. Ensuring project details (e.g., scope of work, deliverables, etc.) are mutually agreed upon before beginning work
   iv. Quality control of the telecommuter's completed product
   v. Maintaining the original approved work agreement, and giving a copy to the Reservist
3. The commander is responsible for approving the use of Government owned equipment and related supplies for use by the telecommuter. The decision to use appropriated funds to pay for equipment, services or supplies for the purposes of telecommuting, rests solely with the commander.

- **Dual Compensation for Federal Employees**

  1. Many reservists also hold separate positions as federal civilian employees. After civilian duty hours, telecommuting as a Reservist to perform IDT should ordinarily be compatible with such employment. However, performing consecutive days of AD, even if such duty transpires after the completion of the civilian workday, will result in a full workday's charge to leave from the federal civilian position.
  2. Military leave, annual leave, leave without pay, accrued compensatory time off, or accrued credit hours may be used to cover the civilian work hour.

- **Safety**

Telecommuters are responsible for ensuring that alternate work locations are safe environments. The Reservist will report any injuries while telecommuting to their supervisor as soon as possible. The supervisor will follow Line of Duty reporting procedures for accidents or injuries.

- **General Obligations**

  1. Reservists are subject to the Uniform Code of Military Justice (UCMJ) while telecommuting. The period of military jurisdiction coincides with the duty hours specified in applicable active duty orders, or the inactive duty hours reflected on the AF Form, *Record of Individual Inactive Duty Training.*

2. Reservists are responsible for providing telecommuting equipment requirements to the supervisor.
3. Reservists should obtain the approval authority's concurrence before performing telecommuting that exceeds the agreed hours.
4. The approval authority, supervisor, or Reservist may terminate participation in telecommuting at any time.
5. Members should not use telecommuting for training purposes.

- **Funding**

1.The approval authority will not authorize travel or per diem for telecommuting.
2.Before beginning a project, approval authorities may authorize reimbursement for incidental and minor out-of-pocket expenses (e.g., postage, long distance telephone calls, consumable supplies). They should include a statement in the telecommuting work agreement allowing the Reservist to use the Standard Form, *Claim for Reimbursement for Expenditures on Official Business*. The normal procedures and dollar limits apply.

- **Agreement**

1. The Reservist and supervisor should sign a work agreement before starting the telecommuting project specifying all terms for the project and before receiving approval authority's signature.
2. The approval authority may authorize a general agreement for the performance of telecommuting projects in four (4) hour increments. However, before each project, the approval authority should document specified project details (e.g., scope of work, deliverables, project completion times, type of participation, resource requirements, reimbursable expenses, and progress report requirements.)
   i. The approval authority should require the Reservist to sign a separate assignment report, or an addendum to the work agreement, acknowledging receipt and understanding of project details.
   ii. The approval authority should give a copy of the work agreement, with any addendum or assignment reports, to the Reservist and supervisor.
   iii.Approval authorities should maintain and dispose of this agreement according to AFMAN *Records Dispositions Schedule*.

SECTION B—EQUIPMENT

- **Government Equipment**

  1. Subject to prescribed rules and limitations, a commander may place government-owned computers, computer software, and telecommunications equipment (hereafter referred to as equipment) in alternative work locations.
  2. The commander or designated representative retains ownership and control of all hardware, software and data associated with, or generated by, government-owned systems. The commander must account for equipment on a hand receipt and inventory annually. The commander must notify the Equipment Control Officer (ECO) of the relocation of the equipment.
  3. Government equipment is **For Official Use Only** (FOUO). Commanders may authorize installation, repair, and/or maintenance of equipment at their discretion and direction. The equipment is for authorized use by the Reservist only.
  4. The Reservist agrees to protect any government-owned equipment from damage, loss, theft and infection with computer viruses.
  5. Before Reservists install any hardware or software on a government system, they must have the permission of the unit designated approval authority (DAA) (commander or designee).
  6. Reservists must follow Report of Survey procedures for damaged, lost or stolen government equipment.
  7. Government information must be protected from modification, destruction, or inappropriate release.

- **Privately Owned Equipment**

  1. Reservists may use privately owned equipment for telecommuting purposes.
  2. Reservists must agree to install, service and maintain (at their own risk and expense) any privately owned equipment.
  3. The government does not incur any liability or assume costs resulting from the use, misuse, loss, theft or destruction (to include computer viruses) of privately owned computer equipment resources.
  4. Government information must be protected from modification, destruction, or inappropriate release.
  5. When using privately owned computer equipment, the member will store all government data on appropriately marked removable media.

6. *Private equipment may not be used to access or view classified material or privacy act data.*

- **Equipment-Related Funding**

  1. Commanders must consider the cost of providing necessary communications and computer systems services before allowing personnel to work from an alternate work location. The commander authorizing the alternate work location must:
     i. Determine the service is necessary for direct support of the agency's mission;
     ii. Fund for necessary equipment, software, LAN access, and phone lines necessary to support the mission;
     iii. Make sure the alternate work location is an economical option to having the individual work in the office;
     iv. Authorize payment for installation and monthly recurring charges;
     v. Certify that adequate monitoring capabilities and safeguards against private misuse exist.
  2. Reservists should use base 800 numbers for remote network access and long distance phone calls, if available.

- **Equipment Obligations**

  1. Reservists using privately owned equipment must sign an agreement outlining the required equipment, software, hardware, data and telecommunication services.
  2. Reservists must ensure that software use conforms to copyright laws and any contractual agreements.
  3. If telecommuting requirements terminate, the Reservist must immediately return government owned hardware, software, data, and cancel all telecommunication services that the government provided.

- **Security**

  1. Reservists must comply with all government security procedures and ensure security measures are in place to protect equipment and data from physical and virus damage, theft, loss or access by unauthorized individuals.
  2. Access to sensitive (e.g. Privacy Act, FOUO material, and classified) documents, data, records, etc. on government equipment must be consistent with Department of Defense (DoD), Air Force and MAJCOM directives and instructions. *Private equip-*

ment may not be used to access or view classified material or privacy act data.

SECTION C—ACCOUNTABILITY

- **Documentation**

  1. The approval authority should sign the work agreement as the approval documentation before the Reservist starts the telecommuting project.
  2. The approval authority documents approval by signing Block III of the Air Force Form *Record of Individual Inactive Duty Training*, Attachment 1, or Section III of the Air Force Form *Application for Active Duty Training*, Attachment 2.
     i. Supervisors should annotate in the remarks section of either form:
        a. Number of anticipated hours of work for the telecommuting project;
        b. The specified time period for the project;
        c. The statement "training to be accomplished by telecommuting." This statement will also be reflected on the order.
     ii. The supervisor must sign Block III of the Air Force Form before starting the telecommuting project, when the Reservist is requesting Inactive duty training.
  3. Upon project completion, the Reservist verifies the project time. The certifying authority indicates agreement by signing Block IV of the AF Form *Request and Authorization for Active Duty Training/Active Duty Tour*.

OREGON OFFICE OF ENERGY
SAMPLE TELEWORKER SELF-ASSESSMENT

A successful teleworker has particular traits, a job suitable for telework and a telework office that's conducive to work. Read each of the numbered sections below, and check the box that most accurately describe you or your situation. Your self-assessment will help you decide whether telework is right for you. See the bottom of page 3 for help in evaluating your self-assessment.

1. Successful teleworkers develop regular routines and are able to set and meet their own deadlines. Are you self-motivated, self-disciplined and able to work independently; can you complete projects on time with minimal supervision and feedback; and are you

productive when no one is checking on you or watching you work?

❏ Always ❏ Usually ❏ Sometimes ❏ Not really

2. Do you have strong organizational and time-management skills; are you results-oriented; will you remain focused on your work while at home, and not be distracted by television, housework or visiting neighbors; do you manage your time and workload well, solve many of your own problems and find satisfaction in completing tasks on your own; are you comfortable setting priorities and deadlines; and do you keep your sights on results?

❏ Always ❏ Usually ❏ Sometimes ❏ Not really

3. Are you comfortable working alone and disciplined enough to leave work at quitting time; can you adjust to the relative isolation of working at home; will you miss the social interaction at the central office on your telework days; do you have the self-control to work neither too much nor too little; can you set a comfortable and productive pace while working at home?

❏ Yes ❏ No

4. Teleworkers should have a good understanding of the organization's 'culture.' Are you knowledgeable about your organization's procedures and policies; have you been on the job long enough to know how to do your job in accordance with your organization's procedures and policies; do you have well-established work, communication and social patterns at the central office?

❏ Yes ❏ No

5. Have you and your supervisor discussed whether co-workers would have additional work when you work at home, and, if so, how the work would be handled; have you determined how to provide support to co-workers while working at home; do you have an effective working relationship with co-workers; and have you evaluated the effects of your telework days and those of your co-workers in maintaining adequate in-office communication?

❏ Yes ❏ No

6. Are you adaptable to changing routines and environments; have you demonstrated an ability to be flexible about work routines and environments; and are you willing to come into the central office on a regularly scheduled telework day if your supervisor, co-workers or customers need you there?

❏ Yes ❏ No

7. Are you an effective communicator and team player; do you communicate well with your supervisor and co-workers; are you able to express needs objectively and develop solutions; and have you developed ways to communicate regularly with your supervisor and co-workers that you can use when you telework?

❏ Yes ❏ No

8. Current job performance is a strong indicator of your potential success as a teleworker. Consider how any problems or developmental needs evident in your last performance evaluation might affect your telework experience. Are you successful in your current position; do you know your job well; and do you have a track record of performance?

❏ Yes ❏ No

9. Do you have the right job for telework? (*check those that apply.*)

   ❏ Job responsibilities that can be arranged so that there is no difference in the level of service provided to the customer
   ❏ Minimal requirements for special equipment
   ❏ Ability to define tasks and work products with measurable work activities and objectives
   ❏ Ability to control and schedule work flow
   ❏ Tasks that include those that could be done away from the central office such as analysis, auditing reports, batch work, calculating, data entry, design work, dictating, drafting, editing, evaluations, field visits, graphics, project management, reading, record keeping, research, telephoning, word processing and writing, etc.

10. Do you have an appropriate home work environment? (*Check those that apply.*)

❏ A safe, comfortable work space where it is easy to concentrate on work
❏ The level of security required by the agency
❏ The necessary office equipment and software that meet agency standards
❏ A telephone, with a separate home office line if required, and an answering machine or voice mail
❏ Household members who will understand you're working and won't disturb you

Are you the right kind of worker? *If your answers to Questions 1-8 are 'always' or 'yes", you're the kind of employee likely to be successful at telework.*

Do you have the right kind of job? You should be able to check every item under question 9.

Do you have the right kind of home environment? You should be able to check every item under Question 10.

STATE OF ARIZONA
TELEWORK PROGRAM EVALUATION

Teleworker Survey

Name _____

Time in current position   ❏ Under 1 yr. ❏ 1-5 yrs. ❏ over 5 yrs.

Your Telework Days   ❏ Mon. ❏ Tues. ❏ Wed. ❏ Thurs.   ❏ Fri.

Message Retrieval   ❏ I call in ❏ Office calls me ❏ Call forwarding
                         ❏ Voice mail ❏ E-mail

Has telework resulted in any changes in your work style?

How could the telework program be improved?

Please indicate with an X whether the fact you are teleworking has had a positive or negative effect on each item listed below (one being most positive, 10 being most negative.) Check only one number per line.

	1	2	3	4	5	6	7	8	9	10
Your relationship with co-workers										
Your co-workers' workload/job content										
Your work unit's performance										
Communications within your work unit										
Overall effect on your work unit										
Relationship with your supervisor										
Communications with your supervisor										
Your supervisor's workload										
Your supervisor's ability to monitor and evaluate your performance										
Establishing expectations and deadlines										
Your job performance										
The content of your job										
Interactions with other work units										
Your personal job satisfaction										

Do you want to continue to telework? ❑ Yes ❑ No

CO-WORKER SURVEY

Name _____

Has telework resulted in any changes in your work style?

How could the telework program be improved?

Please indicate with an X whether Teleworking in your work unit has had a positive or negative effect on each item listed below, 1 being the most positive, 10 being the most negative. Check only one number per line.

	1	2	3	4	5	6	7	8	9	10
Your relationship with teleworkers										
Your personal workload/job content										
Your work unit's performance										
Communication within your work unit										
Overall effect on your work unit										
Your communications with teleworkers										
Your supervisor's workload										
Your supervisor's ability to monitor & evaluate your employee performance										
Interactions with other work units										

Do you want to see telework continue in your work unit? ❏ Yes ❏ No

Would you be interested in Teleworking?   ❏ Yes ❏ No

Manager/Supervisor Survey

Manager/Supervisor _____ Teleworker _____

Was anyone in your work unit rejected for telework? ❏ Yes ❏ No

If YES, explain situation and negative consequences.

Reason for telework   ❏ Regular   ❏ Medical
Has telework resulted in any changes in your work style?

How could the telework program be improved?

Please indicate with an x whether the Teleworking in your unit has had a positive or negative effect on each item listed below, 1 being the most positive, 10 being the most negative. Check only one number per line.

	1	2	3	4	5	6	7	8	9	10
Relationship between teleworkers and her co-workers										
Co-workers workload/job content										
Your work unit's performance										
Communications within your work unit										
Overall effect on your work unit										
Relationship between you and teleworker										
Communications with the teleworker										
Your workload										
Your ability to monitor & evaluate teleworker's performance										
Establishing expectations and deadlines										
Teleworker's job performance										
Teleworker's workload/job content										
Teleworker's interactions with other work units										
Teleworker's job satisfaction										

Do you want this employee to continue to telework? ❑ Yes   ❑ No

STATE OF COLORADO
CO-WORKER SURVEY
[TELEWORK EVALUATION BY
NON-TELEWORKERS]

Indicate if you agree with the following statements.

	Strongly agree	Agree	Neutral	Disagree	Strongly disagree	N/A
I have had to schedule, plan or organize my work differently because co-workers telecommute						
Communication is more difficult on days when co-workers telecommute						
Work interruptions or distractions increased on days when co-workers telecommute						
My workload has not increased as a result of my co-workers telecommuting.						

I have learned new skills as a result of my co-workers telecommuting						
Since telework began, there is less competition for office resources – (printer, fax, copier, etc.)						
I think some people take advantage of telework to work less.						
Telework is having a positive impact on the work group as a whole.						
Management is supportive of telework.						
I believe that telework is good for the firm.						
Overall, the advantages of telework outweigh the disadvantages.						
I want telecommuting to continue in the firm.						
Given the opportunity, I would telecommute.						

ADDITIONAL COMMENTS:

STATE OF COLORADO
SUPERVISOR EVALUATION

This form is to be used 6–12 months after telecommuting begins. If your employee has stopped telecommuting, please complete the survey based on your experience while the employee was telecommuting.

Section A: About Your Organization
How is the equipment and software for telecommuting to be paid for?
Please check all that apply:

- ❑ Out of my normal budget
- ❑ Out of an increase in my budget
- ❑ Out of other budgets in the organization
- ❑ Loaned equipment
- ❑ Varies for each employee
- ❑ No new equipment will be required
- ❑ Surplus equipment in the organization
- ❑ No equipment/software will be provided
- ❑ Other. Please specify _____

Indicate whether you agree with the following statements:

	Strongly agree	Agree	Neutral	Disagree	Strongly disagree	N/A
Upper management is support of telecommuting						
My organization gives me a lot of flexibility in rewarding employees						
I had sufficient influence on who was chosen to telecommute.						
Having employees telework was/will be troublesome for me.						
When teleworking my staff is able to concentrate more on work.						
My organization is reluctant to try out new things.						
Telecommuting improves my firm's ability to retain competent staff.						
I am supportive of my employees' telecommuting.						
When telework began, work group communication was more difficult.						

Because of telework communications in my work group continues to be more difficult.						
I am concerned that my teleworker is less integrated with his/her work group as a result of teleworking.						

Indicate whether you agree with the following statements:

	Strongly agree	Agree	Neutral	Disagree	Strongly disagree	N/A
Handling confidential information is problematic when people telecommute.						
Telecommuting allows people the flexibility to work during their most productive hours.						
It is difficult for telecommuters to supervise other people.						
I let my workers decide how to complete the projects I assign them.						
I think some people take advantage of telework to work less.						

How interested are you in seeing telecommuting continue?

❑ Very interested
❑ Interested
❑ Neutral
❑ Not very interested
❑ Not at all interested

How important are the following methods of communication for successful telework?

	Extremely important	Important	Not important
E-mail			
Voice mail			
Fax machine			

	Strongly agree	Agree	Neutral	Disagree	Strongly disagree	N/A
Employees in our firm are more self-reliant because some are telecommuting.						

It is more difficult to measure the productivity of tele- commuters when they are not in the office than when they are.					
Telecommuters are not around when I need them.					
The right person could telework regardless or her or his job duties.					
It takes a lot of my time to supervise a teleworker.					
Non-teleworkers have been envious of their co-workers who telecommute.					
Telecommuting enhances the job satisfaction of the teleworkers I supervise.					
Overall, the advantages of telecommuting outweigh the advantages.					

What did you feel were the most successful aspects of telecommuting?

What did you feel were the least successful aspects of telecommuting?

What was the most difficult challenge you faced as a supervisor of a telecommuter, and how did you deal with it?

How has telecommuting affected your organization?

Section B: Identifying Telecommuters

How many employees do you supervise directly?

_____ full time

_____ part time

List the names, job titles, and number of telecommuting days per month of all employees you supervise that telecommute.

NAME	JOB TITLE	DAYS

Section C: Job Performance

Fill out a copy of this section for each telecommuter you supervise.

Telecommuter's name _____

How often, approximately, do you currently communicate with your teleworkers?

	At least once/day	2-4 times a wk.	Once a week	Once a month	Less than once a month	N/A
In person- meeting scheduled						
In person- meeting informally						
Formal memos						
Telephone calls						
Faxes or e-mails						
Notes						

Indicate whether you agree with the following statements:

	Strongly agree	Agree	Neutral	Disagree	Strongly disagree	N/A
I closely monitor how this employee uses his/her time						
This employee works best when there is a deadline						
This employee is highly motivated						
This employee's job description fits very well with telework						
Teleworking makes work harder for this employee's coworkers						

Rate this employee's job performance in the following areas:

	Excellent	Very Good	Good	Meets minimum requirements	Needs improvement
Productivity					
Interpersonal skills					
Dependability					
Communication					
Ability to work independently					
Overall performance					

How often, approximately, does this person's job currently require access to resources that are available only at the central office?

	At least once a day	2-4 times a week	Once a week	Once a month	Less than once/month	N/A
Central paper files						
Computers						
Electronic data bases						
Software						
Equipment (copier, fax)						
Professional staff						
Support staff						

Section D: Your Experience with Telecommuting

How interested are you in having your employees continue telecommuting?

❏ Very interested
❏ Interested
❏ Neutral
❏ Not very interested
❏ Not at all interested

How important are the following methods of communication for successful telecommuting?

	Very important	Important	Not important
E-mail			
Voice mail			
Fax machine			

As a **result of telecommuting**, have your employee's work skills changed in any of the following areas?

	Improved greatly	Improved somewhat	No change	Declined somewhat	Declined greatly
Productivity					
Interpersonal skills					
Dependability					

Communication					
Ability to work independently					
Overall performance					
Project management					
Personal time management					
Supervisory skills					
Computer skills					

Please explain:

In general, did you have any problem *obtaining equipment* needed for telework?

❏ No
❏ Yes

If yes, check the statements that apply:

❏ It was difficult for my office to get the funds to buy equipment.
❏ It was difficult finding someone to loan my employee the equipment.
❏ We had problems getting equipment delivered and set up on time.
❏ Other. Please explain.

Please describe any significant change in your work group due to telecommuting.

Has your experience with telecommuting been more or less successful than you anticipated?

    ❏ Much more successful
    ❏ More successful
    ❏ About what I expected
    ❏ Less successful
    ❏ Much less successful

As a result of telecommuting, has there been any change in the workload of the non-telecommuters in the following categories?

	Much more	More	No change	Less	Much less
Management					
Professional Staff					
Support Staff					

In what ways could telecommuting be improved in your organization?

STATE OF COLORADO
TELECOMMUTER SURVEY—AFTER

This form is to be used 6-12 months after telecommuting beings. If you have stopped teleworking, please complete the survey on your experience while you were telecommuting.

Section A: About Your Needs on the Job

How often, approximately, does your job currently require physical access to resources that are available only at the central office?

	At least once a day	2-4 times per week	Once a week	Once a month	Less than once a mo.	Not applicable
Central paper files						
Computers						
Electronic data bases						
Software						
Equipment- (copier,fax)						
Support staff						
Professional staff						

Indicate the importance of each item listed in performing your job effectively:

	Very important	Important	Not important	Not applicable
PC or laptop				
Mainframe computer				
Telephone line for modem				
Fax machine				
Voice mail or answering machine				
Photocopier				

Indicate which equipment you need at home on telecommuting days:

❏ Computer
❏ Software used at central office
❏ Modem
❏ Second telephone line (voice or modem)
❏ Call waiting
❏ Voice mail
❏ Answering machine
❏ Printer
❏ Fax machine
❏ Other. Please list.

Section B. About Your Organization and Co-workers

Do you supervise anyone?

❏ Yes How many people - Part time? _____ Full time? _____
❏ No

How often, approximately, do you communicate with your supervisor?

	At least once/day	2-3 times a week	Once a week	Once a month	Less than once/mo.	Not applicable
In person-scheduled						
In person-informal						
Formal memos						
Phone calls						
Fax or email						
Notes						

Check the box that is the most accurate:

Distractions in the office make it hard to get my work done:

❏ Always
❏ Frequently
❏ Sometimes
❏ Rarely
❏ Never
❏ Not applicable

When working on projects with co-workers, it is difficult to coordinate delivery of timely work products or information:

❏ Always
❏ Frequently
❏ Sometimes
❏ Rarely
❏ Never
❏ Not applicable

Indicate whether you agree with the following statements:

	Strongly agree	Agree	Neutral	Disagree	Strongly disagree	Not applicable
Professional interaction with my colleagues is very important in my job performance						
Telework can improve my firm's ability to retain competent staff						
Upper manage-ment is supportive of telework						
My supervisor is supportive of telework						
I get adequate job performance feedback from my supervisor						
I dislike someone else using my workspace while I am teleworking						

I enjoy social interaction with my colleagues						
It is difficult for teleworkers to supervise others						

Section C: About Your Job Performance

On the average, how many hours do you work at this job?_____

How long have you been in your current job?_____

How stressful is your job in the following respects?

	Very stressful	Some stress	Little stress	N/A
Volume of work				
Scheduling work				
Office politics				
Job security				
Managing multiple projects				

Indicate whether you agree with the following statements:

	Strongly agree	Agree	Neutral	Disagree	Strongly disagree	Not applicable
Most meetings I attend are scheduled a day or 2 in advance						
I am productive when telecommuting						
My work group is highly productive						
I usually decide how to complete the tasks assigned to me.						
Telework allows me flexibility to work my most productive hours						
My family is supportive of telework						

Do you feel that your productivity has changed since teleworking?

❏ No
❏ Yes

If yes, how has it changed?

      ❏ Increased substantially
      ❏ Increased
      ❏ Decreased
      ❏ Decreased substantially

Explain how telecommuting has affected you, either personally or professionally.

Rate your current job performance in the following areas:

	Excellent	Very good	Good	Meets minimum requirements	Needs improvement
Productivity					
Interpersonal skills					
Dependability					
Communication skills					
Work independently					
Overall performance					

Section D: Travel

Miles you commute from home to work, with no added trips _____

Indicate the number of days, approximately, you make additional trips during your commute **to** the office:

	Daily	2-4 days/wk	One day/wk.	Rarely/never
Commute to school				
Shop/run errands				
Social/recreation/dining				
Personal – medical, dental				
Drop off passenger/child				

Indicate the number of days you make additional trips during your commute **from** your office:

	Daily	2-4 days/wk	One day/wk.	Rarely/never
Commute to school				
Shop/run errands				
Social/recreation/dining				
Personal-medical/dental				
Pick up passenger or child				

For travel to and from work, indicate the number of days per week you use the following methods of transportation:

	Daily	2-4 days/wk	One day/wk.	Rarely/never
Drive alone				
Walk to bus				
Drive to bus				
Drive to vanpool				
Carpool				
Motorcycle or moped				
Walk or run				
Bicycle				
Rail				
Ferry				
Other				

If you listed other, please explain. If you listed carpool or vanpool please indicate how many commuters in car or van.

Your usual commute from home to work is_____ minutes.

Your usual commute from work to home is _____ minutes.
  How stressful is your commute?

  ❏ Very stressful
  ❏ Somewhat stressful
  ❏ Slightly stressful
  ❏ Not at all stressful

How congested is traffic during your commute?

  ❏ Heavy
  ❏ Moderate
  ❏ Light

If you drive your car to work, what is its estimated fuel efficiency?

_____ mpg highway   _____ mpg city

Tell us about your use, or desire to use (if provided by the firm), the following:

	Using now	Would use	Not interested
Free parking			
Reduced-price bus pass			
Carpool or vanpool subsidy			
Reduced-price ferry pass			
Reserved carpool or vanpool parking			
Commuter information board			
Commuter transportation coordinator			
Flex-time			
Bicycle racks or storage			

Section E: Your Telecommuting Experience

How interested are you in continuing telecommuting?

❏ Very interested
❏ Interested
❏ Neutral
❏ Not very interested
❏ Not at all interested

How important to telework are the following communication methods?

	Extremely important	Important	Not important
E-mail			
Voice mail			
Fax machine			

As a result of telework, have your work skills changed in the following areas?

	Improved much	Improved some	No change	Declined some	Declined much
Productivity					
Interpersonal skills					
Dependability					

Communication					
Work independently					
Overall performance					
Project management					
Time management					
Supervisory skills					
Computer skills					

Other changes (please explain)

In general, did you have any problems **obtaining** equipment needed for telework?

❑ No
❑ Yes

If yes, check the statements that apply.

❑ It was difficult for my office to get the funds to buy equipment.
❑ It was difficult finding someone to loan me the equipment.
❑ We had problems getting equipment delivered and set up on time.
❑ Other. Please explain.

In general, have you had any problems **using** the equipment?

❑ No
❑ Yes

If yes, check the statements that apply.

❑ It was difficult to get help when the equipment wasn't working.
❑ It was difficult to get help when the software wasn't working.
❑ Other. Please explain.

Did you install additional telephone lines when you began teleworking?

    ❏ No
    ❏ Yes

If yes, who pays the cost?

    ❏ You
    ❏ Employer
    ❏ Other
    ❏ Not applicable

Note below how telework has changed your relationships with the following:

	Improved much	Improved	No change	Worsened	Much worsened	N/A
Management						
Professional Staff						
Support Staff						
Clients						
Family						
Friends						
Neighbors						

Please explain the nature of any significant change due to telecommuting.

Has your telecommuting been more or less successful than you anticipated?

    ❏ Much more successful
    ❏ More successful
    ❏ About what I expected
    ❏ Less successful
    ❏ Much less successful

As a **result of teleworking**, note the degrees of change to the following non-teleworking groups below:

	Much more	More	No change	Less	Much less
Management					
Professional Staff					
Support Staff					

On the days when you telework how often do you typically do the following?

	Often	Sometimes	Rarely	Not suited to telework	N/A
Writing					
Word Processing					
Reading					
Talking on phone					
Design (graphics, etc.)					
Computer programming					
Analysis (quantitative, interpretative)					
Teaching or training					
Record keeping					
Attending meetings					
Problem solving					
Other administrative tasks					

In what ways has telecommuting changed how you feel about your job?

Aside from the commute trip itself, to what extent has telecommuting increased or decreased the distance you travel or the number of trips you make?

     ❏ Much more travel
     ❏ More travel
     ❏ No change
     ❏ Less travel
     ❏ Far less travel

Please explain.

As a result of telecommuting, have you changed your travel modes (bus, carpool, drive alone) on the days you commute to the office?

❏ No
❏ Yes

If yes, explain how.

In what ways could telecommuting be improved in your organization?

STATE OF COLORADO
CO-WORKER SURVEY—BEFORE

(To be completed prior to start of telework program)

Indicate how you feel about the following statements:

	Strongly agree	Agree	Neutral	Disagree	Strongly disagree	N/A
I anticipate having to schedule, plan or organize my work differently because co-workers telecommute						
I anticipate difficulties with communication on days when co-workers telecommute						
I anticipate increased work interruptions or distractions on days when co-workers telecommute						
I do not believe that my workload will increase when co-workers telecommute						
I think some people will take advantage of telecommuting to work less						
I believe that telework will have a positive impact on the work group as a whole						
Management is upportive of telework						
I believe that telework is good for the organization.						

Given the opportunity, would you telecommute?

❑ Yes
❑ No

STATE OF COLORADO
SUPERVISOR SURVEY—BEFORE

(To be completed prior to start of telework program)

Section A: About Your Organization

How is the equipment and software for telecommuting to be paid for? *Check all that apply.*

❑ Out of my normal budget
❑ Out of an increase in my budget

❏ Out of other budgets in the organization
❏ Loaned equipment
❏ Varies for each employee
❏ No new equipment will be required
❏ Surplus equipment in the organization
❏ No equipment or software will be provided
❏ Other. Please specify.

Indicate to what you degree you agree with the following statements.

	Strongly agree	Agree	Neutral	Disagree	Strongly disagree	N/A
Upper management is supportive of telecommuting						
My firm gives me a lot of flexibility in rewarding employees						
I had sufficient influence on who was chosen to telecommute						
Having employees telework will be troublesome for me.						
When teleworking my staff will be able to concentrate more on work						
My organization is reluctant to try out new things						
Telework will improve my firm's ability to retain competent staff						
i am supportive of my employee's telecommuting.						
Because of telework, communications in my work group will become more difficult						
I am concerned that teleworkers will be less integrated with their work group as a result of telework						

Indicate your opinion of the following.

	Strongly agree	Agree	Neutral	Disagree	Strongly disagree	N/A
Handling confidential information will be problematic when people telework						
Telework allows people the flexibility to work during more productive hours.						

It is difficult for telecommuters to supervise other people						
I let my workers decide how to complete the projects I assign them						
I think some people will take advantage of telecommuting to work less						

Which statement best characterizes your decision to supervise telecommuters?

❏ I am enthusiastic about telework and think it will improve how my work group operates
❏ I am interested in telework and I'd like to find out if it will improve how my work group operates.
❏ I am uncertain about telework, but I am willing to give it a try.
❏ I felt pressured into participating.
❏ Other. Please explain.

Did some people in your work group apply to telecommute and not get chosen?

❏ No
❏ Yes

If yes,

❏ It was my decision
❏ It was a joint decision
❏ The decision was out of my hands.
❏ Other. Please explain.

How did those not chosen feel about the decision?

❏ People seemed to accept the reason
❏ There was some resentment
❏ Other. Please explain.

Section B. Identifying Telecommuters

How many employees do you supervise directly? _____Full time

_____Part time

List the names, job title, and number of teleworking days per month of all employees you supervise that will be teleworking.

NAME	JOB TITLE	# DAYS

Section C: Job Performance

Fill out a copy of this section for each telecommuter you supervise.

Telecommuter's name _____

How often, approximately, do you currently communicate with your telecommuter?

	Once a day	2-4 times a week	Once a week	Once a month	Less than Once a month	N/A
In person-meeting scheduled						
In person-meeting informal						
Formal memos						
Phone calls						
Faxes or e-mail						
Notes						

Indicate to what degree you agree with the following:

	Strongly agree	Agree	Neutral	Disagree	Strongly disagree	N/A
I closely monitor how this employee uses her/his time						
This employee works best when there is a deadline						
This employee is highly motivated						

This employee's job description works very well with telework					
Telework will make it harder for this employee's coworkers.					

Rate this employee's job performance in the following areas:

	Excellent	Very good	Good	Meets min. requirements	Needs improvement
Productivity					
Interpersonal skills					
Dependability					
Communication					
Able to work independently					
Overall performance					

How often, approximately, does this person's job currently require access to the following central office resources?

	Every day	2-4 times/wk	Once/ wk	Once/ month	Less than once a month	N/A
Central paper files						
Computers						
Electronic data bases						
Software						
Equipment – (copier, fax)						
Professional staff						
Support staff						

STATE OF COLORADO
TELECOMMUTER SURVEY—BEFORE

(To be completed prior to the start of the telework program)

Section A: About Your Needs on the Job

How often, approximately, does your job currently require physical access to the following central office resources?

	Every day	2-4 times/wk	Once a week	Once a month	Less than Once/month	N/A
Central paper files						
Computers						
Electronic data bases						

Software					
Equipment–copier, fax					
Support staff					
Professional staff					

Rate the importance of each item listed below in performing your job effectively.

	Very important	Somewhat important	Not important	N/A
PC or laptop				
Mainframe computer				
Phone line for modem				
Fax machine				
Voice mail or answering machine				
Photocopier				

Indicate the equipment to be used at home on telecommuting days

	Need to have	Would like to have	Already have	N/A
Computer				
Software used at office				
Modem				
Second phone line				
Call waiting				
Voice mail				
Answering machine				
Printer				
Fax Machine				

Other needs. Please explain

Section B: About Your Organization and Co-workers

Do you supervise anyone?

❏ No
❏ Yes

If yes, how many people - Part time _____ Full time_____

How often, approximately, do you currently communicate with your supervisor?

	Every day	2-4 times/wk	Once a week	Once a month	Less than Once/mo.	N/A
In person – meeting scheduled						
In person – meeting informally						
Formal memos						
Telephone calls						
Faxes or e-mail						
Notes						

Indicate the degree to which you agree with the following statements

	Always	Frequently	Sometimes	Rarely	Never	N/A
Distractions in the office make it hard for me to get my work done						
When working on projects with coworkers, it is diffiult to coordinate delivery of timely work products or info.						
Professional interaction with colleagues is very important to my job performance.						
Telework can improve my firm's ability to retain competent staff						
Upper management is supportive of telecommuting.						
My supervisor is supportive of telework.						
I get adequate feedback on my job performance from my supervisor.						
I dislike the idea of someone else using my workspace while I am teleworking.						
I enjoy social interaction with my colleagues.						
It is difficult for teleworkers to supervise other people.						

Section C: About Your Job Performance

On the average, you work_____ hours at this job.

Appendix B

You have been in your current job _____ years and _____ months

Indicate the degrees of stress in your job in the following respects:

	Very stressful	Somewhat stressful	Not at all stressful	N/A
Volume of work				
Scheduling work				
Office politics				
Job security				
Managing multiple projects				

Indicate the degree to which you agree with the following statements:

	Strongly agree	Agree	Neutral	Disagree	Strongly disagree	
Most meetings I attend are scheduled 1-2+ days ahead						
I am productive when teleworking						
My work group is highly productive						
I usually decide how to complete projects assigned to me						
Telework allows me the flexibility to work my most productive hours						
My family is supportive of my telecommuting						

Do you feel that your productivity has changed in the last year?

    ❏ No
    ❏ Yes

If yes, indicate how it has changed:

    ❏ Increased substantially
    ❏ Increased
    ❏ Decreased
    ❏ Decreased substantially

How will telecommuting affect you, personally and professionally?

Rate your current job performance in the following areas:

	Excellent	Very good	Good	Meets min. Requirements	N/A
Productivity					
Interpersonal skills					
Dependability					
Communication skills					
Able to work independently					
Overall performance					

Section D: Travel

Your commute from home to work, with no added trips is _____miles. Indicate how often you make additional trips during your commute to the office:

	Daily	2-4 days/wk.	1 day/wk	Rarely/Never
Commute to school				
Shop/run errands				
Social/recreation/dining				
Personal-medical/dental				
Drop off passenger/child				

Your usual commute from home to work is _____ minutes.

Your usual commute from work to home is _____ minutes.

Going to and from work, indicate approximately how often you use the following:

	Daily	2-4 days/wk.	One day/wk	Rarely/never
Drive alone				
Walk to bus				
Drive to bus				
Drive to vanpool				
Carpool				
Motorcycle/moped				
Walk or run				
Bicycle				
Rail				
Ferry				

If using other transportation modes, please specify.

If carpooling or vanpooling, how many are in the car or van?

How stressful is your commute?

    ❏ Very stressful
    ❏ Somewhat stressful
    ❏ Slightly stressful
    ❏ Not at all stressful

How congested is traffic during your commute?

    ❏ Heavy
    ❏ Moderate
    ❏ Light

If you drive your own vehicle to work, what is its estimated fuel efficiency?

_____ mpg city   _____ mpg highway

Do you use the following services, or would you use them if your organization provided them?

	Currently use	Would use if available	Not interested
Free parking			
Reduced-price bus pass			
Carpool or vanpool subsidy			
Reduced-price ferry pass			
Reserved car/vanpool parking			
Commuter information board			
Commuter transportation coordinator			
Flex-time			
Bicycle racks or storage			

MITE (MIDWEST INSTITUTE FOR TELECOMMUTING EDUCATION) TELEWORK OFFICE EVALUATION

Personnel conducting home visit _____

Employee name _____ Division _____

Business phone _____ Home phone _____

Address _____

Work Station Set-Up

Located in which room _____

	YES	NO
If in the basement, will there be a problem with moisture?		
Separate from major family activity areas?		
Secure from pets and family members?		
Work area clear of major traffic patterns?		
Background or distracting noise (TV, other people, outside traffic) is minimal?		
Equipment not easily viewed from outside/external areas?		
Desk is 29" high?		
Computer table is 26" high?		
Computer table sturdy enough to handle equipment weight?		
Keyboard reach is 23-26" inches from operators?		
Keyboard slope is a 10-20 degree angle?		
Monitor is arms length from operator?		
The top of the typing line is slightly below eye level?		
Chair provides support to back of waist (15 degree back tilt)?		
Height of chair seat is 15-21" from the floor?		
Phone line situated near desk and computer table?		
The reach to the phone is suitable?		
Lighting is directly behind or to the side of line of vision?		
Supplies and resources such as file drawers close to desk?		

Does the home office comply with lease or association agreement?

❏ Yes
❏ No
❏ Not applicable

Safety

	YES	NO
Are there safe exit paths from the work area?		
Are evacuation plans established?		
Are there any loose rugs on slippery floors?		
Is the smoke detector present, functional and recently checked?		
Is there a fire extinguisher near the work area?		
Is there clear access to the fire extinguisher?		
Are adequate first aid supplies available?		
Are extension and power cords in safe condition?		
Are electrical outlets overloaded?		
Are there any tripping hazards with electrical cords?		
Is equipment out of direct sunlight and away from heaters?		

Are the air quality and ventilation adequate?		
Is the work environment cluttered?		
Are overhead shelves or cabinets in hazardous locations?		

Property Insurance Documentation (Check those available)

❏ Homeowners
❏ Renters
❏ Liability
❏ Business insurance rider

Insurance Company _____

Address _____

Phone _____ Agent _____

Name and number of nearest health care facility:

_____

Security

	YES	NO
Are there locks on the office door and file cabinet drawers?		
Is power surge protection in use?		
Is there protective or secure storage for floppy disks?		
Is there privacy for confidential phone conversations?		

Additional comments or suggestions:

Overall Assessment

❏ Satisfactory
❏ Not suitable at present.

If not suitable, recommendations prior to follow-up are:

Follow-up Date _____

Provide copies of this evaluation to both employee and supervisor

Glossary

ACD. Alternate (or automated) Call Distribution. Primarily used in a call center environment, this provides even distribution of inbound calls to center representatives.

ADA. Americans with Disabilities Act. This 1990 U.S. legislation was designed to establish a clear and comprehensive prohibition of discrimination on the basis of disability, focusing primarily on the areas of employment and public services.

AFMAN. United States Air Force Manual.

ad hoc. For the particular end or case at hand without consideration of wider application. For specific problems or needs. With regard to employment, it generally refers to project-based work.

alternate worksite. Any facility in which the employee works that saves that employee a lengthier distance or time commute to a main work site.

alternative officing. Reconfiguration of a firm's main work site to take advantage of the fact that at least part of the time a significant amount of workspace is not in use, due to telework, and its resulting options—hotelling, desk sharing, etc.

BIND. Berkeley Internet Name Domain; the most widely used implementation of domain name service (DNS), the critical means by which we all locate systems on the Internet by name without having to know specific IP addresses.

BIOS. Basic Input Output System. On PC-compatible computers, the set of essential software routines that test hardware at startup, start the operating system, and support the transfer of data among hardware devices. The BIOS is stored in ROM so that it can be executed when the computer is turned on. Although critical to performance, the BIOS is usually invisible to computer users.

benefits in kind. Employment perquisites paid in goods or services, rather than in cash.

BPR. Business Process Re-engineering. The innovative redesign of business processes to improve efficiency, quality, and customer service. Telework, for instance, offers many opportunities to incur the benefits of round-the-clock working.

broadband. Data transmission speeds in excess of 1 Mbps (megabits per second). This contrasts with modems whose speeds approximate 28.Kbps (kilobytes per second) or ISDNs of 64 Kbps.

CAAA. Clean Air Act Amendment. This 1990 legislation is generally considered the original catalyst for the introduction of telework in the United States.

CAP. Created in 1990, the U.S. Department of Defense Computer/Electronics Accommodation Program has provided the equipment and assistive technology for people with disabilities to work at home or other alternative worksites.

CGI. Common Gateway Interface. An external application that is executed by an HTTP server in response to a request by a client such as a Web browser. Generally, the CGI script is invoked when the user clicks on an element on a Web page, such as a link or image. CGI scripts are used to provide interactivity on a Web page such as feedback forms, links to other Web pages or sites, and to send e-mail to a specific address.

CSCW. Computer Supported Cooperative Work; also referred to as **groupware.** The software tools and working methods used to support teamwork, especially virtual teamwork. It includes the use of computer conferencing, electronic whiteboard systems, and use of intranets.

CTA. Canadian Telework Association, http://www.ivc.ca.org. One of the best online sources of telework news and services.

CTI. Computer telephone integration. The merging of computer and telephony capabilities, usually for SOHO situations.

CWA. Communication Workers of America. U.S. Labor union representing over 740,000 North American workers in telecommunications, printing and news media, public service, health care, cable television, general manufacturing, electronics, gas and electric utilities, and other fields.

call center. A facility or system designed to handle a large volume of telephone calls. Call centers may handle inbound calls (info and referral or 1-800 sales) or outbound calls (outgoing sales calls or research interviews). Call centers may be centralized, with personnel located in a single facility or room) or distributed (with telephone personnel located in a number of locations). Distributed call centers are ideal telework situations.

closet telecommuter. An employee who telecommutes with immediate management approval, but whose organization has no policy in place.

collective agreement. Contracted employment practices and policies as agreed to by employer and unionized workers. In Europe, this often takes the place of legislation in determining employment guidelines.

Communications Decency Act. 1996 U.S. legislation allowing employers to practice reasonable, effective, and appropriate measures to protect themselves against the obscene or harassing use of the employer's telecommunications facilities by employees.

communities of practice (CoP). Informal groups of people sharing information and knowledge.

Commuter Choice Leadership Initiative. Collaboration of the U.S. Environmental Protection Agency, U.S. Department of Transportation, and state and local governments to cut air pollution and improve public health by offering tax benefits to firms implementing or encouraging employee use of alternative modes of transportation. http://www.epa.gov/otaz/transp/comchoic/ccweb.htm

compressed workweek. A forty-hour workweek completed in fewer than five days by increasing the number of hours worked per day.

concentrative teleworking. The switch by many industries (such as banking and insurance) from walk-in office presence to telephone-based sales and support.

constructive dismissal. Occurs when the actions of an employer (e.g., a significant change in duties of employee) effectively terminate an employee. In the area of telework this might occur if an employer suddenly required an employee who had been working on site to work at home.

cookie. A block of data that a server returns to a client as a response to the request of the client. On the Internet, a cookie is a block of data that a Web server stores on a client system. When a user returns to the same Web site, the browser sends a copy of the cookie back to the server. Cookies are used to identify users, to instruct the server, to send a customized version of the requested Web page, to submit account information for the user, and to perform other administrative functions.

core time. In flexible work situations, the period of day when all employees must be present at work. A typical core time might be 9:30 a.m.–4:30 p.m.

cracker. Person proficient at deciphering codes and passwords and breaking security systems for illegal or unethical reasons.

cyberspace. The imaginary "location" where people communicate electronically using e-e-mail and other online services, usually over the Internet.

DLL. Dynamic Link Library; a feature of the Microsoft family of operating systems and OS/2 that allows executable routines to be stored separately as files with DLL extensions (.dll) and to be loaded only when needed by a program.

DM. Deutschmark, Germany's currency. As of this writing, one Deutschmark is roughly equivalent to 47 U.S cents.

DoD. United States Department of Defense.

DSL. Digital Subscriber Line technology that allows data speeds far in excess of the traditional copper pair analog lines.

DTC. Desk Top Conferencing. Videoconferencing where communications is from computer-to-computer, rather than remote video camera to local monitor. Users have a small video camera mounted on top of their computer monitor. Software integrates video images into the desktop environment (Windows, for example). This means that participants can see images of each other alongside other computer-generated information such as documents. Telecooperation takes place by a combination of visual conversation and collaborative document sharing.

DWES. Denmark Working Environment Service. Danish federal department responsible for administration of the Danish Working Environment Act, regulating and inspecting home workplace safety.

defensible space. A room only used by the person concerned, who chooses the technology and how it is used.

denial of service. A computer attack that is nearly impossible to counter. The hacker sends a request to the server to connect to it, but when the server responds with an acknowledgment and tries to establish a session, it cannot find the system that made the request. By inundating a server with these unanswerable session requests, a hacker causes the server to slow to a crawl or eventually crash.

digital divide. In just about every country, there are two groups of people—those with the most powerful computers, the best telephone service, the fastest Internet service, and relevant training, and those without these computers, training, and services. The difference between these two groups of people is what has been called the "digital divide."

digital economy. Also referred to as **network economy**—characterization of the new global economy dominated by digital infrastructures, i.e., electronic or digital networks based upon ICT infrastructures and especially the Internet.

digitalization. The process of conversion away from traditional analog telecommunications technology, based upon the continuous variation of the strength of a signal, to new digital telecommunications technology, where the signal is represented only by its presence (ones) or absence (zeros) as bits. Digitalization enables telecommunications systems, like telephones, to converge and interact directly with digital computers and other information technology hardware and software.

discrete task. One with finite, distinct, countable components; the ideal job for telework.

distributed team. A group of employees working on the same project and/or in the same organizational unit who are based at two or more locations. The distribution can be as extensive as each team and/or department member working at a different location. The group can also be spread worldwide.

docking station. Sometimes used as a synonym for **port replicator,** this computer hardware is a box that contains slots in which to place interface cards and space in which to put a hard disk, etc. This box can be permanently attached to a PC.

domain name. These are easily remembered names that are used in place of IP addresses.

duty station. An employee's primary work location. In a telework situation it would be the place where the teleworker reports for work when not teleworking—typically the employer's main office.

ECPA. Electronic Communications Privacy Act. U.S. legislation prohibiting unauthorized interception of electronic communications and unauthorized access to stored electronic communications.

EDI. Electronic Data Interchange. The exchange of structured electronic messages, such as orders or invoices, over special telecommunications networks, replacing paper transactions.

EPA. U.S. Environmental Protection Agency.

ETO. European Telework Online. Supported by the European Telework Development Commission, this site provides information, ideas, connections, and discussion covering aspects of telework, teletrade (e-commerce), and telecooperation. http://www.eto.org.uk

EU. European Union, formerly known as the European Community. Created after World War II to unite the nations of Europe economically, EU membership now includes fifteen countries, representing 370 million people. The first steps toward European integration began in1952 when the founding members pooled their coal and steel industries. In January of 1993 the member countries set about creating a single market in which goods, services, people and capital would move as freely as within one country. EU's focus, originally in the areas of foreign trade, agriculture, and transportation, now also encompasses research, technology, energy, the environment, foreign aid, education and training. On January 1, 2002, the European Union fully launched the Euro, Europe's single currency. The member countries are Austria, Belgium, Denmark, Finland, France, Germany, Greece, Ireland, Italy, Luxembourg, the Netherlands, Portugal, Spain, Sweden, and the United Kingdom.

ecash. Electronic cash. Currency that exists as information. It may be held in smart cards or on disk storage and can be traded through special terminals or over networks.

ecommunity or **evillage.** Master-planned community (residential housing development) pre-wired for broadband access.

e-lancer. Electronically connected freelancer.

electronic commerce (e-commerce). The handling of formal transactions over electronic networks, often directly computer to computer. Early electronic commerce took place over proprietary networks using EDI, but the scope is now considerably wider, including trading over open networks such as the Internet.

electronic community. Usually refers to a virtual community in the electronic commerce or electronic market context. (See **virtual community.**)

electronic market. Locations on the Internet that facilitate connections and trading between buyers and sellers. These may be in the form of virtual shopping malls, trade directories, electronic communities, or online auctions.

e-mail bombs. Usually a personal attack. Someone sends you the same e-mail hundreds or thousands of times until your e-mail system cannot accept any more messages.

Employment Standards Act. Ontario, Canada, legislation that sets the minimum wage for home workers at 110 percent of the regular minimum wage.

episodic telework. Informal work-at-home employee arrangement existing temporarily due to illness or injury, or when a specific assignment is better completed away from the office and its distractions.

ework. Telework with an electronics communication component.

extranet. see **VPN**.

extreme telecommuting. Work wholly unfettered by physical location. Also referred to as nomadic telework.

FHWA. The U.S. Federal Highway Administration.

FLSA. The U.S. Fair Labor Standards Act provides for minimum standards for both wages and overtime entitlement and spells out administrative procedures by which covered work time must be compensated. Included in the act are provisions related to child labor, equal pay, and portal-to-portal activities. In addition, the act exempts specified employees or groups of employees from the application of certain of its provisions. First passed in 1938, the act began applying to federal employees in 1974.

FOUO. U.S. military acronym, indicating " For Official Use Only."

FTP. File Transfer Protocol. The process for transferring binary files (documents or software) across a network.

facetime. Work time spent not telecommuting (i.e., time spent at the office, interacting with coworkers and supervisors).

fast company. A U.S. term for an organization somewhere in the middle between the extremes of free agency and the traditional career path. As the name implies, a fast company tends to be rapidly constructed and rapidly transformed or dismantled as need or wishes direct, but it still provides a greater sense of belonging and continuity than free agency. A fast company is a stable, if temporary, organization where mutual commitment can build relationships and social glue.

Federal Employees Compensation Act. 1993 U.S. legislation that determined that federal employees are covered by workers compensation for work-related injuries that happen when they are working from home.

firewall. A set of related programs designed to protect computer systems from unauthorized access.

flexband. In a flexible work situation, the time periods wherein an employee chooses an arrival and a departure time (e.g., your firm's arrival flexband may be 6:30–8:30 a.m., your departure flexband 4:30–6:30 p.m.).

flexible work. Working practices defined by employers and documented in employment policies, offering employees latitude for accomplishing assigned tasks. Examples are flexible hours (the policy states a minimum number of hours to be worked and parameters for when those hours can be), flexible work location (various permissible work locations are defined), and flexible work contracts (the employee's role may vary within defined parameters).

flexiplace. U.S. federal government's term for working from a remote location.

free-address workspace. Permanent workspace designed to be shared by remote workers on a first-come, first-served basis; also referred to as a landing pad.

free agent. Individual who shuns the traditional corporate career path.

GIF. Graphics Interchange Format. Compression algorithm for computer images in 256 colors. The most commonly used format for images on the Internet, although JPEG compression is considered better for high-quality photographs and usually compresses smaller.

GSA. General Services Administration. A central management agency that sets federal policy in such areas as federal procurement, real property management, and information resources management.

gateway. Point of access between your computer and the Internet.

Gil Gordon & Associates. This telework pioneer offers an organization and site consolidating a wide variety of information from around the world, and from many different perspectives, on the subjects of telecommuting, teleworking, the virtual office, and related fields, at http://www.gilgordon.com

green commute. Alternative, environmentally positive forms of transport such as walking, cycling, carpooling, and mass transit.

group-address workspace. Workspace designated for a work team for a specified period of time.

HK. Denmark's Union of Commercial and Clerical Employees. The country's largest trade union, with over 370,000 members. http://www.hk.dk (available in English).

HTML. Hypertext Markup Language. The code used on World Wide Web pages to instruct the browser how to display the text. It adds different types of tags and pairs of tags to delineate blocks of text. For example, <b> indicates bold, <i> indicates italics. HTML indicates how browsers should respond to user actions such as key press or mouse click.

HTTP. Hypertext Transfer Protocol. The client/server protocol used to access information on the World Wide Web.

HASH. In many FTP (File Transfer Protocol) programs, a command that instructs the FTP client to display a pound (#) sign every time it sends or receives a block of data.

Health and Safety at Work etc. Act. United Kingdom 1974 legislation stating that employers have a general duty, as far as reasonably practicable, to protect the health, safety, and welfare of their employees, whether employees are working in a conventional office or remotely.

home office. Professional space designated in the home.

hop and skip. An innovative mass transportation program in the Boulder, Colorado, area designed to facilitate travel to downtown, work, and school. For further information, see http://www.ci.boulder.co.us/goboulder/pubs/hopskip_menu.html.

hot-desking. Depersonalizing workspace by tearing down traditional walls and personal office or desk space and replacing it with group space, where individuals book or find space as they need it.

hoteling. Flexible workspace in an office where desks are assigned to employees by the day. A telecommuting program that enables employees who don't maintain a specific office at the employer's facility the opportunity to make reservations in advance for a number of offices or cubicles on the days that they commute.

ICT. Information and communications technology.

ICMP. Internet Control Message Protocol. Used by a router to exchange information with other routers.

IIS. A Microsoft product, Internet Information Server is the Web server software found on most Web sites deployed on Windows NT and Windows 2000 servers.

IP. Internet Protocol. The main delivery system for information over the Internet.

IP address. Each machine on the Internet is assigned a unique address. The addresses are 32-bit numbers, usually expressed as four "octets" in a dotted decimal number. A typical IP address might read 212.38.81.436.

IPR. Intellectual Property Rights. Rights to intellectual material normally in the form of content on electronic networks, where it can be difficult to control copying and use without the IPR holder's knowledge and/or permission.

IRS. Internal Revenue Service. The U.S. agency responsible for federal taxation legislation and collection.

ISAPI. Internet Services Application Programming Interface allows developers to extend the capabilities of an IIS server using DLLs.

ISDN. Integrated Services Digital Network. A system of digital phone connections that allows data to be transmitted simultaneously across the world using end-to-end digital connectivity. ISDN supports simultaneous voice, data and video connections over the same circuit and offers speed and flexibility to the telecommuter.

ISP. Internet Service Provider (AOL, MSN, etc.).

IT. Information technology.

ITAC. International Telework Association and Council, whose mission is to drive the growth and success of work, independent of location. ITAC studies, develops, and recommends tools, techniques, and processes that promote the benefits of telework; see http://www.telecommute.org.

incubator. Incubators "quick start" businesses and have them grow at a rate 7 to 22 times faster than for businesses started otherwise. Incubators maintain an inventory of business experts, consultants, advisors, procedures, methodologies, state-of-the-art technologies, and total resources that businesses are likely to use in the growth process.

intelligence productivity. One of the job types most likely to thrive in telework, this terms indicates job functions resulting in the creation or enhancement of intellectual property rather than material goods.

intelligent agent. A piece of software using artificial intelligence techniques that operates autonomously using a set of rules. A common type of agent is one that roams the Internet and searches out information. Other types filter incoming information and messages for items of relevance to particular users.

Internet. The worldwide collection of networks and gateways that use the TCP/IP suite of protocols to communicate with one another. At the heart of the Internet is a backbone of high-speed data communication lines between major nodes or host computers, consisting of thousands of commercial, government, educational, and other computer systems that route data and messages.

intranet. A computer network designed for information processing within a company or organization, which usually employs applications associated with the Internet, such as Web browsers, Web pages, newsgroups, e-mail, etc. An intranet is accessible only to those within the company.

JPEG. Joint Photographic Experts Group. An image format widely used on the Internet for compressed photographic images (.jpg).

knowledge management. The supervision of an organization's knowledge, both explicit (information or knowledge that can be codified) and tacit (the knowledge in people's heads). It involves a systematic approach to managing knowledge processes—creation, identification, gathering, classifying, storing, disseminating, and using—as well as creating the environment for knowledge creation and sharing to flourish. Collaborative technologies such as the Internet, intranets, and groupware play an important part in most knowledge management initiatives.

LAN. Local Area Network. A data communications network geographically limited (typically under two miles), allowing easy interconnection of terminals, microprocessors and computers within adjacent buildings. Ethernet and FDDI are examples of standard LANs.

LMRA. Labor Management Relations Act. U.S. legislation stating that employees have the right to engage in concerted activities for the purpose of collective bargaining or other mutual aid or protection and that an employer must not interfere with the rights of covered employees.

list server. A server that redistributes electronic mail to those that have subscribed to the list. Commonly used software for list servers are Listserv and MajorDomo.

locally fixed. A job that requires the personal presence of the employee at a particular place. Not a good candidate for telework.

location-independent. A job that can be done anywhere, to suit the employer or the person doing the work.

MATAC. Metro Atlanta Telecommuting Advisory Council, http://www.matac.org

MIME. Multipurpose Internet Mail Extensions. A standard format for encoding files for sending over the Internet. It is able to handle special character codes and symbols, which the Internet (with a limit of 7-bit ASCII codes) is unable to do. It can be used to send files as varied as word processing documents, spread sheets, and image and video files.

MPEG. Moving Picture Expert Group. A group that defines compression standards for video (moving) images.

MSF. Manufacturing, Science, and Finance. One of the largest unions in the UK, MSF refers to itself as the union for skilled and professional people.

macros. In computer applications, a set of keystrokes and instructions recorded and saved under a short key code or name. When the key code is typed or the macro name is used, the program carries out the instructions of the macro. Users can create a macro to save time by replacing an often-used or lengthy series of keystrokes with a shorter version.

Management of Health and Safety at Work Regulations. 1992 UK legislation requiring employers to do a suitable and sufficient risk assessment of all work activities carried out by those working at the employer's office or remotely. The risks assessment needs to identify the hazards present and then to assess the extent of the risks.

Massachusetts Telecommuting Initiative. During 1994 the Massachusetts Division of Energy Resources and the Massachusetts Highway Department undertook a project to study what specific impacts telecommuting has on companies, individuals, and society. The Federal Highway Administration and the Commonwealth of Massachusetts provided funding for the project. http://www.state.ma.us/doer/programs/trans/telecomm.htm

mixed-use telecommuting. A combination of the use of the main or central office, telecenters, and home offices.

modem. Modulator-demodulator. A device that connects your computer to the telephone network to access remote computers and online services. Most can send and receive faxes, while later models also handle incoming voice messages.

moteling. Telework employees who don't maintain a specific office at the employer's facility are assigned on a first-come, first-served basis to one of a number of offices or cubicles on the days that they commute.

mount. To make a physical disk or tape accessible to a computer's file system. Most commonly refers to accessing disks in Apple Macintosh and UNIX-based systems.

Mountd. Controls and arbitrates access to NFS mounts on UNIX hosts.

NAAQ8. The United States' health-based national air quality standard for ground-level ozone, the primary constituent of smog. The new U.S. standard is 0.08 parts per million (ppm), defined as a "concentration-based" form, specifically the 3-year average of the annual 4th-highest daily maximum 8-hour ozone concentrations.

NC. Network computer. A computer having the hardware and software necessary to be connected to the Internet.

NEPI. National Environmental Policy Institute. A Washington, D.C., nonprofit, bipartisan organization of environmental leaders. It fosters the growth of new ideas for developing environmental policies that contribute to genuine environmental progress. http://www.nepi.org

NTI. National Telecommuting Initiative. Implemented by the President's Management Council, its mission was to boost, primarily, the number of federal teleworkers and, secondarily, the number of teleworkers in other sectors of the U.S. workforce. It was the first government-wide telework initiative to set numerical goals—60,000 federal teleworkers by October 1998 and 160,000 by the end of 2002.

neighborhood center. A telecenter is merged into a housing development, uniting employees of various firms. Typically, they are equipped with workstations and PCs with long distance data transmission capabilities.

network. A group of computer and associated devices that are connected by communications facilities. A network can involve permanent connection such as cables or temporary connections such as telephone or other communications links. This can be as small as a local area network (LAN) consisting of a few computers, printers, and other devices or as large as numerous computers linked over a vast geographic area.

nexus. A causal link.

newsgroups. Bulletin boards, where users post messages that can be accessed by others using a "news reader." Each newsgroup has its own unique address, such as dk.business.network. These are organized into hierarchies, where the prefix indicates types of newsgroup—e.g., biz. for business, job. for employment, sci. for science, etc. and into countries, using Internet 2-character codes (dk, uk, us, etc.).

noncompete covenant. Commonplace practice before the prevalence of e-mail and telework, this agreement constrains the employee from employment with and thus sharing of employer information with a competitive firm within a specified time and geographic area after leaving the first firm's employ.

NOx. Oxides of nitrogen. The sum of nitrogen oxide and nitrogen dioxide.

null session connection. Also known as **anonymous logon,** this is a mechanism that allows an anonymous user to retrieve information over the network or to connect without authentication.

OEN. Open Electronic Networking. The use of open systems like the Internet, for telecooperation. This contrasts with proprietary online services, such as AOL, and uses a variety of methods including electronic mail, distribution lists, and the World Wide Web.

OLR. Off-line reader. Software that allows users of e-mail and the Internet to download new information into their local computer and browse it while not connected. This saves significantly on telephone charges.

OSHA. Occupational Safety and Health Administration. A division of the U.S. Department of Labor, whose mission is to save lives, prevent injuries, and protect the health of America's workers. http://www.osha.org.

offshore telework. Tasks are split across several countries, and jobs are shifted from one region, town, or country to another.

outwork. Denmark's term for work performed out of the home.

PC. Personal, rather than networked, computer. Also has come to mean any computer or terminal that is IBM, rather than Macintosh, compatible.

PGP. Pretty Good Privacy. Developed privately to overcome U.S. regulations on the export of encryption technology, PGP is a method of encrypting messages, so that they can only be read if the recipient applies the appropriate decryption method. Encryption and decryption rely on a combination of a private "key," known only to the sender, and a public "key" known to the recipient. Since messages are encoded using cryptographic algorithms, they are extremely difficult to decode if intercepted. Encryption is at the heart of secure electronic transactions (see **SET**).

PoP. Point of Presence. Indicates an access point to an Internet Access Provider. Many providers now provide PoPs on a national or international basis, through agreements with other IAPs or ISPs. This gives their clients Internet access for the cost of a local telephone call from many locations, a boost to reducing the cost of location-independent working (see **LIW**).

packet. A grouping (subdivision) of data sent over the Internet.

packet sniffers. Invade computers by inspecting and grabbing all packets in their range, even though the packets don't match their IP address.

pilot program. A designated time period and documented process for introducing telework.

plug and play. A set of specifications that allow a PC to configure itself automatically to work with peripherals such as monitors, printers, and modems. A user can "plug" in the peripheral and "play" it without manually configuring the system.

port replicator. This piece of computer hardware is a copy of the laptop ports that may be connected permanently to a PC.

POTS. Plain old telephone system.

printer time. A relatively recent term to describe productive time lost, usually in conversation, when employees wait for either print jobs to be output or someone to fix a non-functioning or jammed printer. Rapidly replacing "water cooler effect."

Prohibition of Labor Market Discrimination Act. In Denmark an employer must not discriminate against employees due to race, color, religion, political belief, sexual orientation, or national, social, or ethnic origin. The act guarantees employees equality with respect to recruitment, dismissal, transfer, and promotion as well as pay and working conditions. The act prohibits discrimination of employees with respect to access to telework, vocational guidance, training, or retraining measures

project-based telework. Work from a remote location of a temporary nature, for a definite time period, for the purpose of completing a specified project.

protocol. The predefined way that someone who wants to use an Internet service talks with that service. Protocols are often text, and simply describe how the client and server have their conversation. The **http**, for instance, is the World Wide Web's protocol. Some others, defined separately in this glossary, are **IP, TCP, FTP, UDP, ICMP, SMTP, SNMP**, and **Telnet.** A company might set up only one or two machines to handle a specific protocol and ban that protocol on other machines.

puppy. Generally used in telework center, this is a one-drawer, lockable, metal file cabinet on rollers that is assigned to one telework center user.

push technology. A way of delivering technology to an Internet user in background mode. While the user is browsing or accessing e-mail, "channels" of information, according to user selection, are sent into their local computer invisibly. They may be viewed later by user selection or activated as a screen saver.

RPC. Remote Procedure Calls allow programs on one computer to run programs on a second computer.

R commands. In UNIX these enable someone to access a remote system without supplying a password.

reactive transportation demand management. A new area of transportation that serves to market alternative forms of transportation. RTDM efforts are being implemented in urban areas across the United States in order to reduce traffic congestion and air pollution and to increase efficiency of the transportation system.

remote access. Access of an employer's computer system from any off-site location. Refers to both the telephone dial-up of an employer's LAN or use of the Internet to communicate with the employer's computer network.

remote work centers. Workspace and equipment available to the general public and rented for specific periods of time.

remote workers. Employees whose work location is other than the location of management.

road warrior. An employee who typically operates from a virtual office such as a sales executive or field service technical support engineer

SBA. Small Business Administration. Offering tips on starting, expanding, and financing your business from the U.S. government, this federal organization's site includes an outstanding directory of information and links for local services. http://www.sba.gov

SET. Secure Electronic Transactions. A protocol standard that uses key encryption for transmitting information as part of a teletrade transaction. It may be used to authenticate buyers and transfer funds. The standard is backed by major finance clearing organizations (VISA and MasterCard) and will increasingly be incorporated into commercial electronic commerce servers and client browser software. An important aspect of the practical use of such a standard is that of "trusted third parties" who hold the private parts of the keys of buyers and sellers. (See also **PGP**.)

SIP. State implementation plan. Refers to procedures embraced by U.S. states for air quality improvement.

SMB. Server Message Block protocol. Also known as the Common Internet File System (**CIFS**), enables file sharing over computer networks.

SME. Small and Medium Enterprises. Generally defined as fewer than 250 employees and less than 25 percent owned by large companies.

SMTP. Simple Mail Transport Protocol. Used to send text-based information (e-mail)

SNMP. Simple Network Management Protocol widely used by network administrators to monitor and administer all types of network-connected devices ranging from routers to printers to computers.

SOHO. Small office/home office.

Sadmind. Allows remote administration access to Solaris systems, providing a graphical user interface for system administration functions

satellite offices. Permanent offices located in the suburbs where data can be transferred to a central office. Typically set up and used by a single employer, they are not necessarily geographically convenient or designed specifically for telework use.

scalability. The ability to upgrade existing software to accommodate more users, as a cost-effective alternative to the purchase of additional equipment.

search engine. A facility and an Internet site (URL) that lets you search for information on the Internet from an index that typically holds references to all the text on World Wide Web pages. Commonly used engines are Excite, Yahoo, Lycos, InfoSeek and AltaVista.

Sendmail. The program that sends, receives, and forwards most electronic mail processed on UNIX and Linux computers.

severe ozone attainment level. Air that is approaching the ozone and pollutant level of a health hazard.

smart growth. Community and business development that strives to maintain a balance between fiscal health, economic growth, protection of limited environmental assets, and quality of life with a goal of building community livability, providing access to a qualified workforce and promoting regional competitiveness.

sniff. An electronic software concept that means to search through.

social partners. Organized representatives of labor market interests such as employers associations and trade unions.

sound control. Protection of the telecommuter from household noise and the household from the telecommuter.

spamming. The frowned-upon practice of posting messages indiscriminately into newsgroups and individual emails, e.g., for unsolicited advertising.

summary judgment. A request for a decision by a court of the matters submitted to it, based upon legal arguments only, where no material facts are in dispute.

TA. Terminal adapter. Hardware that allows ordinary analog phone equipment to be used over an ISDN line, eliminating the need to purchase special ISDN lines.

TCP. Transport Control Protocol. Used to break apart and rebuild information that travels over the Internet.

TIPS. Transportation Improvement Plans. May be telework, mass transit, flexible work schedules, compressed workweeks, carpooling, tax incentives, etc.

telecooperation. The application of information and communication technologies by individuals and organizations to enhance communications and access to information.

telecottage. Originating in Sweden, and primarily found in Europe, the telecottage aims to provide under one roof a range of local services based around computers and telecommunications, with staff to help you use the equipment. Varying with each telecottage, some of the integrated services may include training, a computerized workplace, childcare, business services, business incubation, and IT support, marketing and subcontracting, social events, and networking opportunities. The original focus of telecottages was to bring technology and relevant skills to people in remote villages who lack opportunities to gain these skills by working for "hi-tech" employers, who have generally clustered in and around urban centers.

telehealth. The use of communication and information technologies to deliver medical diagnosis and patient care over large and small distances. Also referred to as telemedicine.

telehubbies. Male spouses who work from home.

telemanagement. Frontline supervision of teleworkers.

teletrade. Doing business over networks. The use of advanced information and technologies such as the Internet to market and sell goods and services, enhance customer service, and reach distant markets without the overhead of a physical presence.

technomad. The cutting edge of telework. Someone whose technology, connectivity, work methods, and lifestyle are so evolved that they literally need no base of operation. Many technomads work out of either recreational vehicles or a series of short-term habitations and are able to combine a professional career with a perpetual vacation.

telecommuting. The International Labour Office defines the concept of telecommuting as the combination of information and communication technologies with the concept of a flexible workplace. Work is carried out in a location that is remote from central offices or production facilities, where employees have no personal contact with coworkers. They communicate with colleagues using technology.

telefficiency. The process of improving organizational efficiency through the use of telecomputing technology.

telework. Periodic work out of the principal office, one or more days per week, either at home, a client's site, or in a telework center; the partial or total substitution of information technologies for the commute to work. The emphasis here is on reduction or elimination of the daily commute to and from the workplace. Telecommuting is a form of teleworking.

Telework America. Part of ITAC, a public/private partnership whose mission is to encourage acceptance and growth of telework arrangements through a nationwide program of public awareness, education, and active public-private participation focused on employee, employer, community, and environmental benefits. http://www.telecommute.org/twa/twa1999/workshop1.shtml.

telework center. An alternate worksite that contains workstations leased by a variety of employers for the use of teleworkers in their organizations. Generally, telework centers are set up in "geographically convenient" locations. Have been established by cooperative ventures or partnerships, private sector organizations, and public sector agencies.

telework connection. Web site devoted to telecommuting job opportunities, best practices, products, services, and teleworker resources. http://www.telework-connection.com.

Telework Guys. Bob Fortier, Ottawa-based CEO of InnoVisions Canada (telework consultants); president of the Canadian Telework Association, and director for the International Telework Association and Council; and

John Edwards, Virginia-based CEO of Telework Analytics International and its president. Both sit on the board of the International Telework Association and Council (John Edwards is its past president).

Telnet. Used to perform commands on a remote computer.

time shifting. The use of flexible and staggered office hours to reduce peak travel time congestion. Time shifting occurs where an employee is permitted to carry out her or his duties under certain circumstances at any time, day or night, weekends, holidays or religious holidays—in other words, fully flexible hours of work.

tour of duty. A teleworking employee's scheduled workdays, hours, and location(s).

Trojan horse. A destructive program that is disguised as a game, utility, or application. When run, it does something harmful to the computer system while appearing to do something useful.

UDP. User Diagram Protocol. Used for information that requires no response, such as streaming audio and video.

UK. United Kingdom. Consisting primarily of the countries and areas of England, Northern Ireland, Scotland, and Wales.

UK Online. The Web site portion of a partnership between government, industry, the voluntary sector, trade unions, and consumer groups whose mission is to enable everyone in the UK to gain access to the Internet by 2005 and to make the UK one of the world's leading knowledge economies. Much information on UK telework is available at http://www.dti.gov.uk/ministers/speeches/hewitt130900.html and http://www.ukonlineforbusiness.gov.uk/Advice/publications/teleworking/home.html

UNI. Union Network International represents over 15 million workers in 800 unions from 140 countries worldwide.

URL. Uniform Resource Locator. It defines an Internet location and type of resource.

Usenet. Also known as Net News. A large distributed bulletin board system consisting of over 12,000 newsgroups. Each newsgroup is propagated around the Internet on a daily or more frequent basis. Internet Access Providers hold copies of a large portion of these for local access by their users.

VDU. Video Display Unit (computer monitor).

VMT. Vehicle miles of travel.

VOC. Volcanic Organic Compounds. This generally refers to gaseous, non-methane organic compounds with vapor pressure.

VPN. A network using Internet protocol, that allows external organizations, such as suppliers or customers, access to selected internal information. In essence, it is an intranet that gives external users restricted access (for example, password protection) to particular information through the firewall.

vaporware. New software anticipated, but not delivered by the manufacturer on its promised delivery date.

videoconferencing. The use of camera, microphone, and monitor to allow visual communications over a high-speed communications link (typically 1 Mbps or higher) instead of proximity face-to-face communications. Videoconferencing equipment ranges in size from person-to-person, to large group. Users can control camera direction and angle of vision, so that remote users may be shown images other than the user's face. Person-to-person communications is increasingly being incorporated as another channel in computer communications, while use of compression techniques means reasonable quality video over much slower links than traditionally.

virtual community. A community developed around an area of common interest, using online techniques to sustain itself. It may use electronic bulletin boards, the World Wide Web or e-mail distribution lists to share information and maintain communications. As well as volunteer-run communities, others are being developed by commercial ventures, to create a focal point for electronic marketing.

virtual company. Merger of legally independent and spatially separated teleworking individuals or small businesses into a network to form a firm, which on the market acts as a single unit with one company name.

virtual/mobile office. In this option, workers are equipped with the tools, technology and skills to perform their jobs from anywhere the person has to be—home, office, hotel room, airport, customer's location, etc.

virtual organization. Group composed of employees or independent contractors affiliated with separate organizations or firms, who sometimes work together to accomplish a specific, defined result.

virtual team. Employees from the same or different departments in the same company, working out of the same or varying locations, who operate as a structured team under a designated team leader to accomplish a specific, defined result.

virtualization. A blanket term used to embrace the many types of virtual activity or structure, where those taking place remotely over networks replace traditional forms. Telework, for example, is the virtualization of work, while teletrade is the virtualization of products and services.

virus. An intrusive program that infects computer files by inserting copies of itself in those files. The copies are usually executed when the file is loaded into memory, allowing them to infect still other files, and so on. Viruses often have damaging side effects—sometimes intentional, sometimes not—such as destroying a computer's hard disk or taking up memory space.

WAH. Work at home.

WAN. Wide Area Network. Unlike LANs (Local Area Networks), WANs are not limited to a single location. Many wide area networks span long distances via telephone lines, fiber-optic cables, or satellite links. They can also be composed of smaller LANs that are interconnected. The Internet is a WAN.

water-cooler effect. A phrase used to describe the productive time lost by employees when they socialize during work hours at their offices.

Web weaver. Someone with a good understanding and interest in current technologies and in new ways of communicating with people and organizations.

Webcasting. Broadcasting live video and audio data over the Internet.

work area. In a work-at-home situation, the home space dedicated to the employee's work tasks.

workers' compensation. A U.S. government state-regulated insurance program that pays medical bills and replaces some lost wages for employees who are injured at work or who have work-related diseases or illnesses.

worm. A destructive program containing code that replicates itself until it fills the target drive or network, causing it to malfunction.

Index

About the Authors

BILL FENSON has been a leader in improving employee performance through individual career alignment for over twelve years. Through his workshops and counseling services, provided most recently through his own consulting firm, The Skills Emporium, LLC, in Binghamton, New York, he has helped thousands of people.

SHARON HILL is co-owner of De Scribe, offering business writing, editing, and advertising copywriting services from a base near Atlanta, Georgia. She specializes in career and recruitment issues.

BILL FENSON has been a leader in improving employee performance through individual career alignment for more than a decade. He has helped thousands of people through his workshops and counseling services, provided most recently through his own consulting firm, The Skills Emporium, LLC, in Binghamton, New York.

SHARON HILL is co-owner of De Scribe, offering business writing, editing, and advertising copywriting services from a base near Atlanta, Georgia. She specializes in career and recruitment issues.

ISBN: 1-56720-614-X

Praeger Publishers
88 Post Road West
Westport, CT 06881
www.praeger.com